EXPLORING
Christian Spirituality

EXPLORING
Christian Spirituality

Essays in Honor of
Sandra M. Schneiders, IHM

Edited by
Bruce H. Lescher
Elizabeth Liebert, SNJM

Paulist Press
New York/Mahwah, N.J.

Cover design by Trudi Gershenov
Book design by Lynn Else

Library of Congress Cataloging-in-Publication Data

Exploring Christian spirituality : essays in honor of Sandra M. Schneiders / edited by Bruce H. Lescher, Elizabeth Liebert.
    p. cm.
  Includes index.
  ISBN 0-8091-4216-3 (alk. paper)
  1. Schneiders, Sandra Marie. 2. Spirituality—Study and teaching. 3. Spirituality—Catholic Church—Study and teaching. I. Schneiders, Sandra Marie. II. Lescher, Bruce H. III. Liebert, Elizabeth, 1944-
  BV4511.E96 2006
  248—dc22

          2005035834

Published by Paulist Press
997 Macarthur Boulevard
Mahwah, New Jersey 07430

www.paulistpress.com

Printed and bound in the
United States of America

CONTENTS

v

Contents

INTRODUCTION

Bruce H. Lescher and Elizabeth Liebert, SNJM

In recent years Christian spirituality has emerged as a rich and dynamic player among the academic disciplines, claiming as its focus the critical exploration of religious experience in its many facets. Sandra M. Schneiders commands respect as one of the most significant and influential figures in the emergence of the study of Christian spirituality. This volume has two purposes. It commemorates Schneiders's contributions to the foundation and maturing of this vital young discipline. And it offers its own contribution to the development of the discipline through a collection of essays that push the boundaries of the discipline. Happily, these two purposes coincide. How appropriate to honor Schneiders's foundational contributions by building on her foundations as these nine authors do in this collection.

SCHNEIDERS'S CONTRIBUTIONS TO THE DISCIPLINE OF CHRISTIAN SPIRITUALITY

Three main contributions to the discipline of Christian spirituality emerge from Sandra Schneiders's scholarly pursuits: the doctoral program at the Graduate Theological Union, her writings on defining the field, and her involvement in the Society for the Study of Christian Spirituality. She might well be honored for her contributions in just one of these areas, but her involvement in all three renders her achievements all the more remarkable.

1

Doctoral Program at the Graduate Theological Union

Schneiders arrived at the Jesuit School of Theology at Berkeley, a member school of the Graduate Theological Union (GTU), in January 1976. At that time interest in spirituality was widespread among several GTU faculty members as well as some at the University of California Berkeley (UCB). Interested GTU faculty included Michael Buckley, James Empereur, Daniel O'Hanlon, Mary Ann Donovan, Donald Gelpi, and William Fulco of the Jesuit School; Joseph Chinnici, Anita Caspary, and James Liguri of the Franciscan School; William Herzog and Eldon Ernst of the American Baptist Seminary of the West; Wilhelm Wuellner and Durwood Foster of the Pacific School of Religion, Max Pearse and Massey Shepherd of the Church Divinity School of the Pacific; Antoninus Wall of the Dominican School; and Robert Goeser of the Pacific Lutheran School of Theology. Interested UCB faculty included William Bouwsma and William Slottman (history), Robert Bellah (sociology), and Mark Juergensmeyer and Lewis Lancaster (religious studies). Schneiders served as a catalyst to bring these faculty members together and to launch a doctoral program in Christian spirituality under the disciplinary umbrella of history of religions. The doctoral council of the GTU approved this move on May 5, 1976, and Schneiders served as the first program facilitator.[1] In 1992 Christian spirituality became a separate area of study within the GTU, with its own distinct faculty and protocol.

While Schneiders's scholarship would become a major influence in the field, she herself was influenced by the academic environment in which she taught and did research. In an interview with the editors of this volume on November 5, 2004, she noted that her own approach to the discipline evolved out of a need to address the requirements of a doctoral program at the GTU. For example, one of the first questions with which the faculty struggled was where to locate Christian spirituality within the academic areas of the GTU. Possible candidates included systematic or moral theology, but Schneiders argued that it be located within a phenomenological area, the history of religions. Thus, from the

2

beginning, she sought to articulate spirituality's independence, as a study of lived experience, from the traditional divisions of theology. Further, because the doctoral program in Christian spirituality was originally located within the history of religions, its protocol had to address the requirements of that area. As a result, the study of foundational texts (in this case, the Bible) and the historical development of a tradition (in this case, the history of Christian spirituality) became the two constitutive disciplines in Schneiders's explanation of spirituality, and they have been embedded in the GTU doctoral program from its outset.

Launching the doctoral program in Christian spirituality constituted a major contribution to the academic discipline. The first generation of scholars in Christian spirituality were trained in other disciplines, such as biblical studies, systemic theology, or history of theology. Now, a new generation of scholars could be trained in Christian spirituality as a field in its own right. Prof. Schneiders has directed many of the dissertations completed in the GTU program and mentored several graduates into faculty positions in other institutions.

The ecumenical and interfaith context of the GTU meant that the discipline would develop in ways that differed from other programs, such as those at the Pontifical Gregorian University in Rome, the Institut Catholique in Paris, and Fordham University in New York. For example, in addition to the two constitutive disciplines of Bible and history of Christian spirituality, the GTU curriculum requires the study of a spirituality other than Christian as a way of grounding the study of Christian spirituality in a wider interfaith context.

Writings Defining the Field

One of the first challenges facing this new field of Christian spirituality was how to define itself. What was its object of study? Its methodology? Writing in 1986, Schneiders noted that "spirituality is, in a sense, a phenomenon which has not been defined, analyzed, or categorized to anyone's satisfaction."[2] More than a decade later, in 1998, she observed: "In the space of a couple of decades a new discipline has emerged. Spirituality is by no means a full-grown participant in the academy. Neither its self-definition nor its relationships with other disciplines is clearly established."[3] As this volume will demonstrate, the effort to delineate this discipline, perhaps no longer emergent but still in its youth, continues today.

As the new discipline took root, Prof. Schneiders wrote several seminal articles setting out her vision of its contours. The bibliography (Part III) of this volume demonstrates the depth and breadth of her scholarship to date in this area. Here we will summarize her writing in broad themes; the essays that follow will delve more deeply into various facets of her work. For each of these themes Schneiders has advanced the conversation among scholars by articulating her position with great clarity. While some of her peers have disagreed with her conclusions, they are nonetheless indebted to her spirited engagement in advancing the conversation.

Prof. Schneiders's writings about the academic discipline of Christian spirituality fall into five broad areas. First, she has consistently argued that spirituality is an academic discipline in its own right, not a subdiscipline within theology. Traditionally, spiritual theology, with its branches of ascetical and mystical theology, was a subdivision of moral theology. Schneiders has articulated a position that spirituality, as the study of lived religious experience, precedes theology, which is a second-level reflection on experience. Theology, as a reflective discipline, "has the ability and the responsibility to criticize spirituality," to judge its adequacy as an expression of the Christian tradition.[4]

Second, an academic discipline needs to define its object of study. What is it that spirituality studies? Schneiders has delineated spirituality's object as "the spiritual life as experience."[5] Spirituality seeks to understand lived experience "as it actually occurs, as it actually transforms its subject toward fullness of life in Christ, that is, toward self-transcending life-integration within the Christian community of faith."[6] Because of this focus on experience, Schneiders, following Paul Ricoeur, argues that spirituality studies the individual

> precisely as an individual. Spirituality is characteristically involved in the study of individuals: texts, persons,

particular spiritual traditions such as Benedictinism, elements of spiritual experience such as discernment, interrelations of factors in particular situations such as the mutual relation of prayer and social commitment, concrete processes such as spiritual direction.[7]

Third, an academic discipline also needs to delineate the method or methods by which it studies its object. Schneiders's contribution here is to argue for a hermeneutic approach to spirituality. This is to say, a given study of lived religious experience is likely to include three phases: description of the experience being investigated, analysis leading to explanation and evaluation, and finally appropriation (what this experience means to us today).[8]

Fourth, while arguing for a hermeneutical approach to spirituality, Schneiders also contends that spirituality is a "field-encompassing field."[9] It does not have one methodology; rather, it employs whatever methodologies are relevant to understanding the topic being researched. Lived religious experience can be studied from the viewpoint of many disciplines. Nearly any study would include biblical studies and the history of spirituality, but other disciplines could be involved as well: theology, psychology, sociology, literary criticism, artistic theory, architecture, ecology, and so on. The choice of methodology depends upon the topic being studied.

Finally, Schneiders posits that the discipline of spirituality has a triple finality: research into religious experience adding to cumulative knowledge, assisting the researcher's own spiritual life, and assisting in the lives of other people.[10] Within the academy this threefold goal raises a tangle of issues around the self-implication of the researcher. Schneiders has courageously explored these areas and articulated a position that honors both the integrity of research and the self-involvement of scholars in their research. She has also posited differing ends between the study of spirituality for research (academia) and for purposes of training people in a spiritual tradition (formation), a move that further clarifies the distinct role of the academic discipline of Christian spirituality.

The Society for the Study of Christian Spirituality

Prof. Schneiders's third contribution stems from her involvement in the founding and organizing of the Society for the study of Christian Spirituality. The founding of the Society in 1992 was a major step in the development of the discipline, because it gave scholars a forum to discuss issues affecting their rapidly developing field and established an organ through which their research could be published. The society quickly became a major locus for advances in the field.

Under the leadership of Prof. Bradley Hanson of Luther College in Decorah, Iowa, the American Academy of Religion (AAR) sponsored a Consultation in Christian Spirituality in 1982–83 and a Seminar on Modern Christian Spirituality, 1984–88.[11] Hanson and other colleagues were seeking ways to continue the conversation but were not successful in getting further program units within the AAR. At the AAR's 1991 annual meeting in Kansas City, these scholars decided to form an affiliated society that would meet immediately prior to the AAR sessions. Schneiders was involved in these initial discussions, and she and Prof. Hanson began recruiting others. The AAR approved the group's application to become an affiliated society. A steering committee consisting of Bradley Hanson, Sandra Schneiders, Douglas Burton-Christie, Mary Elizabeth Moore, and Don Saliers was appointed, and the society held its first meeting in San Francisco in 1992. From these small beginnings the society now has a membership of 450 members.

Schneiders served on the steering committee and also on the first governing board. She recruited Douglas Burton-Christie to be editor of the *Christian Spirituality Bulletin,* which began publication in 1993. Burton-Christie developed the *Bulletin* into an attractive and quality publication that came to be widely respected in academic circles.[12] Schneiders was elected president of the society in 1996 and delivered the presidential address in November 1997. She was also instrumental in the evolution of the *Bulletin* into a refereed journal, entitled *Spiritus,* which began publication in 2001 under the auspices of Johns Hopkins University Press. She continues to serve on the editorial board of *Spiritus.* This refereed journal provides a forum for a wide range of scholars to publish within the discipline of Christian spirituality.

ADVANCING THE CONVERSATION

In light of Schneiders's influence on the formation of the discipline, it seems most appropriate to honor her contributions to the field by continuing to advance the study of Christian spirituality, addressing issues that emerge at present at the "edges" of the discipline. At these borders lie significant questions of content and method that will set the course of the discipline for the next decade; here matters are being debated and the field is being refined as it is explored. In this volume colleagues and students of Dr. Schneiders and other collaborators in the academic discipline of Christian spirituality articulate issues for the field from their various disciplinary and methodological perspectives. The focus is not so much on what these disciplines and methods say about Christian spirituality as an academic discipline, but on how scholars working in the field fruitfully *employ* them in pursuing the academic study of Christian spirituality itself.

Methodological Essays

The volume begins, as is appropriate for a new discipline, with three essays that examine issues of methodology. From the perspective of a historical theologian, Philip Sheldrake argues that spirituality is—and must remain—a provocative presence within theology, as well as a distinct discipline, but that spirituality may very well be the key to the contemporary theological problematic. Spirituality's role, claims Sheldrake, is to remind theology not to separate itself from the wisdom found in lived experience and practice, even as the discipline of spirituality itself must move more fully into these very commitments that constitute its self-identity.

We have noted Schneiders's use of the phrase "field-encompassing field" to describe the academic discipline of Christian spirituality. That is to say, scholars of spirituality employ other disciplines as they pursue their distinctive work. From her vantage point as a scholar of "interdisciplinarity," Judith Berling addresses the claim that Christian spirituality is inherently interdisciplinary. She pushes beyond the structural aspects of interdisciplinarity to probe precisely how the scholar goes about interdisciplinary scholarship. As Berling proceeds, she raises questions about constitutive and problematic disciplines (as Schneiders defines these terms) and about how broadly or narrowly the discipline defines its boundaries, issues that the developing discipline is now in a position to address.

The person of the scholar is inevitably and overtly drawn into the study of Christian spirituality—the discipline is inherently self-implicating. Not only is the researcher's own experience relevant to the research project, but what the researcher studies implicates the researcher. Belden Lane probes this controversial aspect of the discipline, inquiring precisely how the scholar's self is both effectively and ineffectively exercised in the practice of spirituality as a critical discipline. He illustrates helpful and problematic examples of authorial presence in classical texts, at the same time modeling appropriate authorial presence in contemporary scholarship in Christian spirituality. The point, he reminds us, is not, after all, about ourselves.

Essays at the Edges of the Discipline

The remaining essays serve as "reports from the field." From their various content and disciplinary perspectives, six scholars report on their work at the edges of the discipline. New Testament scholar John Donahue traces the development of biblical spirituality, particularly in Sandra Schneiders's work. He begins with the wider context in the discipline of spirituality, summarizing Schneiders's understanding of spirituality and the academic discipline that critically studies the phenomenon of spirituality, as well as the developments within the Roman Catholic Church after Vatican II in which biblical spirituality developed. He concludes with remarks on the evolution of Christian spirituality from the perspective of biblical studies. Readers unfamiliar with the discussions of the scope of the discipline may wish to begin with this essay.

Moving beyond the binary use of gender terms—man versus woman, male versus female—Lisa Dahill explores the rich and often overlapping levels of gender in relation to Christian spirituality. Gender, she demonstrates, is far more than a basic form of classification; it is, in fact, a hermeneutical category. Unpacking meaning inevitably entails unpacking multiple gender categories and levels: of the person being studied; of the scholar doing the study; and indeed, of the very perceptions of God that ground the religious experience being studied.

At first blush the methodologies of the natural sciences appear largely incompatible with those of theology and spirituality in their cultures of evidence and their use of scientific and mathematical languages. Robert John Russell, director of the Center for Theology and the Natural Sciences in Berkeley, goes to the heart of the apparent disjuncture, revealing the rich possibilities for mutual influence between spirituality and the natural sciences. By introducing the concept of a hierarchy of disciplines and expanding it to include spirituality, Russell demonstrates how the discussion can be carried on in terms admissible in each discipline.

Given the pervasiveness of questions of suffering and the presence of evil, Douglas Burton-Christie believes it is not surprising how frequently they surface in contemporary experience. Although the genre of nature writing is not necessarily overtly religious, it nonetheless supplies a theater where these questions are dealt with as a matter of course. Burton-Christie uses two contemporary authors to press the issues of suffering and evil. Mary Kerr's work raises the questions: Is there any center to the cosmos? Can there be a God who cares? Czeslaw Milosz struggles with how to cope with both the beauty and the mathematical cruelty of the universe. Burton-Christie probes these authors for clues about the ways that such questions of God's justice surface as matters of spirituality in contemporary discourse.

The contemporary world is marked by religious pluralism; we are perhaps more aware of the astounding complexity of religious traditions in the United States in the aftermath of 9/11. This pluralism poses a challenge to traditional understandings of Christianity as "the one true religion." As a scholar deeply engaged in Christian-Jewish dialogue, Mary C. Boys asks scholars of Christian spirituality to acknowledge the inaccurate and destructive history in which Christians discount and denigrate Judaism as a legitimate spiritual tradition. Not only does Judaism have much to contribute to Christian spirituality, but scholars of Christian spirituality will consistently misinterpret their own tradition if they omit or subsume Judaism. She asks, "If Christians were to regard Judaism as a partner in waiting and working for the world's full redemption, what difference would it make both in our self-understanding and in our understanding of the religious 'other'?"

Alejandro García-Rivera sets very different interlocutors together in a promising border-crossing exercise. Putting inter-faith dialogue in conversation with aesthetics allows García-Rivera to develop an *interfaith aesthetics,* where participants in interfaith dialogue come together in mutual appreciation and love of beautiful artifacts from each other's traditions. This aesthetic experience can engender a love for each other's traditions, deeper than articulating truths, that propels the participants into an interfaith "looking at by looking through." Interfaith aesthetics, García-Rivera believes, is the point where theology and spirituality meet, the place where "faith finds faith in faith itself."

Although we recognize that it is somewhat unusual to include an essay by the honoree in a volume of this type, we have chosen to do so. Sandra Schneiders's essay addresses a critical question that continually resurfaces: the relationship between the academic disciplines of Christian spirituality and theology. This essay contains Prof. Schneiders's latest thinking on this issue. She moves beyond the language of "problematic" disciplines to describe a role that theology can play in spirituality research to address the similarities and differences in the way that theology and spirituality approach a similar subject from differing viewpoints.

We hope that this collection of essays will provoke students and scholars of Christian spirituality, as well as practitioners who rely on Christian spirituality to fund their ministries, to continue critically thinking, discussing, writing and practicing Christian spirituality, moving it into its next decade. What will we be able to say in ten more years about this developing discipline? What will the leading questions be then? Who will emerge as the next generation of scholars? Whoever they may be, their debt to

Sandra Schneiders will continue to be profound. She has served as a major architect of the very discipline.

Notes

1. Log of the Doctoral Council, May 5, 1976. Office of the President and Dean. Claude Welch, 1971–82 Collection, Graduate Theological Union Archives, Berkeley, California.

2. Sandra M. Schneiders, "Theology and Spirituality: Strangers, Rivals, or Partners?" *Horizons* 13 (1986): 253.

3. Sandra M. Schneiders, "Spirituality in the Academy," *Theological Studies* 50 (1989): 696.

4. Schneiders, "Theology and Spirituality," 270.

5. Sandra M. Schneiders, "A Hermeneutical Approach to the Study of Christian Spirituality," *Christian Spirituality Bulletin* (Spring 1994): 9.

6. Sandra M. Schneiders, "The Study of Christian Spirituality: Contours and Dynamics of a Discipline," *Christian Spirituality Bulletin* 6 (Spring 1998): 3.

7. Schneiders, "Spirituality in the Academy," 694.

8. Ibid., 695.

9. Schneiders, "Theology and Spirituality," 274. Schneiders borrows the phrase from Van A. Harvey, *The Historian and the Believer: The Morality of Historical Knowledge and Christian Belief* (Philadelphia: Westminster, 1966), 54–59.

10. Schneiders, "Spirituality in the Academy," 695.

11. Historical references here are contained in an email message from Bradley Hanson to Bruce Lescher, September 20, 1997.

12. Seminal articles in the *Bulletin* and the early volumes of *Spiritus,* including two essays by Schneiders, have been reprinted in *Minding the Spirit: The Study of Christian Spirituality,* ed. Elizabeth A. Dreyer and Mark S. Burrows (Baltimore: Johns Hopkins University Press, 2005).

PART I

Methodological Essays

1

Spirituality and Its Critical Methodology

Philip Sheldrake

Since Descartes's *Discourse on Method,* Western thought has been preoccupied with method. Since the nineteenth century, theology has been specifically exercised by the emergence of historical consciousness. Within the Catholic tradition the struggle to return to the classic sources of theology in their historical and cultural contexts provoked a movement away from an a priori dogmatic theology in the decades leading to Vatican II. Philosophical concepts were supplemented by history and the social sciences and a theory of interpretation or hermeneutics became necessary.[1] The development of academic spirituality, especially in the English-speaking world, has been influenced by these movements and shares their preoccupation with method.

Sandra Schneiders has led the debate about methodology in the English-speaking world with a succession of seminal articles. Whatever position we take on the overall relationship between spirituality and theology, Prof. Schneiders has rightly questioned the imperialism of dogmatic theology as the nonnegotiable determinant of spirituality. Spirituality is not reducible to a second-order application of doctrine to life. It involves the study of "felt experience" and "lived practice" in ways that, while not detached from theological tradition, overflow the boundaries that positivist theology tends to set.

The study of Christian spirituality owes so much to Prof. Schneiders that it is a particular pleasure to base my comments on the foundations she has laid. In this essay I address three main themes in the area of fundamental methodology and of technical methods: first, the problem of historical consciousness in contemporary Western culture; second, the impact on spirituality of new perspectives from critical disciplines; and finally, spirituality as the meaning and future of theology. In some respects the last point is the most controversial. Yet, in my estimation, it is critical. On the one hand, I believe that the academic discipline of spirituality has reached a sufficiently advanced stage that, methodologically, it should no longer need to concentrate its energies on self-defense. On the other hand, the nature of theology and its raison d'être is an increasingly contentious issue. In my view, the developed discipline of spirituality now has a unique capacity to help in the renewal of theology in constructive and refreshing ways.

SPIRITUAL EXPERIENCE

The emphasis that contemporary spirituality often places on experience reflects a sense that there is something deeper than conceptual approaches to religion. We are continually reminded of the widespread openness to "the spiritual" among people who are uninvolved in organized religion.[2] The concept of spirituality is increasingly used outside religious contexts (often in relation to social issues such as health care) to designate a quest for depth and purpose in life as a whole—a vision of the human spirit and what enhances it.

Hanging over the debate about the nature of spiritual experience, whether this is generic and separable from faith traditions, is the legacy of William James's *The Varieties of Religious Experience*. This book is a brooding presence, if no longer an unquestioned influence.[3] James's desire to establish a science of religion on the same empirical, epistemological, and methodological grounds as the natural sciences, detached from the specifics of religious language, is questionable. There are linguistic-conceptual problems—in what sense is there "naked" experience prior to interpretation and language? There are also phenomenological ones—detailed study of "religious experience" in different cultures, different locales, and different historical contexts reveals only particularity and difference. A cross-cultural and interreligious approach to spirituality can never escape into a realm of "contextless," generic definition.

THE WISDOM OF HISTORY

The centrality of context and therefore of historical method in spirituality is no longer a matter of debate.[4] However, historical consciousness more broadly understood is in question. How we think about the past is a complex issue in Western culture and has an impact on how people approach the subject of spirituality. We exist in a time of cultural change when there is an evident weariness with history and with the notion of being involved in a stream of tradition through time. To hark back to the past seems a distraction. It is common for people to believe that history signifies only the past rather than something that enables our present to exist or that invites us to consider the future and what we aspire to.

In Booker Prize–winner Pat Barker's novel, *Another World*, Geordie, the centenarian veteran of the Somme, is dying. He has particularly close relationships with two people. Helen, the professional historian who has recorded interviews with him and other veterans, represents a strong historical consciousness. She has a fervent commitment to preserving memories for the sake of posterity. Geordie's grandson, Nick, represents a generation that not only believes that history has no message but in fact does not really believe in history at all:

> "Well, you see the first thing is I don't believe in public memory. A memory is a biochemical change in an individual brain, and that's all there is."...And secretly, what he wants to say is that raking about in the detritus of other people's memories is a waste of time and energy. The only true or useful thing that can be said about the past is that it's over. It no longer exists.[5]

This weariness with history relates to several factors. Rapid social change and the decline of traditional communities have broken many people's sense of a living connection with the past. History and tradition are perceived as conservative forces from which we need to break free if the world is to be more rational. The power of history-as-myth to sustain entrenched social, religious, and political divisions tends to reinforce this negative view.

So, is history dead? The French Christian philosopher Paul Ricoeur is greatly preoccupied with the importance of reconstructing a "historical consciousness." He argues that this is vital to our identities, and thus, implicitly, to our spiritual well-being: "Time becomes human time to the extent that it is organized after the manner of a narrative; narrative, in turn, is meaningful to the extent that it portrays the features of temporal existence."[6]

At first glance Ricoeur is something of a paradox. On the one hand, he shares a postmodern skepticism for meta-narratives and attempts by history to decipher the supreme plot.[7] However, Ricoeur also rejects a tendency to deconstruct history as a form of narrative. If we reject mediating narratives altogether, this is not liberating but profoundly oppressive. Without narrative we undermine a vital element of human solidarity and remove a key incentive for changing the status quo as well as a means of bringing this about. "We tell stories because in the last analysis human lives need and merit being narrated. The whole history of suffering cries out for vengeance and calls for narrative."[8]

We all need a story to live by in order to make sense of the disconnected events of life. It is only by enabling alternative stories to be heard that public history can offer a place for the oppressed who have otherwise been excluded: "Without a narrative, a person's life is merely a random sequence of unrelated events: birth and death are inscrutable, temporality is a terror and a burden, and suffering and loss remain mute and unintelligible."[9] Rather than abolish narrative, we need to ask, Whose narrative is told? Who belongs within the story?

Ricoeur attempts to retrieve history as more than a set of objective "events" emptied of the warmth of human stories. History once again has something to do with people's vision. It is an act of interpretation and all interpretation is necessarily an act of *commitment*. History implies continuities that in turn imply responsibilities. Commitment and responsibility point to the important fact that history is not merely about the past but also about the present and future. A historical consciousness opens us to possible action rather than to a passive acceptance of the way things are. In this way of understanding, a sense of history remains a critical spiritual issue.[10]

METHOD AND METHODOLOGY

In the remainder of this essay I focus on two other central themes: that both spirituality and theology are now engaged with perspectives that would once have been considered alien and that spirituality is actually the key to the future of theology. First, there is a simple but important distinction to be made between method(s) and methodology. As we shall see, the study of Christian spirituality may involve a range of methods. However, there are a few fundamental principles that constitute a methodological theory of the field as a whole. It is to the area of methodology that I now turn.

CRITICAL THEORY

Several theologians have recently highlighted the impact on theology of two closely related conversations: with critical theory and with cultural analysis. Broadly speaking, these conversations remind us that the study of theology cannot be separated from the cultural contexts within which it takes place.

Since the end of the Second World War critical theory has been largely associated with French philosophers, influenced by social analysis, such as Michel Foucault, Jacques Derrida, Paul Ricoeur, Emmanuel Levinas, Jean-Luc Marion, and Michel de Certeau. These writers attack the rationalism of the Enlightenment, "the mechanization of reality," and promote two important standpoints.[11] First, hard disciplinary boundaries give way to interdisciplinarity. Second, and arising from this breakdown of closed systems of analysis, the ways we think are bound up with issues of power.

English theologian Graham Ward rightly reminds us that "theology's business has always been the transgression of boundaries," precisely because it requires a multiplicity of disciplines for its very possibility as a subject.[12] Sadly, the fragmentation of "theology" into several discrete discourses over the last couple of hundred years tends to obscure this fact. However, the role of interdisciplinary study has become a central methodological principle of spirituality and one of Sandra Schneiders's important legacies. The criticism used to be leveled at spirituality that it sought to use as many methods and tools as possible only because there was no adequate sense of disciplinary identity. There is certainly a "cheap" interdisciplinarity—plundering the *vocabulary* of different disciplines without developing a sufficient literacy in them. Despite this potential weakness, at its best interdisciplinarity is not a matter of expediency but is a principled position.[13]

Equally, the political dimension of our approach to history, to texts, to interpretation, to application and appropriation, is something that spirituality has struggled with for a long time. Critical theory emphasizes that margins and boundaries, in academic study as in the whole of life, are political realities. The emphasis in interpretation is no longer on the finished text— written texts, the text of "the self," or the text of life as a whole—but on a quest for meaning that forever pushes us beyond the temptations of final conclusions.

Students of spirituality learn to exist in the world of borderlands—between theory and practice, theology and other disciplines, the sacred and the secular, interiority and exteriority. Indeed, spirituality as reflection on "felt experience" and "lived practice" is necessarily, in Graham Ward's words, "a venture into the ambivalent"[14] because of its fundamental horizon of otherness and transcendence. In this, as in so much else, spirituality reminds theology of its task of crossing thresholds and questioning human absolutes.

There is an ascetical aspect to interdisciplinary work because such encounters make us vulnerable. What was taken as simple and neat is shown to be multifaceted and messy; what was assumed to be fixed proves to be the starting point for another journey. This is not a question of continual deferral or refusing commitment. Interdisciplinarity is a *discipline (askesis)* of learning to live with the provisional.

Critical theory reminds us that the issue for spirituality is not simply a question of content or of tools (what are the constitutive disciplines and what are the problematic disciplines?)[15] but involves larger methodological questions. *Why* do we approach this material? *What happens* when we approach this material in these ways and for these reasons? In other words, our way of studying a mystical text, a spiritual tradition, a significant personality involves more than the use of certain techniques. We operate from our own cultural horizons, which, while they include blind spots that need to be exposed, are also the only means through which interpretation is possible.[16] The impact of critical theory, with its emphasis on broader interpretative questions, accords well with the establishment of *hermeneutical methodology* at the heart of academic spirituality—another of Sandra Schneiders's legacies.

CULTURAL ANALYSIS

Cultural analysis has had a particular impact on theology in North America.[17] Like critical theory, on which it is partly based, it promotes interdisciplinarity and takes a political view of all thought forms. So, religious traditions are both cultural expressions and producers of culture. We should remember that anthropologists no longer understand culture as homogeneous but as a plural, often-contested reality associated with issues of dominance and exclusion.[18]

Cultural analysis leads theology to address *particularities* rather than be a detached "reflection on perennial questions in their most general forms."[19] Theology is embedded within a complexity of particular historical, cultural, and social worlds. We experience and come to know *in context*. Equally, theology is no longer the exclusive domain of elites. "Ordinary Christians" are not merely passive consumers of values derived from the powerful. They are also producers of religious meaning. Consequently, theology is more than complex ideas or written texts. Its sources are also to be found in non-discursive, even non-linguistic, social practices. Because theology is culturally embedded, it is inevitably implicated in issues of power negotiation. Otherness, difference, struggle, and contestation are its surrounding realities and influences, and also critical sources of theological reflection.

Arguably, the study of spirituality, at least in the English-speaking world, has been promoting culturally sensitive methodological principles for some time. However, I sense that awareness of the issues is sometimes theoretical rather than realized in the construction of syllabi and in methods of teaching and learning. Evidence on the ground in the English-speaking world suggests that the study of spirituality still tends to privilege contemplative-mystical-monastic traditions. Definitions of spirituality *explicitly* favor the notion that it encompasses all aspects of human existence, viewed through a particular lens, yet methodologically academic study still *implicitly* tends to locate the context of transformation away from everyday life. Although liberationist and feminist theologies have a substantial impact on spirituality's engagement with social transformation, more broadly it is only slowly moving beyond classic paradigms to delve into everyday life as spiritual practice. As it does so, a rich range of subject matter opens up for serious study. Michel de Certeau's two-volume project, *The Practice of Everyday Life,* is an exercise in social history and cultural studies rather than spirituality.[20] Yet, at a time when de Certeau is being recovered as a religious thinker, it is not too far-fetched to see his concern for everyday practices (the city, travel, food) as grounded in spiritual as well as social and political values.

Academic spirituality needs to draw regularly on sources other than written ones. One of the great riches of Christian spirituality is the range of genres in which it is expressed: art, music, architecture, practices such as pilgrimage, communitarian ways of life, and rituals. Yet, interestingly, an ecumenical study of research and teaching of Christian spirituality in North America only a few years ago noted that the dominant approaches remained historical and theological. The role of the social sciences, for example, is still peripheral, whatever the theoretical belief in interdisciplinarity and breadth.[21]

METHODOLOGY AND PURPOSE

Hermeneutical methodology moves the study of spirituality beyond matters of content toward a quest for wisdom to live by, rather than technical information held at a distance. Sandra Schneiders has consistently portrayed academic spirituality as self-implicating, and this phrase has almost become a truism. What distinguishes the discipline of Christian spirituality in its fullest sense is that it is not only *informative* but *transformative*. When we approach our sources we clearly seek *information*: historical data, a detailed analysis of texts, an understanding of theological frameworks, and an identification of the kind of spiritual wisdom being presented. However, beyond information lies a quest for wisdom embodied in traditions, texts, or practices, and how to gain access to it. This confronts us with questions such as what difference does this make? or what could or should our response be? This is the *transformative* dimension of the method and involves *judgment* (this is important) and *appropriation* (we seek to make this wisdom our own). A number of contemporary scholars actually refer to an "appropriative method" in relation to Christian spirituality. In other words, study favors *application* and the purpose of application is *appropriation*.[22] Understanding is concerned with meaning but also with purpose and values.

SPIRITUALITY AND THE MEANING OF THEOLOGY

Self-implication, transformation, and appropriation draw our attention to my final methodological principle. An integrated study of Christian spirituality is always *theological in purpose* even when it is not explicitly employing theological tools.

David Tracy, an important methodological voice in English-speaking theology, highlights theology's task of being a public discourse and his belief that there can be no theology without spirituality. For Tracy, the meaning of theology and its methods are determined in part by its audience.[23] He delineates three audiences: society, academy, and church. However, these overlap and are rarely exclusive in the life of the particular theologian or scholar of spirituality. Unlike some theologians influenced by cultural analysis, Tracy does not posit three entirely separate theologies.[24] Nor, unlike post-liberal theologians such as George Lindbeck or Stanley Hauerwas, does Tracy suggest a kind of separatism where church theology would be better off if it retreated into the ghetto. Such a retreat would not aid theology's purpose as a form of public, prophetic speech. Theology (and implicitly, spirituality) is always "in public."

An important link between Tracy's public, prophetic theology and his emphasis on the importance of mystical language is his sense of God as radically "other" and disruptive. Such a God must be contemplated rather than imprisoned by our definitions. "We may now learn to drop earlier dismissals of 'mysticism' and allow its uncanny negations to release us."[25] This God is strange and elusive rather than familiar or domestic; one who is and does more than we can conceive. To practice a theology rooted in spirituality involves the risk that knowledge may transform us. "'Saying the truth' is distinct from, although never separate from, 'doing the truth.'...More concretely, there is never an authentic disclosure of truth which is not also transformative."[26] Such transformation is a prerequisite of effective public, prophetic utterance.

It is sometimes asserted that spirituality is in danger of further fragmenting theological discourse by adding another ingredient to an already overloaded multidisciplinary framework and threatening the "objective rigor" of theology. I see things differently. There are two valid meanings of *spirituality* in relation to theology. In most discussions the emphasis has been on academic spirituality as a specific discipline and the degree to which this is congruent with theology. I will call this *Spirituality 1*. While this has coherence, we also need to recover spirituality as a central, not incidental, dimension of every theological discipline— *Spirituality 2*. By extension, *Spirituality 2* is a synthetic discipline as far as theology is concerned. It holds the varied elements

24

together and prevents the theological enterprise from dispersing into a collection of semi-autonomous disciplines, biblical, historical, systematic, or practical. *Spirituality 2* is the holistic heart of the broad field of theology that gives it its shape and meaning.

"Doing theology" is self-implicating and shapes the theologian. Theologians or spirituality scholars undoubtedly need social scientific tools but do not embrace a social scientific finality by "bracketing out" commitments in favor of "pure" observation. Theology is a spiritual practice because it involves "an improvement, or is tied to an improvement, of the spirit."[27] To put it another way, theology involves becoming a *theological person.* Thus, theologians are those who *live* theology rather than "do" it as an activity divorced from who they are and from the vision of the world by which they seek to live. In the aftermath of modernist distinctions between theory and experience or practice, we should recall that *theory* in its origins does not concern the abstract but *theōria,* that is, contemplation. To think *about* God is to think *of* God and therefore to become involved *with* God.

Undoubtedly, the contemporary discipline of spirituality depends on some kind of distinction from doctrine, but this is not the same as a distinction from *theology.* However, spirituality is a critical and provocative presence within theology. It is too complacent to assert (as I have heard said) that all good theology is already spiritual theology, as if this might keep at bay the Trojan horse of contemporary spirituality! Spirituality makes space within the theological enterprise for at least two important things. First, it leaves space for what is called *intertextuality*—that is, for God's "speech" or self-revelation that takes place "in the space between" different Christian traditions and between Christian discourse and other discourses, whether religious or nonreligious. Second, and in relation to the first, spirituality leaves room for religious, social, and cultural realities that have not readily found a place within traditional systematic theology. For example, spirituality scholars are used to studying the aesthetic—literature, the arts, music—as an important medium for the human relationship with God.[28] The study of spirituality must also now engage with the impact on our understanding of human life of developments in science such as cosmology, quantum mechanics, ecology, genetics, neuroscience, artificial intelligence and the birth of cyber-space.[29] Christian spirituality is just beginning to make a contribution to discussions outside religious circles about the spiritual dimension of such critical public themes as health care, education, citizenship, the future of cities, the future of work, and so on. All these involve unfamiliar theoretical and practical disciplines. These conversations bring into the arena of spirituality new descriptive and analytical tools without compromising spirituality's broader methodological principles.

I am cautious about viewing spirituality *solely* as a discrete discipline—whether alongside or within theology. I worry about separating "pure" and "applied" disciplines within theology. An assumption exists, for example, that doctrinal theology is a "pure" discipline with its own integrity. The danger here is a reductionist view of theology as abstract and definitive. "Applied" disciplines (for example, liturgy, pastoral studies, ethics, spirituality) are then supposed to touch areas that "pure" theology cannot or does not wish to reach—the level of "felt experience" or "lived practice." The danger, however, is that this approach marginalizes the "applied" out of harm's way where it can do no significant damage to "pure" theology.

A CONTEMPLATIVE METHOD?

Contemporary theories of interpretation in the study of spirituality point to a form of contemplative practice that challenges exclusively analytical methods. Letting a text speak demands an intense presence to whatever we study. This sense of contemplative attention is reinforced by the vulnerability opened up by interdisciplinarity and the transformation implied by self-implication.

Taken together, is it possible to understand this in terms of *method*? In her work on the spirituality of John's Gospel, *Written That You May Believe: Encountering Jesus in the Fourth Gospel*, Sandra Schneiders suggests that the patristic-monastic theory of scriptural exegesis, allied to modern scholarly sophistication, offers a way to practice the study of scripture—and, by extension, of other theological or spiritual texts—in terms of the ultimate purpose of application and transformation.[30] This method of study is known as *lectio divina*—a fourfold process (later systematized over-rigidly as four stages) of *lectio* (careful meditative reading of a text), *meditatio* (deep rumination on its meaning), *oratio* (a personal, prayerful response to meaning), and *contemplatio* (surrender to the action of God drawing one into the divine mystery *in and through* the meaning of the text). The importance of the contemplative method in spirituality is underlined when we consider what is involved if we attempt to "explain" apophatic language or to fill in the open referent—to say what the text really meant to say, but didn't! If you like, such texts sharply focus the hermeneutical conundrum when we study *theologically* in the full sense—how to read texts without *exclusively* applying discursive reasoning and analysis.[31]

My point is that contemplative engagement is demanded not simply by spirituality but by the theological enterprise as a whole. Reflecting on the writings of Johannes Baptist Metz, contemporary Basque theologian Gaspar Martinez comments:

> Theology begins in prayer and ends in prayer. Prayer, says Metz, in its flexibility and complete freedom is a limitless language, a language that knows no barriers, a language that goes, at least inchoately, well beyond what is being explicitly expressed and into the inexpressible. In this sense, everything can be said to God in prayer, from rage, frustration, and accusation, to downright denial of God's existence. Beyond being such an all-flexible language, prayer is a discourse suffused with experience, with concreteness; it is a living discourse and, hence, the very matrix, the natural setting of a biographical theology. In the last analysis, theology stems from prayer, talk about God from talk to God. Negative theology [an emphasis in Metz] is also a result of intensification. The language of prayer is more suffused with negative theology than the official language of theology itself. Theology is nothing other than reflexive prayer language.[32]

Finally, in a brief but pregnant essay, "Theological Integrity," Rowan Williams explicitly links the power of contemplation to theological language in terms of "integrity." For Williams, contemplation is concerned with honesty in what we say *about* God as well as in what we seek to do *in the name of God*. Christianity involves speaking out—but our words must have integrity. Part of theology's "honest discourse" is to admit that it does not claim to be, in and of itself, final.[33]

This notion is difficult for people who, in using religious language, make claims "about the context of the whole moral universe, claims of crucial concern for the right leading of human life."[34] The point is that theology does not merely expound theory but speaks of what God seeks, *wills*. Yet, because it claims to speak about the nature of God's desire, theological language "declares itself to be...dealing with what supremely *resists* the urge to finish and close what is being said."[35] Thus, what Williams calls "communicative" and "critical" theological styles must interact with the "celebratory"—grounded in "praise of God."[36] For "the integrity of a community's language about God, the degree to which it escapes its own pressure to power and closure is tied to the integrity of the language it directs *to* God."[37]

Rowan Williams fundamentally suggests that theological language is only honest if it is *surrendered to God*. The rigor of theology is not simply the rigor of explanation but also of *askesis*—a realization that theology embodies commitment in need of continual testing. Without testing, theology confuses faithfulness with dogmatism, engagement with what de Certeau called "the totality of the immense" with an ability to define a "total perspective."[38] Williams suggests that this involves a "dispossession of the human mind conceived as central to the order of the world, and a dispossession of the entire identity that exists prior to the paschal drama, the identity that has not seen and named its self-deception and self-destructiveness."[39] At the heart of dispossession is *apophasis*—deferral to what Williams calls the prior actualities of God. "The fruition of the process [of contemplation] is the discovery that one's selfhood and value simply lie in the abiding faithful presence of God, not in any moral or conceptual performance."[40] Contemplation is a state in which "the self acts out of an habitual diffused awareness that its centre is God."

> To act from its centre *is* to give God freedom in the world, to do the works of God. The self, we could say, has attained integrity: the inner and outer are no longer in tension; I act what I am, a creature called to freedom, and leave behind those attempts at self-creation which in fact destroy my freedom. As Teresa [of Avila] puts it, Martha and Mary unite: truthful, active and constructive love issues from and leads into patience and silence, or, better, is constantly *contemporary* with patience and silence.[41]

CONCLUSION

My sense that spirituality is the key to our contemporary theological problematic partly reflects a British perspective. In Britain, so-called secular universities still have theology departments, nowadays with an ecumenical membership. There are sometimes Christian foundations within universities or denominational seminaries linked to them. Broadly speaking, academic theology and spirituality (where they exist) find their home in a public, non-confessional higher education system. Theology, therefore, is not exclusively ecclesially committed. Its properly religious dimension is held in creative tension with critically committed reflection in which no question can in principle be excluded. Most theologians recognize this situation as challenging but important and would consider it a loss to theology and to the academy if theology were forced to retreat into purely church settings. However, this particularity does not, I believe, undermine my general perceptions about the future of theology.

A recent discussion among colleagues at the University of Durham on the study of spirituality revealed not only that most believed that spirituality should be a dimension of *all* theological disciplines but also elicited the thought that spirituality is actually the future of theology! In simple terms, there is an increasing weariness with the viability and attraction of a purely detached approach to theology. In that sense the emergence of spirituality may prove to be a powerful reform movement within theology, just as theology's engagement with truth claims is a provocative presence within the wider academy. The "vocation" of spirituality is to remind theology not to separate from the wisdom found in lived experience and practice, even though academic theology must proceed in a properly critical way, interpreting and evaluating living traditions using a wide range of technical methods.

Does this mean that spirituality as a separate discipline actually needs to *die*? Not immediately, I am sure. In practice, much of the typical subject matter of spirituality is still not adequately addressed in other parts of theological syllabi. However, we should remember that the emergence of academic spirituality cannot be separated from context. Its creation over the last thirty years was a contingent process. Its existence reflects a particular moment in Western culture, in the relationship between traditional religious traditions and culture, and in the state of theology. Spirituality as a distinct discipline is currently a necessary, provocative, and disruptive presence in the academy, but in its present form, it may prove to be transitional as the hard boundaries between the subdisciplines of the theological enterprise, between theology and other disciplines, and between theory and practice become even more mobile and fluid.

Notes

1. For a summary of these developments, see William L. Portier, "Interpretation and Method," in *The Praxis of the Reign of God: An Introduction to the Theology of Edward Schillebeeckx,* ed. Mary Catherine Hilkert and Robert L. Schreiter (New York: Fordham University Press, 2002), 9–36.

2. See Douglas Burton-Christie, "The Weight of the World: The Heaviness of Nature in Spiritual Experience," in this volume.

3. William James, *The Varieties of Religious Experience* (London: Penguin, 1982; originally published 1902).

4. For a justification for this statement, see Philip Sheldrake, *Spirituality and History: Questions of Interpretation and Method,* rev. ed. (Maryknoll, NY: Orbis Books, 1998).

5. Pat Barker, *Another World* (London: Penguin Books, 1999), 85, 87.

6. Paul Ricoeur, *Time and Narrative,* 3 vols., trans. Kathleen Blamey and David Pellauer (Chicago: University of Chicago Press, 1984–88), 1:3.

7. Ibid., 3:103.

8. Ibid., 1:75.

9. Mark Wallace, "Introduction," in Paul Ricoeur, *Figuring the Sacred: Religions, Narrative and Imagination,* trans. David Pellauer (Minneapolis: Fortress Press, 1995), 11.

10. For further reflection on these points, see Philip Sheldrake, "The Wisdom of History," *The Way Supplement* 96 (Autumn 1999): 17–26.

11. For a study of the impact of critical theory on theology, see Graham Ward, *Theology and Contemporary Critical Theory,* 2nd ed. (London: Macmillan; New York: St. Martin's Press, 2000).

12. Ibid., ix.

13. See Judith Berling, "Christian Spirituality: Intrinsically Interdisciplinary," in this volume.

14. Ward, *Theology,* ix.

15. On "constitutive" and "problematic" disciplines, see Sandra Schneiders, "The Study of Christian Spirituality: Contours and Dynamics of a Discipline," *Christian Spirituality Bulletin* 6, no. 1 (Spring 1998): 1–12.

16. See Philip Sheldrake, "Interpreting Texts and Traditions" in *Spirituality and Society in the New Millennium,* ed. Ursula King (Brighton: Sussex Academic Press, 2001), 19–34.

17. For useful essays on cultural analysis and theology, see Delwin Brown, Sheila Greeve Davaney, and Kathryn Tanner, eds., *Converging on Culture: Theologians in Dialogue with Cultural Analysis and Criticism* (Oxford: Oxford University Press, 2001).

18. For a summary of the issues, see the editors' introductory essay "Culture, Power, Place: Ethnography at the End of an Era," in *Culture, Power, Place: Explorations in Critical Anthropology,* ed. Akhil Gupta and James Ferguson (Durham, NC: Duke University Press, 1999), 2–29.

19. Brown, Davaney, and Tanner, *Converging on Culture,* vi.

20. See Michel de Certeau, *The Practice of Everyday Life* (Berkeley and Los Angeles: University of California Press, 1988); and Michel de Certeau, Luce Giard, and Pierre Mayol, *The Practice of Everyday Life,* vol. 2, Living and Cooking (Minneapolis: University of Minnesota Press, 1998).

21. Arthur Holder and Lisa Dahill, "Teaching Christian Spirituality in Seminaries Today," *Christian Spirituality Bulletin* 7 (Winter 1999): 9–12.

22. See Michael Downey, *Understanding Christian Spirituality* (New York: Paulist Press, 1997), 129–31; Sandra Schneiders, *Written That You May Believe: Encountering Jesus in the Fourth Gospel* (New York: Crossroad, 1999); Rowan Williams, *On Christian Theology* (Oxford: Blackwell, 2000), chap. 4.

23. See David Tracy, *The Analogical Imagination: Christian Theology and the Culture of Pluralism* (New York: Crossroad, 1991), chap. 1.

24. In this, Tracy differs from some other theologians who have written on the role of cultural analysis as a theological partner. See, for example, Delwin Brown, "Refashioning Self and Other: Theology, Academy, and the New Ethnography," in Brown, Davaney, and Tanner, eds., *Converging on Culture,* 41–55.

25. Tracy, *The Analogical Imagination,* 360.

26. Ibid., 77–78.

27. Eric O. Springsted, "Theology and Spirituality: Or, Why Theology Is Not Critical Reflection on Religious Experience," in *Spirituality and Theology: Essays in Honor of Diogenes Allen,* ed. Eric O. Springsted (Louisville, KY: Westminster/John Knox Press, 1998), 49.

28. On a theology of interreligious conversation deeply informed by Christian spirituality, see Michael Barnes, *Theology and the Dialogue of Religions* (Cambridge: Cambridge University Press, 2002). On the spiritual foundations of politically engaged theologies, see Gaspar Martinez, *Confronting the Mystery of God: Political, Liberation, and Public Theologies* (New York: Continuum, 2001). On the dimension of aesthetics in theology and spirituality, see the classic twentieth-century treatment in Hans Urs von Balthasar, *The Glory of the Lord: A Theological*

Aesthetics, 7 vols., various translators (San Francisco: Ignatius Press, 1982–89). Also see Jeremy S. Begbie, *Voicing Creation's Praise: Towards a Theology of the Arts* (Edinburgh: T & T Clark, 1991); Frank Burch Brown, *Good Taste, Bad Taste, and Christian Taste: Aesthetics in Religious Life* (New York: Oxford University Press, 2000); and Nicholas Wolterstorff, *Art in Action: Toward a Christian Aesthetic* (Grand Rapids, MI: Eerdmans, 1980). See also the essays by Douglas Burton-Christie, "The Weight of the World: The Heaviness of Nature in Spiritual Experience," and Alejandro García-Rivera, "Interfaith Ethics: Where Theology and Spirituality Meet," both in this volume.

29. See, for example, the contribution of Robert John Russell, "Spirituality and Science," in *The New Westminster Dictionary of Christian Spirituality,* ed. by Robert John Russell (London: SCM Press; Louisville, KY: Westminster/ John Knox Press, 2005); idem, "The Contributions of the Natural Sciences for the Academic Discipline of Christian Spirituality," in this volume; and his longer study, in "Natural Sciences," *The Blackwell Companion to Christian Spirituality,* ed. Arthur Holder (Oxford: Blackwell, 2005), 325-44.

30. Schneiders, *Written That You May Believe,* esp. 16–18. Also Sandra Schneiders's comments on Christian spirituality as a self-implicating enterprise in "The Study of Christian Spirituality: Contours and Dynamics of a Discipline," *Christian Spirituality Bulletin* 6, no.1 (Spring 1998): 9–11 and *The Revelatory Text: Interpreting the New Testament as Sacred Scripture* (Collegeville, MN: The Liturgical Press, 1999), esp. 11–26. See also the classic study of monastic exegesis, Jean Leclercq, *The Love of Learning and the Desire for God: A Study of Monastic Culture* (New York: Fordham University Press, 1982).

31. See Michael Sells, *Mystical Languages of Unsaying* (Chicago: University of Chicago Press, 1994), 4.

32. Martinez, *Confronting the Mystery,* 87.

33. Rowan Williams, "Theological Integrity," in *On Christian Theology* (Oxford: Blackwell, 2001), 5.

34. Ibid.

35. Ibid.

36. Williams, *On Christian Theology,* xii–xvi.

37. Williams, "Theological Integrity," 7.

38. Michel de Certeau, *The Mystic Fable* (Chicago: University of Chicago Press, 1992), 299.

39. Williams, "Theological Integrity," 10–11.

40. Ibid., 11.

41. Ibid., 12.

2

CHRISTIAN SPIRITUALITY
Intrinsically Interdisciplinary

Judith A. Berling

DEFENSE OF THE DISCIPLINE

Sandra Schneiders has been a devoted champion of the discipline of Christian spirituality, seeking to establish its place in the academy and to dispel the clouds of confusion that have surrounded it. She has written articulately to argue what Christian spirituality is not: not theology (although it does have a theological moment),[1] not anthropology (although it may at times borrow anthropological approaches),[2] not religious studies (although it often studies the same phenomena).[3] Schneiders stipulates what Christian spirituality is not in order to demarcate this discipline from other disciplines, establishing a distinctive niche in the academy.

The distinctive niche has enabled the institutionalization of Christian spirituality: as a field of doctoral study and as a professional society (Society for the Study of Christian Spirituality) with its own journal.

Schneiders has also articulated the material object of Christian spirituality (lived Christian faith) and its formal object (experience).[4] She writes, "[Christian] spirituality as a discipline...seeks to understand [Christian experience] as it actually occurs, as it actually transforms its subject toward fullness of life in Christ, that is, toward self-transcending life-integration within the Christian community of faith."[5] She has identified its methodology as "a hermeneutically governed interaction of description,

35

critical analysis, and constructive interpretation for the purpose of the fullest possible understanding of the phenomenon."[6]

In all of her essays Schneiders has characterized Christian spirituality as interdisciplinary: "essentially an interdisciplinary discipline,"[7] "the interdisciplinary study of Christian religious experience as Christian, as religious, and as experience,"[8] "necessarily interdisciplinary, cross-cultural, and inter-religious,"[9] and "intrinsically and irreducibly interdisciplinary."[10] These are strong and unambiguous claims.

The purpose of this chapter is to unpack those claims, exploring more precisely in what respects Christian spirituality is "intrinsically interdisciplinary." I probe these claims closely against the backdrop of interdisciplinary theory, bringing to light dimensions not yet addressed and highlighting the implications of the claims.

DISCIPLINES AND INTERDISCIPLINARITY

The term *interdisciplinary* is used in a number of senses: to delineate a new discipline that has emerged from the interface of two others (for example, biophysics), to "mark off" an emerging conversation among scholars from various disciplines (for example, performance studies), to characterize or denigrate research and writing that does not fit neatly into a single category (for example, gender studies). Whether the word is used for the creation of a new entity (an *interdiscipline*[11]), a collaborative endeavor, or subversive boundary crossing, the word *interdisciplinary* is dependent on the notion of the *discipline*. But the notion of discipline itself is complex and problematic.

In part, the idea of academic discipline is predicated upon history: a discipline is a longstanding division of the university. Christian spirituality is, as disciplines go, one of the new kids on the block. Like the many "studies" (American studies, religious studies) Christian spirituality emerged as a separate discipline in the second half of the twentieth century. All of these late disciplines have been challenged on historical grounds; they do not have the claim of a long-established history.

The second dimension of an academic discipline is its institutional identity. Disciplines are institutionalized as academic departments, professional societies, and professional journals. They function as "guilds." The departments train future members, setting the standards of knowledge and practice; the professional societies are guild fellowships; and the journals establish guild standards by what they accept for publication.

The third dimension of an academic discipline is intellectual: epistemological assumptions; a distinctive lens for defining, selecting, and interpreting what is to be known; accepted ways of knowing; a range of methodologies; specialized language; literature representing both debates within the field and consensus that delineates it from other disciplines; standards and rules for legitimate argument. That is to say, an academic discipline represents a range of intellectual practices and assumptions.[12]

None of these dimensions of the academic discipline is unproblematic. The historical sense of the disciplines ignores the dramatic changes in universities since the Enlightenment, and particularly in the development of the research university in the twentieth century. Important scientific fields (for example, computer science and cognitive science) did not exist before the middle of the twentieth century.

The institutional aspect of the university changes more slowly, but virtually all university disciplines, including those in the human sciences, are now internally diverse and in contention. Historians who study written texts and archives work in very different ways and with different assumptions from those who use computer models to analyze data sets. There is no longer a single set of assumptions, warrants, and data for all historians; rather, there is a set of internal debates and discussions about how best to study history.

Not only are there diverse established practices within each of the disciplines, but there is also an enormous amount of crossing over into other disciplines. Julie Thompson Klein has written of such boundary crossings:

> John Higham describes the academy as "a house in
> which the inhabitants are leaning out of the many open

windows gaily chatting with the neighbors, while the doors between the rooms stayed closed" (*Challenge of Connecting Learning* 1990, 15). A great deal more, in fact, is going on. Some are happily chatting. Some are arguing with their neighbors, and others have fallen out of the windows. Many doors remain closed. Yet other doors have been broken down, and in some cases entirely new buildings have been constructed.[13]

The tidy institutionalized picture of the disciplines, then, is more than a little misleading. Yet, despite the internal heterogeneity and boundary crossings, the institutionalization of departments is still powerful. To take but one example, jobs are still listed by department. There are numerous jobs listed as theology, history, or biblical studies, and very few jobs listed as Christian spirituality. In sum, while disciplines are internally divided and have increasingly porous boundaries, the academic world is still organized in terms of the disciplines.

The discussion of disciplines lays the groundwork for a fundamental distinction between two aspects of interdisciplinarity: structural versus dynamic or operational.[14] The structural dimension of interdisciplinarity consists of the disciplines or fields brought together in an interdisciplinary field and their relative weights and roles. Schneiders offers a structural analysis of the interdisciplinarity of Christian spirituality, which I discuss below. Dynamic or operational interdisciplinarity pertains to the practices of the interdisciplinary scholar, analyzing the operations and boundary crossings that make up the work. Dynamic or operational interdisciplinarity requires a different level and mode of analysis.

THE STRUCTURAL INTERDISCIPLINARITY OF CHRISTIAN SPIRITUALITY

Constitutive Disciplines

Sandra Schneiders has offered a structural analysis of Christian spirituality as an academic discipline. She begins her analysis by specifying the material object (*what* Christian spirituality studies) as "lived Christian faith," and its formal object (*particular aspect* under which it is studied) as "experience."[15] She goes on to specify layers of interdisciplinarity in the study of Christian spirituality. First, she specifies two constitutive disciplines: scripture and the history of Christianity. These are constitutive, in her view, "because they supply the positive data of Christian religious experience as well as its norm and hermeneutical context."[16] All scholars of Christian spirituality, she argues, must have a basic grounding in these two constitutive disciplines, by which she means a broad or deep familiarity with the Bible and Christian history and the methodological competence to handle materials responsibly.[17] Is she arguing that scholars of Christian spirituality must also be biblical scholars and historians of Christianity? Not exactly. In order to better understand what she is claiming and not claiming, we need to examine her statements more closely.

The claim that biblical studies and history of Christianity "supply the positive data" does not in itself entail a specific commitment to the disciplines. For example, Freud used "the data" of the story of Moses for his psychoanalytic theory in a way that owed nothing to biblical studies or to the history of Judaism. Schneiders, however, makes a more specific claim: these disciplines "supply the positive data of Christian religious experience." This claim invokes the traditions and assumptions of the disciplines (as well as of the Christian tradition). The biblical stories are not merely tales to be studied and analyzed; they are the "meta-story into which each individual and communal Christian story is integrated and by which it is patterned."[18] Likewise, history is not merely a congeries of events, movements, and incidents; it is "the general hermeneutical framework for the interpretation of every phenomenon of Christian experience, past or present."[19] While these clarifications tie the study of Christian spirituality more closely to biblical texts and Christian history, these ties are primarily to a hermeneutical or interpretive context. These two fields provide the necessary background, context, and basic training for studies of Christian spirituality. To understand the force of this point, substitute Buddhist spirituality for Christian spirituality. Scholars of Buddhist spirituality will turn to

Buddhist texts and history for their positive data, norms, and hermeneutical contexts; they need background and grounding in both textual studies and history, but the extent of their required expertise in textual studies or history will depend on their particular scholarship. This analogy suggests that these two disciplines are constitutive of the curriculum (general training) of Christian spirituality, and therefore of the discipline as institutionalized. The role they play in any particular study of Christian spirituality will vary.

Schneiders argues that biblical studies and history of Christianity are constitutive because of their centrality to the hermeneutic context. Her argument holds for the centrality of these disciplines for the understanding of spirituality *as Christian*. However, for the understanding of Christian spirituality *as spirituality* I would argue that comparative religions is also a constitutive discipline. Other religious traditions have traditions of spiritual practice that supply positive data for understanding and interrogating, and developing various categories of religious experience. Schneiders admitted something very close to this point when she wrote:

> Spirituality is ecumenical, interreligious, and cross-cultural. This does not mean that every investigation in the field is comparative in nature but rather that the context within which spiritual experience is studied is anthropologically inclusive. Even the study of Christian spirituality as such does not proceed on the assumption that Christianity exhausts or includes the whole of religious reality or that only Christian data is relevant for an understanding of Christian spiritual experience. A study of Christian mysticism, for example, must be carried on within and in terms of the ongoing cross-cultural and interreligious discussion of mysticism, religious and nonreligious, as a human experience.[20]

Thus, comparative religion supplies important comparative data and analytical categories that make the understanding of Christian spirituality possible. The hermeneutical context, then, is not only Christian experience (past, studied for present meaning), but also human religious experience as a resource for understanding Christian spirituality. The role of comparative studies is not to "contribute to" the spirituality or practice of Christians, but to contribute to the *understanding* of Christian spirituality by offering an additional hermeneutical resource.

Thus, extending her logic, biblical studies, history of Christianity, and comparative religion all become "constitutive disciplines" insofar as they supply positive data and the hermeneutical contexts for understanding Christian spirituality. This is not to claim, however, that scholars of Christian spirituality must be experts in all of these disciplines. They are part of the curriculum designed to train scholars of Christian spirituality. Scholars in the field must have a solid background and sufficient methodological competence to handle materials competently.

Putting this point in terms of interdisciplinary theory, we might say that Christian spirituality builds upon or borrows extensively from the disciplines of biblical studies, history of Christianity, and comparative religion. Interdisciplinary scholarship often builds upon and borrows from a variety of disciplines. Responsible interdisciplinarity takes seriously what is called "the burden of comprehension" in the act of borrowing.[21] At the very least, the burden of comprehension requires a "basic understanding of how something is used in its original context."[22] Schneiders's explanation of scholarly responsibility to the constitutive disciplines is a very strong form of the burden of comprehension. In the case of biblical studies and history of Christianity, the scholar is building upon a foundation of these two disciplines; in the case of comparative religion, the scholar borrows as necessary to aid understanding, but does so responsibly.

Problematic Disciplines

Schneiders's description of Christian spirituality as an academic discipline also includes a broad range of what she calls problematic disciplines, "called into play and integrated into the methodology of a particular study because of the problematic of the phenomenon being studied."[23] Her concept of problematic disciplines invokes the model of "problem-based interdisciplinarity." The problem-based model stems historically from team-based interdisciplinary projects, often in the social sciences or the health field. Complex problems (urban planning, care of a patient with multiple medical conditions) are deemed to require a team approach, pulling together experts from many disciplines.[24]

The problem-based model is extended from the team-based projects to academic research by a single scholar on problems or objects of study so rich and complex that no single discipline can exhaust them. Schneiders argues that the object of spirituality or religious experience is one such object. Christian spirituality, she writes, "is interdisciplinary because of the complex and multi-faceted character of spiritual experience as such."[25] The choice of particular problematic disciplines in each case is more properly a matter of dynamic or operational spirituality, to be discussed below. The structural point is that religious experience, the object of study of Christian spirituality, is so multifaceted that it requires utilizing multiple disciplines.

Let us examine more closely the object of study and its inter-disciplinary entailments. Schneiders wrote in 1989 that "spirituality is interested in the experience *as* experience, i.e., in its phenomenological wholeness."[26] There is a significant problem with studying experience as such; namely, the scholar does not have direct access to the object of study. This has been recognized as the limit of phenomenology.[27] Lacking direct access, the scholar explores its various intersubjective dimensions[28] in a hermeneutical process that seeks to move toward ever greater understanding. This is why Schneiders argues that Christian spirituality requires a hermeneutical approach and methodology.[29] The intersubjective dimensions (texts and human reports, as well as the analysis of those dimensions by means of various disciplines) are all partial and indirect approaches toward what is intended as an understanding of the religious experience itself.

While this may appear to be shaky ground, it is familiar ground to interdisciplinary scholars. Interdisciplinary scholars tend to be "broad gauged" and "interested in problems of wide latitude and complexity." They are interdisciplinary "collators," gifted in exercising the hermeneutical function.[30] When facing problems of wide latitude and complexity, scholars rely on colla-

tions and employ hermeneutical methods to create a viable interpretation from disparate and indirect fragments.

There are two significant implications of the hermeneutical
problem-based approach of Christian spirituality. First,
Schneiders is arguing against a reductive interpretation beholden
only to a single discipline. For example, a psychologist might
study the experiences of Teresa of Avila using only the assumptions and analytical categories of psychology to explain her experiences in psychological terms. This would not be a study of
Teresa's religious experience, much less her Christian religious
experience; it would be a study of her psychological experience.
To study religious experience as such, both the religious dimensions and the particular experience need to be addressed. A
scholar of Christian spirituality might use psychological methods
to help interpret Teresa's religious experience. Such a study would
put into conversation (and tension) the psychological and religious dimensions of the experience in order to seek a fuller understanding.

The second implication of the hermeneutical problem-based
interdisciplinarity of Christian spirituality is that studies can offer
simply an interpretation of the phenomenon under study: no
instance of Christian religious experience can ever be fully and
finally understood, for several reasons: (1) it has so many aspects
that they could not be included in a single interpretation; (2) it
cannot be known in and of itself; and (3) interpreters bring to the
act of interpretation their own experiences and assumptions that
shed new light on the phenomenon studied.

DYNAMIC OR OPERATIONAL
INTERDISCIPLINARITY

In a given research project the scholar of Christian spirituality will use both constitutive and problematic disciplines in order
to study the phenomenon at hand. Depending on the topic, a constitutive discipline may emerge from its background role in the
curriculum to become the lead discipline, as biblical studies would
in a study of the spirituality of discipleship in Mark's Gospel.[31]

Likewise, a problematic discipline may take the lead, as in literary studies framing a study of the metaphor of water in the writings of Teresa of Avila.[32] Schneiders appropriately argues that graduate students need to be adequately trained in those disciplines they intend to use as their scholarly toolbox. She writes, "Mentors have to insure that the interdisciplinary methodology which students develop to pursue their research is sufficiently broad and sufficiently focused that the student will be neither a shallow generalist nor an academic lone ranger."[33]

Yet, the picture is not quite as neat as the quotation suggests. Schneiders' depiction works very well in terms of mentoring graduate students in Christian spirituality toward and through their doctoral dissertations. The dissertation topic selected (an issue, or problem) will define the depth of background and methodological training needed in each of the constitutive and problematic disciplines. So far, so good. But what about the next major project after the dissertation? Will the choices students make in preparation for the dissertation serve as a sufficient base for future topics of research? Are they locking themselves into a particular model of interdisciplinarity, a particular combination of disciplines, seriously delimiting the topics they may pursue?

Granted, every scholar must make choices and specialize. As Schneiders writes, "No one is, or ever will be, a universal expert in spirituality. Rather the scholar becomes a specialist in some area or aspect of spirituality and continues to learn throughout his or her career."[34] As Schneiders also notes, "Method no longer dictates what can be studied or how. Rather, methods are tools in service of research that is increasingly dictated by the interests of researchers and the needs of society rather than by the agendas of the academic guilds."[35] Scholars of Christian spirituality with lively minds will move beyond the confines of what they studied as doctoral students and move in new directions, crossing boundaries and entering territories hitherto little explored by them.

The likelihood of new interests developing in lively scholars suggests a footnote to Schneiders's principles of mentorship. As she writes, "What we need to avoid in ourselves and prevent in our students is, on the one hand, an 'undisciplined' mixing of methods used without sufficient attention to the demands of the disciplines involved and, on the other hand, imprisonment in narrow disciplinary enclaves through fear of being less than expert."[36] This is a fine principle, but putting it into practice means not only grounding students in what they need to get through the doctoral program and the work they already envision, but also instilling a sense of interdisciplinary responsibility so that they will have both the imagination and courage to cross boundaries and the knowledge of how to do so responsibly.

Let us consider also the practical dimensions of specialization. Scholarship in Christian spirituality requires competence in the language and historical context of one's sources; this is where history of Christianity and biblical studies are clearly seen to be constitutive disciplines. Thus, while it is possible to conceive of a scholar attempting to build a career on a certain sort of psychological approach to understanding Christian spirituality, scholars in the field are likely to suspect any study not competent in the language and context of its source material. The authority of linguistic and historical competence will tend to bind a scholar to a particular period or linguistic group of texts or phenomena, with the "freshness" of approach deriving from the issue explored in each particular study. And, as we have seen, the issue explored will determine the problematic discipline brought into play. Thus, while scholars may spend years researching Benedictine spirituality, they will presumably ask a number of different questions about Benedictine practices across their careers. This dynamic may tempt them to stretch too far, to engage in "undisciplined" boundary crossing. Scholars in Christian spirituality require rigorous training in how to cross boundaries responsibly.

The most fundamental question about the dynamic interdisciplinary practices of the scholar of Christian spirituality has to do with how the actual practices function in an interdisciplinary way. Christian spirituality follows the problem-based model of interdisciplinary research. Historically, this model derives from projects done by teams of experts from a variety of fields. The major challenge of such projects is how to transcend the multidisciplinary approach, in which each expert studies the problem and contributes a solution in the terms of one specific expertise. In multidisciplinarity, each discipline contributes its findings, but there is no way to reconcile or integrate the findings. Schneiders has claimed that Christian spirituality is "not only multidisciplinary, but explicitly interdisciplinary."[37] In terms of interdisciplinary theory, this would imply that the "findings" of various disciplines brought into play are somehow reconciled or integrated.[38] Schneiders is not entirely clear about how the integration happens, except to say (1) that Christian religious experience is never entirely explained by or reduced to the explanation of another discipline, and (2) understanding Christian religious experience is a hermeneutical process that draws on many sources of analysis.

In her discussion of the problematic disciplines, Schneiders suggests three examples to illustrate how other disciplines might function in the study of Teresa of Avila's spirituality: role of humanity, using theology; the metaphor of water, using literary studies; the role of achievement and self-esteem, using psychology or feminist theory.[39] Each of these projects could be done purely as a project of the "other" discipline: the role of humanity in Teresa's religious thought; the metaphor of water in her writings; the role of achievement and self-esteem in her life. In the case of Christian spirituality, however, these analyses are used in service of understanding her spirituality, her religious experience, rather than as ends in themselves; hence, the theological role of humanity in Teresa's religious experience; what the water metaphor in her writings reveals about her religious experience; how issues of achievement and self-esteem shape, contribute to, or inhibit her religious experience. The problematic disciplines are used instrumentally (to serve the ends of understanding religious experience) rather than "synoptically" (to claim that all study of religious experience must include a theological, literary, or psychological dimension; that the discipline is incomplete or insufficient without those additions).[40] Christian spirituality research uses these other disciplines as an aid to understanding religious experience.

The instrumental use of other disciplines in the practice of Christian spirituality raises yet another issue. Are scholars of Christian spirituality simply "raiders," border crossers who take what they need and give nothing in return? Or does the use of other disciplines in Christian spirituality also contribute to those disciplines? Interdisciplinary theory frequently refers to trading zones (between disciplines), interlanguages (new pidgins developed to promote interdisciplinary thinking), and hybrid fields.[41] These metaphors suggest ongoing interactions, conversations, and mutual enrichments. Schneiders's writings on Christian spirituality seem to suggest a one-way instrumental borrowing, a "raiding" of other disciplines when they are useful. However, I suspect that this impression is misleading and is caused by the fact that her articles seek to define the field, its boundaries, and its practices over against other disciplines. It would be useful for Christian spirituality scholars to consider not only what they take or gain from other fields, but also what and how they can contribute to them. This is fairly self-evident in terms of the constitutive disciplines; every study of Christian spirituality contributes something to the history of Christianity and/or biblical studies and to comparative religion's study of religious experience. Christian spirituality scholars also need to consider what they can contribute to literary studies, psychology, sociology, and other disciplines of which they avail themselves. Attention to contributions to other disciplines would deepen and nuance the sense of responsibility and accountability paid to those disciplines. The "instrumental" use of other disciplines would also become "dialogical" or "relational."

I have to this point evaded a discussion of the relation of Christian spirituality to theology. This is a complex issue. Schneiders argues that theology is related "to both the constitutive and the problematic layers" of Christian spirituality, but primarily to the problematic as "an analytical and critical tool, among other tools, for the understanding and criticism of spirituality phenomena."[42] Theology's role as a problematic discipline is, if I may say so, unproblematic. However, its putative role as a constitutive discipline rests on a very broad definition of theology ("the Church's reflection on both Scripture and Christian experience"[43]) rather than on a strict definition of it as a discipline with its distinctive categories and habits of analysis. She also argues, "Although spirituality and theology in the strict sense are mutually related in that theology is a moment in the study of spirituality and vice versa, theology does not contain or control spirituality."[44] The most

47

important point of this statement is to establish spirituality as a field independent of theology as a discipline. However, the claim that "theology is a moment in the study of Christian spirituality" does not refer to theology as a discipline, but rather to a reflexive movement that stems from the location of Christian spirituality in a theological school or department. Scholars of Christian spirituality reflect theologically on the meaning and implications of their work much as all scholars in theological disciplines do, and much as all Christians reflect theologically on their lives of faith and practice. That is not to say that Christian spirituality is a subdiscipline of systematic theology, or that only professional systematic theologians may reflect theologically on Christian spirituality by means of their established systematic categories. The word *theology* is relevant in the more general sense and not in the professionalized disciplinary sense.

Schneiders argues that the study of Christian spirituality, as any hermeneutical operation, has three moments: descriptive, analytical, and constructive.[45] The issue is, of what does this constructive moment consist? It will, as she rightly notes, transform the subject, the interpreter. Following her definition of the field, that should mean that the scholar's understanding of religious experience (not just this instance, but of the nature and possibilities of religious experience) is transformed. It should also mean that the possibilities of Christian religious experience—indeed of "the Christian"—are transformed. Thus scholars not only describe and critically analyze the particular subject at hand but come to an understanding of that particular object that broadens and transforms their general understanding of religious experience and of "Christian." And this broader understanding opens the scholar to new possibilities of religious experience and "Christian" in their own life experiences.

When the scholar is studying in a Christian theological school or department, that broader understanding will entail theological reflection, broadly conceived. Such theological reflection is the constructive or reflexive moment in all theological scholarship; it is not a disciplined reflection of the systematic theologian.

If, however, scholars of Christian spirituality were to be located in the religious studies departments of secular universities, the understanding might be "theological" only in the sense that they would understand the Christian tradition more deeply than before; the reflexive appropriation of understanding in those cases might have more to do with a fuller appreciation of the possibilities of human religious experience.

Since Christian spirituality is in fact practiced almost exclusively within theological schools and departments of theology, the above argument may seem moot. But it is an important point, for it shows that the location of Christian spirituality, its audience, and its communities of accountability shape the reflexive move and the hermeneutical appropriation that derives from the discipline. They also shape the understandings of each of the discipline's normative parameters.

Schneiders has argued that biblical studies and the history of Christianity provide the resources, norms, and hermeneutical context of Christian spirituality. Yet there is more than one way to construe each of these norms and contexts. Global, contextual biblical interpretations, for instance, draw on cultural and religious resources that introduce spiritualities that would seem to many borderline or foreign, but they are "Christian" in certain contexts. Likewise, the global history of Christianity can include within its purview a broad sweep of movements, practices, and traditions that seem borderline or "non-Christian" to some. The breadth or narrowness by which these two norms and contexts are construed will shape future dimensions of Christian spirituality.

CONCLUSION

Given her agenda of establishing Christian spirituality as an autonomous discipline distinct from several fields with which it is sometimes confused, Sandra Schneiders has articulated the objects, structures, and practices of the discipline that locate it clearly in the academy and the theological school or department. To her credit, as she has drawn the boundaries of the field, she has also attempted to clarify its fundamental interdisciplinary nature, distinguishing between "constitutive" and "problematic" disciplines, borrowed for instrumental purposes. Her depiction establishes the structural interdisciplinarity of the discipline, although—given the location of Christian spirituality—she somewhat underplays the role of comparative religion in that structural picture.

Her writings can be extended to explore the dynamic or operational interdisciplinarity of the scholar of Christian spirituality. Probing the operational dimensions raises a number of questions that the discipline is now in a position to address.

Notes

1. Sandra M. Schneiders, "Spirituality in the Academy," *Theological Studies* 50 (1989): 687, 689.

2. Sandra M. Schneiders, "Spirituality as an Academic Discipline: Reflections from Experience," *Christian Spirituality Bulletin* 1, no. 2 (Fall 1993): 13–14.

3. Sandra M. Schneiders, "A Hermeneutical Approach to the Study of Christian Spirituality," *Christian Spirituality Bulletin* 2, no. 1 (Spring 1994): 9.

4. Sandra M. Schneiders, "The Study of Christian Spirituality: Contours and Dynamics of a Discipline," *Christian Spirituality Bulletin* 6, no. 1 (Spring 1998): 2.

5. Schneiders, "The Study of Christian Spirituality," 3. First bracket mine; second in text.

6. Schneiders, "A Hermeneutical Approach to the Study of Christian Spirituality," 14.

7. Schneiders, "Spirituality in the Academy," 692.

8. Schneiders, "Spirituality as an Academic Discipline," 15.

9. Schneiders, "A Hermeneutical Approach to the Study of Christian Spirituality," 14.

10. Schneiders, "The Study of Christian Spirituality," 3.

11. Interdiscipline describes new fields that emerge from interdisciplinary research. See Julie Thompson Klein, *Crossing Boundaries: Knowledge, Disciplinarities, and Interdisciplinarities* (Charlottesville: University Press of Virginia, 1996), 78–84.

12. Judith A. Berling, "Disciplines, Disciplines-in-Becoming, and Methodologies," Handout for IDS6000, Seminar on Interdisciplinarity.

13. Klein, *Crossing Boundaries,* 19.

14. See Judith A. Berling, "Models of Disciplinarity," handout for IDS6000, Seminar on Interdisciplinarity.

15. Schneiders, "The Study of Christian Spirituality," 2–3.

16. Ibid., 3.

17. Ibid., 4.

18. Ibid.

19. Ibid.

20. Schneiders, "Spirituality in the Academy," 693.

21. Julie Thompson Klein, *Interdisciplinarity* (Detroit: Wayne State University Press, 1990), 85–94, esp. 88.

22. Ibid., 88.

23. Schneiders, "The Study of Christian Spirituality," 3–5.

24. Klein, *Interdisciplinarity,* 121–39.

25. Schneiders, "A Hermeneutical Approach to the Study of Christian Spirituality," 12.

26. Schneiders, "Spirituality in the Academy," 692.

27. See Gavin Flood, *Beyond Phenomenology: Rethinking the Study of Religion* (London: Cassell, 1999), 91–116.

28. Ibid., 108–13.

29. Schneiders, "A Hermeneutical Approach to the Study of Christian Spirituality."

30. Klein, *Interdisciplinarity,* 186, citing Henry Winthrop, "Methodological and Hermeneutic Functions in Interdisciplinary Education," *Educational Theory* 14 (April 1964): 118 –27.

31. Schneiders, "The Study of Christian Spirituality," 4.

32. Ibid., 5.

33. Ibid., 6.

34. Ibid., 7.

35. Ibid.

36. Ibid.

37. Schneiders, "A Hermeneutical Approach to the Study of Christian Spirituality," 9.

38. See Klein, *Interdisciplinarity,* esp. 121–39. The importance of integration cannot be overstressed. For example, the major society of interdisciplinary scholars is called the Association of Integrative Studies.

39. Schneiders, "The Study of Christian Spirituality," 5.

40. Klein, *Interdisciplinarity,* 41ff.

41. Klein, *Crossing Boundaries,* esp. 1–37.

42. Schneiders, "The Study of Christian Spirituality," 4.

43. Ibid.

44. Schneiders, "Spirituality in the Academy," 687.

45. Schneiders, "A Hermeneutical Approach to the Study of Christian Spirituality," 12–13.

3

WRITING IN SPIRITUALITY AS A SELF-IMPLICATING ACT
Reflections on Authorial Disclosure and the Hiddenness of the Self

Belden C. Lane

Learning to get out of the way is the most difficult task in spiritual writing. Yet in a genre of literature that dares to speak of God, readers expect the author's unconcealed presence. Credibility depends on resolute, transparent honesty. There are times when we judge writers' reliability, not only by the thoroughness of their scholarship, but by the evidence they give of having experienced something of which they speak. Yet in hinting at this experience, authors must also disappear. If they do not excuse themselves quickly, they run the risk of intruding too long on a subject that, having been raised to consciousness, can be distorted by an over-self-consciousness. In short, authors must dance lightly and leave. It is not, after all, about them.

Sandra Schneiders calls attention to the importance of this insight, modeling it in her own writing and reflecting on the demands it makes of researchers in the field of spirituality as an academic discipline. She argues that the methodological style that characterizes work in spirituality is inherently participative.

> Like psychology, spirituality deals with material that often cannot be understood except through analogy with personal experience. Spirituality deals with spiritual experience as such, not merely with ideas about or

principles governing such experience (although these certainly have a role in the research).[1]

She adds that work in this highly participative field of spirituality must also submit itself to the appropriate objectivity of the discipline. Scholarship should be both rigorously critical and self-implicative. The writer, in other words, has to become alternately transparent and opaque. The well-timed presence and absence of the authorial self are essential in the writing of spirituality, especially in areas of research where the analysis of experience crosses over into practice and performance.

Achieving this balance between academic and personal credibility requires the use of multiple methodological approaches. Researchers in the field of spirituality wrestle with problems similar, for example, to those faced by ethnographers of religion. These social anthropologists explore the lived experience of religious ideas within a particular cultural matrix. A recent, field-defining book, *Personal Knowledge and Beyond: Reshaping the Ethnography of Religion,* explores this perennial question of ethnographers' personal involvement in their research.[2] To what extent does one allow one's life to be touched by one's work, even to participate in the shaping of one's research?

The question has never been simply an academic one. The problem of the self recurs repeatedly in the great spiritual texts of Western religious thought. Authors continually struggle with how to use their own spiritual experience in pointing the reader to the Divine without drawing undue attention to the one doing the pointing. From Augustine to Julian of Norwich to Thomas Merton, the spiritual writer regularly engages in a delicate dance of revealing and concealing the authorial self.

Researchers in spirituality are caught in a similar dilemma of bridging the distance between a given historical and cultural expression of spirituality and the world view of their contemporary readers. In overcoming this distance writers may sometimes use their own experience of the "other" as a heuristic device, inviting readers into a deeper understanding of the phenomenon described. But even when they keep themselves at a distance, they invariably encounter what Schneiders describes as the "self-implicating" character of the discipline of spirituality.[3] As much as the scholar aspires for neutrality, the self inevitably "gets in the way" and/or "helps" in the process of facilitating the reader's comprehension of the unfamiliar.

This is particularly apparent in ethnographic fieldwork among religious scholars. The possibilities and problems of research in religious ethnography are exemplified in Robert Orsi's studies of Italian Catholic piety in East Harlem and American Catholic women's devotion to Saint Jude, in Thomas Tweed's description of Cuban refugees and their attachment to a Marian Shrine in Miami, and in Karen McCarthy Brown's compelling analysis of Mama Lola, a Vodou priestess in Brooklyn.[4] In each case the authors become inescapably a part of their descriptive analysis. While this is what makes their work so readable, the still prevalent notion of the self as a "contaminant" in social and religious research raises questions about the "objectivity" of their inquiry.

Stories from these researchers demonstrate how their critical distance as objective scholars is often challenged or compromised. In the midst of his research on the devotion to Saint Jude, for instance, Orsi tells of being invited to present a paper in New York City. As his plane was caught in a circling pattern over LaGuardia an hour before he was to speak, the pilot announced over the intercom that they would not be able to land. They were being rerouted to Philadelphia. Orsi admits to suddenly praying almost unconsciously in that moment, "Help me, Saint Jude." To his amazement, the pilot's voice returned, saying a slot had unexpectedly opened and that they would be on the ground in five minutes. "I am not a devout," Orsi confesses in his book, "but I promised to tell this story at the time, and here it is."[5] In this instance, Orsi—as critical ethnographer—came face to face with the extraordinary intersubjectivity evoked by the nature of his research.

Similarly, Thomas Tweed speaks of attending Cuban Catholic events in Miami where he is regularly mistaken for one of the faithful. On one occasion he found himself inadvertently praying to Our Lady of Charity of Cobre for the well-being of Mother Cuba.[6] Karen McCarthy Brown admits to becoming so attached to Alourdes (the woman known as Mama Lola) that she considers her an adopted mother. On holidays when she is not with her own family, she is likely to be in Brooklyn with her friend. She gives credit to Alourdes for help in shaping her research and even shares the profits from the book with her. These narratives reveal the inevitable ambiguities that arise as a result of ethnographers' personal investment in their research.

Scholars in spirituality frequently find themselves pulled between historical and ethnographic approaches, between meticulous work in archival collections and unpredictable work in the field. Tweed admits to feeling frustrated by the "muteness of the dead" when he focuses more or less "safely" on the historical traditions of the past. But when he engages in the give-and-take of fieldwork, the disturbing subjectivities of his exchange with living practitioners make him wish for the controlled security of the library. "Messy entanglements with the living" (*and* the dead) are intrinsic to the task of actively engaging the reader through the researcher's own participation in what he or she studies.[7]

Problems arise when authors pretend perfect objectivity, able to trust only knowledge obtained in ways wholly divorced from themselves. Readers may find their work lifeless, clinical, and unimaginative. Yet when the researcher in spirituality "goes native," inserting the authorial self to such an extent that scholarly distance is dissolved, the reader learns as much about the writer as the subject under investigation. The representation of spirituality runs the risk of becoming invention.[8]

The history of ethnography readily demonstrates this longstanding dilemma. Ethnographic studies emerged in the late nineteenth century as a response to governmental needs for knowledge about marginalized groups. The British Foreign Office wanted to understand its colonial subjects (like the Nuer in Sudan), while the American Bureau of Indian Affairs sought information about the Sioux Ghost Dance and other Native American practices. Hence, they hired pioneering anthropologists like Edward Evans-Pritchard and James Mooney. In a similar way sociological ethnography grew out of the Chicago settlement houses in the early twentieth century, as researchers like William

F. Whyte studied immigrant poverty for the purpose of assimilating the "socially disadvantaged" into American society.[9]

The early history of ethnography is thus rooted in recognizably imperialistic and paternalistic points of view. The question of objectivity has been a bothersome one from the beginning. How do researchers maintain a clear social and intellectual distance from those with whom they work? Is that even possible or desirable? On the other hand, does joining the group being studied, erasing this critical distance, allow for an increase or decrease in usable knowledge? These are questions that bring to the fore the basic problem of the authorial self.

This essay asks how the disclosure and concealment of the researcher's self is effectively (and ineffectively) exercised in the practice of spirituality as a critical discipline. I argue that the problem of the authorial self can be illuminated by comparing patterns of self-indication in classic spiritual writers as they reflect on their own experience, to the work of scholarly interpreters as they analyze the experience of others. Subsequently, I turn to a particular example of engaged scholarship from my own work, asking how ancillary disciplines like literary and rhetorical criticism can help in articulating and critiquing various strategies of self-presentation.

REVEALING AND HIDING THE AUTHORIAL SELF

The author's self is always inescapably present. To pretend otherwise, out of a zealous commitment to the imagined purity of scholarship, is no less dangerous than uncritically inviting the reader into the writer's own private world. In dealing with this dilemma of the self, I propose a threefold pattern for clarifying the role of the researcher's authorial identity in the writing of spirituality. This involves:

1. The need to identify openly the authorial self, that is, the writer's own perspective and multilayered relationship to the spiritual figure, tradition, or text under examination.

This addresses the problem of the *absent author* whose biases are present but undisclosed.

2. The need to recognize the instructive potential of the authorial self as a bridge figure in providing the reader a deeper understanding of the world of the "other." This recognizes the possibilities and difficulties of the *engaged author* whose experience becomes admittedly a part of the analysis.

3. The need subsequently to conceal or deconstruct the authorial self, keeping the researcher's identity in the background so as to focus on the research itself. This points, in turn, to the problem of the *interfering author* whose subjectivity abandons methodological rigor, risking a dangerous self-indulgence if not a new colonialism with respect to the subject(s) being studied.

A particularly important area for analysis is the relationship between the second and third steps of this pattern. In lifting the veil of the author's imagined invisibility, a methodological self-effacement has to screen the ego in the process of addressing deep concerns of the soul. Among classic works, examples include the deliberately anonymous author of the fourteenth-century *Cloud of Unknowing* or the late-fifth-century pseudonymous writings of Dionysius the Areopagite. Obliterating, disguising, or diminishing the authorship of a spiritual work is a practice often required of those who draw most heavily on their own experience. Julian of Norwich emphasized her authorial role as "a woman, ignorant, weak and frail" in deflecting the criticism of her visions that she expected from others. Søren Kierkegaard alternately hid and revealed himself as he wrote for multiple audiences, from the Danish public of his day to Regina Olsen, the woman he secretly loved.[10]

Identifying the rhetorical strategies of the absent, engaged, and interfering author helps to clarify the extent to which authorial disclosure (and/or disguise) can increase the honesty and effectiveness of one's writing. Examples of the absent author often appear in works that claim an unabashed authoritative objectivity in presenting their subject matter. One thinks of Adolphe

Tanquerey's *The Spiritual Life,* a classic text that catalogued an intensive range of spiritual states for generations of priests and seminarians prior to Vatican II. This French Sulpician theologian defined asceticism as "the science of the spiritual life," insisting that Christian perfection is simply "the logical outcome of dogma." While the author admits to a "preference for the spirituality of the French School of the seventeenth century," he proceeds to lay out an impartial "study of the facts" of ascetical and mystical theology.[11] The study claims an unquestioned orthodoxy, free of controversy and personal bias.

Yet this "science of the saints" clearly favors a pessimistic view of human nature, emphasizing the self-annihilation and conformity to the divine will that characterized Sulpician spirituality in particular. In a lexical pattern of 1,599 points the book classifies spiritual phenomena in comprehensive detail—from penance and mortification to the practice of levitation and the supernatural perception of fragrant odors. It offers a stylized model of Christian growth by which faithful Catholics can anxiously plot their progress (or regress) in the spiritual life. The author's reluctance to acknowledge his own frame of reference gives the book its impression of being a final and definitive description of spiritual experience.

Effective models of the engaged author appear in Martin Luther's "Commentary on the Psalms" and William James's *The Varieties of Religious Experience.* In each of these texts the writer sustains the reader's interest by making his own experience a part of the analysis. Luther's highly engaged writing comes tumbling out of his own desperate search for a gracious God in his early years at Wittenberg. Under the surface of the text lies the struggling believer, plodding at times through the dark night of doubt and temptation (Luther's *anfechtungen*). Those who dare to write of holy things, he urges, must endure the depths of spiritual longing. "It is not by reading, writing or speculation that one becomes a theologian. Nay, it is rather by living, dying, and even being damned." "Experience alone makes the theologian," Luther declares.[12] The risk of one's very being is the sole foundation of worthwhile spiritual writing. To read Luther's "Commentary" is to enter into the heart of the Psalmist himself, crying out of the depths.

William James readily identifies himself as an exemplar of what he calls the "sick soul," one who wrestles in an angst-ridden world, natively suspicious of the sky-blue optimism of the "healthy-minded soul." As he worked on his Gifford Lectures, James labored under a severe heart condition, contending with fragile nerves and a brooding anxiety. His scientific study of religious experience, therefore, is preeminently concerned with his own healing and recovery. His whole life is an effort to deal with the severe depression he had known in his late twenties. Indeed, the book's most poignant expression of religious dread is drawn from his memory of that period. He "thanks the sufferer" for permission to share an example of "the worst kind of melancholy," presenting an account of his own depression as if it came from one of his informants.[13] The power of James's vivid prose is due in large part to his deeply personal investment in his writing.

One discerns a prototype of the interfering author in Richard Rolle's fourteenth-century classic, *The Fire of Love*. Rolle was a free-lance English mystic who followed his own sense of divine leading and rarely sought the advice of others. Self-assured to the point of arrogance, he writes of himself as one of those "rare souls" who "cannot wander into a false path."[14] His writing is often full of himself. He regularly presents his experience as paradigmatic, dismissing his detractors and those who slandered his name. Both Walter Hilton and the author of *The Cloud of Unknowing* warned people of the excesses of Rolle's emotionalism. Known as the Hermit of Hampole, he lived on a perpetual "high"—speaking continually of being "aglow, transfigured...snatched up to the highest peak of contemplation." He reports feelings of physical burning in his chest, transports of divine sweetness, even the ability to hear heavenly angelic music. Receiving this gift of superior melodies in his ecstasies, he found it hard to lower himself to singing psalms along with others in church. Self-referential disclosures of this sort recur frequently in his work. He acknowledges his unusual behavior with women—touching them inappropriately, making comments on the size of a woman's breasts, and being scolded on occasion for conduct unbecoming a hermit.[15] Rolle's authorial self strayed toward an egotistical absorption, as distracting as it was illustrative of his spiritual attainments.

PARAMETERS FOR USING
THE WRITER'S EXPERIENCE

Having identified various patterns of self-indication in classic spiritual texts, I want to compare contemporary researchers in spirituality who similarly draw on their own experience in their scholarly writing. Albert Raboteau's disclosure of his family background and conversion to Eastern Orthodoxy is an example. In pointing readers to the diversity of African American spirituality, he draws attention to himself for the purpose of giving life to a larger, diversified tradition.[16] The opening and closing of the writer's experience serves a higher end that eclipses the importance of the writer himself.

Scholars like Karen McCarthy Brown recommend employing the authorial self "only where there is some difference or misunderstanding that needs explaining." Her stories, for instance, reveal her mistakes in the unfolding of her research, inviting readers to laugh at her naiveté and, in the process, to identify their own.[17] Acknowledging the foibles of analysis and interpretation in this way allows the author simultaneously to insert and withdraw herself. It also models what the reader, in turn, is expected to do: join an engagement of the self with a hermeneutics of suspicion in the creative work of rendering meaning.

There are enormous differences, of course, in comparing the problem of the self in classic spiritual writings and in the contemporary exercise of religious research, whether ethnographic or otherwise. The investment of the author's personhood is resolute and central to the one but guarded and peripheral to the other. The former may risk everything in seeking a direct apprehension of the holy; the latter enlists the self in a controlled effort to instruct.

How, then, do contemporary writers in Christian spirituality (those rooted in the academy as well as those writing along its margins) make use of their own experience in providing their readers deeper access to the material they explore? Aware of the risks involved, various researchers employ different approaches in attempting to balance participative understanding with critical insight. Among scholarly researchers, Roberta Bondi addresses a larger public audience than church historians usually address, assuming the pastoral voice of one of the desert fathers or mothers in relating patristic scholarship to the contemporary practice of prayer.[18] My own work in probing the experience of "place" in the history of spirituality employs multiple levels of discourse in juxtaposing analysis and experience. Alongside theoretical chapters on the religious and cultural perception of place, I invite the reader into specific encounters of sacred places through personal essays. More often than not, my vulnerability as a person rather than my expertise as a scholar is what opens the work to the experience of others.[19]

The most widely read spiritual writers of recent generations—from Thomas Merton and Henri Nouwen to Frederick Buechner and Kathleen Norris—have regularly contended with this dilemma of the self. How does one write about spirituality in the first person while still remaining hidden? How does one reveal oneself, touching what is most universal and deeply human in the reader, while also concealing what belongs only to God and avoiding what simply distracts by focusing on the author's idiosyncratic experience?

Merton wrote more or less openly of his difficulties with Abbot James Fox at Gethsemani, even about falling in love with a nurse in Louisville. Nouwen wrestled publicly with his demons, trying to write his way into a freedom he never quite realized. Buechner spoke the unspeakable in disclosing his father's suicide. Norris has written guardedly of her husband's mental illness. Each author struggles with knowing how much to say and what *not* to say in modeling a spirituality to which they invite their readers' entrance.[20] They walk a narrow edge, trying not to step outside of the hiddenness that necessarily protects them, their families, and their readers.

Negotiating the differences between the writing of "scholarly work" in spirituality and "popular writing" in the field is never easy. The history of Christian spirituality is full of instances where critical analysis and personal experience creatively overlap. Jonathan Edwards, for example, served both as field researcher and preacher of the 1734–35 revival in Northampton, Massachusetts. His "Faithful Narrative of the Surprising Work of God" described the recent awakening in his hometown and constitutes "a kind of early modern ethnography."[21] The eighteenth-century theologian's account includes a geographical, historical, and astutely psychological analysis of the community and its response to the new religious movement. Based on direct observation, including case studies of actual converts, the author emphasizes the importance of field research and personal experience in getting at the deeper realities not immediately manifest to those witnessing the events from afar.[22] At the same time, however, Edwards tries to minimize the impact of his authorial intrusion by discounting his importance as minister, stressing God's role in the awakening and his reluctance in authoring the narrative. The result is a paradigmatic illustration of the possibilities and problems one faces in rendering any "thick" description of religious experience.

RHETORICAL STRATEGIES AND THE SELF

Having articulated the problem of the self as it appears in the primary and secondary literature of the field of spirituality, it may help to examine various perspectives on self-disclosure and self-concealment as these arise from the ancillary disciplines of spirituality. The task of dissecting the interplay among multiple "authors" and "readers" of any given work is enormous. It requires the literary critic's sensitivity to the whole process of reading and writing, the historian's critical analysis of multilayered texts, and the psychologist's study of the process of identity formation, not to mention the theologian's cautiousness about the limits of all speech concerning God.

Literary and rhetorical critics, for example, pay careful attention to the intricate relationships among author, reader, and text. Writers sometimes create fictional or "implied versions" of themselves, Wayne Booth observes, in order to startle, entice, or overcome resistance in their readers. The "implied author" or "second self" operating as a guiding personality behind the work is not necessarily synonymous with the actual author.[23] Indeed, the device can suggest things about which the actual author might prefer to keep silent, not feeling competent to speak.

Margaret Miles has argued, for instance, that Augustine (in his *Confessions*) employed a textual strategy of multiple selves, projecting alternately his youthful persona as a prurient seeker of pleasure and his mature role as celebrant of higher enjoyments. This produced a sustained "increment of erotic energy" in his readers, moving them, it is to be hoped, toward an experience of being ravished by Divine Beauty themselves.[24] Coleman Barks, a poet in his own right, has been one of the most effective twentieth-century translators of Jelaluddin Rumi, the thirteenth-century Sufi mystic. One is continually aware of multiple voices in his presentations of Rumi's mystical yearnings. Rumi, Shams (his teacher), Allah (the Alluring One), and Barks himself—each of these plays across the page, seducing the reader on various levels.[25] This fluidity of perceived authorship enhances the reader's involvement with the text, even as it runs the risk of obscuring what it represents.

In writing *The Solace of Fierce Landscapes,* my own struggle as church historian and student of landscape was to make the apophatic spirituality of the early desert Christians accessible to contemporary readers. This involved inviting them into multiple perspectives of an unfamiliar reality, making use of a continually shifting authorial voice. The subject matter itself required this. How, after all, does one attempt to put into words what is wholly beyond language? How does one carry the reader into an experience of loss that approximates the monastic encounter of the desert in Late Antiquity? How can the desert landscape be allowed to speak for itself?

On one level I address the reader with a scholar's voice, unfolding an argument about the use of landscape images in the history of the apophatic tradition. Apophatic spirituality rejects all analogies of God as ultimately inadequate. God is greater than any language we might ever use to speak of God. In the history of the tradition, however, I had noticed that a few austere landscape images were frequently employed to challenge the very use of images themselves. These include desert, mountain, and cloud—spare "aniconic images" used to question the overconfidence in words that often characterizes theology, as well as to suggest metaphorically the ultimately indescribable human experience of God.[26]

The book develops this argument, historically and geographically, in six principal chapters. But, from the beginning, I avoid any confusion about the narrator as absent author by acknowledging myself as "a self-identified Christian...one burned out (like a lot of people) on shallow religion." I place myself alongside those potential readers for whom theological discourse has ceased to carry significant meaning.

On another level I move more fully into the posture of an engaged author, speaking with the voice of one personally stripped of language. In brief personal essays inserted between the main chapters, I speak of accompanying my mother through her "desert experience" of death by cancer with Alzheimer's disease. I juxtapose her experience of losing memory and language with my own exposure to harsh desert terrain in New Mexico and the Sinai region. Expressing a "voice of loss" in this oblique way serves to exemplify (and to challenge) the claims asserted by the scholar's "voice of control" in other parts of the book. This alternative voice can say:

> I sat beside my mother's bed on that first day in the nursing home, seeing her as grotesque, almost unrecognizable....Black spots and purple splotches covered her hands and feet where needles had searched for shriveled veins. A feeding tube hung from her nose. Her lips were dry and peeling, her breath foul. She'd been tied to the bed because she didn't know where she was and repeatedly tried to get up to leave. Yet there in the twisted shape of my mother's body I stumbled upon an unguessed wholeness.[27]

This description of my mother's physical appearance and mental disorientation is echoed in a later account of Antoine de

Saint-Exupery's survival of a plane crash in the Libyan Desert in 1935. After walking 124 miles over three days in the desert, his features and behavior were exactly like those of my mother. Sharing a similar experience of abandonment, he too had encountered a desert that whispered with its own silent, insistent voice.

On yet a third level I know the desert terrain has to speak for itself—not as metaphor, but as place—receiving the last word in the book. Whenever the voice of personal vulnerability threatens to dissolve into sentimentality, that is, when the engaged author runs the risk of becoming an interfering author, I try to give the desert's harsh, indifferent voice free rein. This throws author and reader alike into a deeper embrace of silence. "Throughout this book, the desert [functions] as a kind of Greek Chorus, never speaking but always present, offering its own critique of everything said, silently deconstructing every naive and romantic notion."[28]

As the book juxtaposes these authorial voices, the historian invites readers to evaluate the monastic experience of desert emptiness in the history of spirituality. The son, coping with his mother's dying, points readers to their own limit experiences for which there are no words. Finally, the desert itself periodically calls a halt to all other speech in a shared moment of sustained silence. What is said, then, in scholarly discourse is subsequently twisted into personal meaning through an anguished discourse and finally unsaid again by the desert's apophatic language. Along the way, it is to be hoped, the reader is carried through the same process.[29]

When this happens, a book has the possibility of becoming a performative text. The meaning of any text never permanently resides within it as an absolute quality readily abstracted from the page. Its meaning has to be enacted, finally realized only in performance.[30] Readers complete, in their experience of performative reading, what the voice (or voices) of the author had only begun to suggest. Indeed, the readers' incorporation of their own vulnerability into the experience of the text through active reading creates not only new insights but a new reality, something that had not previously existed. This act of participation is what often allows readers to suggest far deeper understandings of the text than anything the author might initially have envisioned.

Most academic writing in the field of spirituality will follow the usual canons of historical and theological research. The writer's predisposition should always be acknowledged, but disclosures of the authorial self may remain, at least ostensibly, fairly minimal. Yet there are times when a deeper investment of the writer's experience is required, especially in writing that probes the remote edges of human language and experience itself. While this divulgence of the self's struggle for meaning is inevitably "messy," it also is necessary.

"Theologians are worthy of the title," writes Karl Rahner, "only when they do not seek to reassure themselves that they are providing clear and lucid discourse, but rather when they are experiencing and witnessing, with both terror and bliss, to the analogical back and forth between affirmation and negation before the abyss of God's incomprehensibility."[31] To the extent that the study of spirituality is a theological enterprise, writing in this field inevitably places authors in that deep humility of self where terror and bliss are most rigorously exercised. If writers wish to touch this humility in their readers, they will first have to have touched it in themselves. In proceeding, then, to expose this awareness of limit and vulnerability in their writing, they must dance as lightly as possible, pointing their readers beyond themselves to a truth finally comprehended in their own disappearance. It is not, after all, about them.

Notes

1. Sandra Schneiders, "Spirituality in the Academy," *Theological Studies* 50 (December 1989): 694.

2. James V. Spickard, J. Shawn Landres, and Meredith B. McGuire, eds., *Personal Knowledge and Beyond: Reshaping the Ethnography of Religion* (New York: New York University, 2002).

3. Schneiders, "Spirituality in the Academy," 695.

4. Robert A. Orsi, *The Madonna of 115th Street* (New Haven, CT: Yale University, 1985) and *Thank You, St. Jude* (New Haven, CT: Yale University, 1996); Thomas Tweed, *Our Lady of*

the Exile (New York: Oxford University, 1997); Karen McCarthy Brown, *Mama Lola: A Vodou Priestess in Brooklyn* (Berkeley and Los Angeles: University of California, 1991).

5. Orsi, *Thank You, St. Jude,* xxi.

6. Spickard, Landres, and McGuire, *Personal Knowledge and Beyond,* 63–74.

7. Ibid., 63.

8. James Clifford and George E. Marcus, eds., *Writing Culture: The Poetics and Politics of Ethnography* (Berkeley and Los Angeles: University of California), 2.

9. See Spickard, Landres, and McGuire, *Personal Knowledge and Beyond,* 7–8.

10. See Belden C. Lane, "Saints and Writers: On Doing One's Work in Hiding," *Theology Today* 59 (January 2003): 607–17.

11. Adolphe Tanquerey, *The Spiritual Life* (Tournai, Belgium: Desclée and Co., 1932), vii, 12–14.

12. Martin Luther, "Commentary on the Psalms," *Luthers Werke* (Weimar: Hermann Bohlau, 1892), 5:163.

13. William James, *The Varieties of Religious Experience* (New York: New American Library, 1958), 135–36.

14. See Karen Armstrong, *Visions of God: Four Medieval Mystics and Their Writings* (New York: Bantam, 1994), 21.

15. Ibid., 23.

16. Albert J. Raboteau, *A Fire in the Bones: Reflections on African-American Religious History* (Boston: Beacon, 1995).

17. Spickard, Landres, and McGuire, *Personal Knowledge and Beyond,* 127–33.

18. See Roberta C. Bondi, *To Love as God Loves: Conversations with the Early Church* (Philadelphia: Fortress Press, 1987).

19. See Belden C. Lane, *Landscapes of the Sacred: Geography and Narrative in American Spirituality* (Baltimore: Johns Hopkins University, 2001).

20. See *The Journals of Thomas Merton,* 7 vols., ed. Patrick Hart (San Francisco: HarperCollins, 1996–98); Michael Ford, *Wounded Prophet: A Portrait of Henri J. M. Nouwen* (New York: Doubleday, 1999); Frederick Buechner, *Telling Secrets* (San

Francisco: HarperCollins, 1991); and Kathleen Norris, *Amazing Grace* (New York: Riverhead, 1998).

21. Finbarr Curtis, "Locating the Revival: Jonathan Edwards's Northampton as a Site of Social Theory," in *Embodying the Spirit: New Perspectives on North American Revivalism,* ed. Michael J. McClymond (Baltimore: Johns Hopkins University, 2004), 47–66.

22. See Jonathan Edwards, "A Faithful Narrative of the Surprising Work of God" (1737), in Jonathan Edwards, *The Works of Jonathan Edwards,* vol. 4, *The Great Awakening,* ed. C.C. Goen (New Haven, CT: Yale University, 1972), 152.

23. Wayne C. Booth, *The Rhetoric of Fiction* (Chicago: University of Chicago, 1961), 74–75.

24. Margaret Miles, *Desire and Delight: A New Reading of Augustine's Confessions* (New York: Crossroad, 1992), 26, 96.

25. See Coleman Barks, *The Essential Rumi* (San Francisco: Harper, 1997).

26. Belden C. Lane, *The Solace of Fierce Landscapes: Exploring Desert and Mountain Spirituality* (New York: Oxford University Press, 1998), 4.

27. Ibid., 31.

28. Ibid., 231.

29. On readers' responses to fictionalized roles into which authors invite them, see Walter Ong, "The Writer's Audience Is Always a Fiction," *Proceedings of the Modern Language Association* 90 (1975): 9–22.

30. See John L. Austin, *How to Do Things with Words* (Cambridge: Harvard University, 1975), 6–12.

31. Karl Rahner, "Experiences of a Catholic Theologian," *Theological Studies* 61, no. 1 (March 2000): 7.

PART II

Essays at the Edges of the Discipline

4

THE QUEST FOR BIBLICAL SPIRITUALITY

John R. Donahue, SJ

Among the kaleidoscope of important theological specialties emerging after the Second Vatican Council, biblical spirituality is assuming its rightful place. No scholar in the last three decades has written so extensively or thoughtfully on this topic as Professor Sandra M. Schneiders, IHM. She has both shaped and chronicled the discipline of Christian spirituality and, from her earliest work on John's Gospel until the present, has defined and practiced a creative biblical spirituality. She also brought to this project qualities possessed by few scholars—excellent training in contemporary philosophy, wide theological knowledge and reading, a lifetime of creative exposition of biblical texts, and sophisticated feminist hermeneutics—all presented in elegant and eminently readable prose.[1] Though her contributions to the delineation and practice of biblical spirituality merit a thorough chronological and critical exposition, limitations of space preclude this endeavor. Rather, with her work as my guide, I will survey her different presentations of *spirituality,* and *biblical spirituality.* Then, perhaps rushing in where angels fear to tread, I will offer some random suggestions from the perspective of biblical studies on the continuing evolution of the vital discipline of spirituality.[2]

WHAT IS SPIRITUALITY?

The English term *spirituality* has a somewhat quaint history. The *Oxford English Dictionary* lists a number of usages. The first and one of the earliest is "the body of spiritual or ecclesiastical persons," quoting a document from 1441, "I come before the spiritualite, Two cardynals and byshoppis fyve." Other early usages describe "a spiritual society" or "ecclesiastical things or possessions." A usage akin to modern understandings appears in the early sixteenth century: "Sum spark of licht [light] and spiritualitie Walkins [wakens] my wit, and ressoun [reason] bids me rys [rise]." By the nineteenth century the term has a contemporary nuance, for example, "No spiritual man ever claims that his spirituality is his own."[3]

In a superb essay Walter Principe notes that the term is rooted in the Pauline writings.[4] Following the Old Testament heritage, *spirit* connotes the power and presence of the living God. In Paul, "spirit" is the presence and action of the loving God manifest in the Christ event, which summons Christians to be "spiritual" persons or to walk "in the spirit." When Paul contrasts spirit to flesh, he is not reflecting a dualistic anthropology but speaks of the whole person as either open to the action of God or turning away from it. For example, he exhorts the Romans, "Do not lag in zeal, be ardent in spirit, serve the Lord" (Rom 12:11), and tells the Galatians, "If we live by the Spirit, let us also be guided by the Spirit" (Gal 5:25).[5]

In a number of places Principe and Schneiders discuss the various meanings and evolution of *spirituality*. From the first abstract use of *spiritualitas* in the fifth century until the present, it has been a rather protean term, variable in its meaning. In the modern period the term *spirituality* emerges in seventeenth-century France in reference to "the interior life, especially in relation to its affective relationship with God,"[6] and later as a branch or subdivision of theology where the debate was primarily over whether the "continuity or discontinuity between the life of ordinary virtue and the mystical life, and especially concerned over whether all Christians or only some are called to the mystical life."[7] These authors both note that spirituality begins to emerge as a self-conscious discipline in mainly French works of the late nineteenth and early twentieth centuries (especially those of Adolphe Tanquerey and Pierre Pourrat),[8] and Principe calls attention to their influence on the definition of *spiritualité* in the 1964 edition of the *Dictionnaire...de la langue française,* as "ensemble des principes qui règient la vie spirituelle d'une personne, d'un groupe" [the entirety of principles which regulate the spiritual life of a person or a group], a definition he found unequalled in any English dictionary of the time.[9] Principe also set the agenda for future discussion by suggesting three levels of the term *spirituality:* lived experience, teachings, and the academic study of experience or teaching.[10]

In her extensive writings Schneiders clarifies the different descriptions and divisions of spirituality, an analysis that provides a prerequisite to any discussion of biblical spirituality.[11] In attempting "a phenomenology of the contemporary definition of spirituality," Schneiders first lists four things that it is *not:* (1) no longer "an exclusively Roman Catholic phenomenon"; (2) neither dogmatic nor prescriptive by "the application to concrete life principles derived from theology"; (3) not concerned with "perfection" but with growth that is not reserved to a select few; and (4) not limited to "the interior life" in opposition to the whole social and human context of a person's life.[12] She concludes that "spirituality has something to do with the unification of the human person by reference to something beyond the human person." The following paragraph offers a definition of Christian spirituality as "that particular actualization of the capacity for self-transcendence that is constituted by the substantial gift of the Holy Spirit establishing a life-giving relationship with God in Christ within the believing community."[13]

Throughout her writings Schneiders is concerned to lay claim to spirituality as an academic discipline independent from but related to other branches of theology. The relation is dialectical. Theology itself, as a discipline, arises in relation to religious experience (spirituality) but then assumes a critical and reflective function with respect to spirituality, much as literary criticism arises from literature and returns to it as its subject. Theology "renders judgment on the adequacy of a particular spirituality to the Gospel and Tradition."[14] When theology is understood in its broadest and critical sense, "the discipline of Christian spirituality belongs under the heading of theology as one field of revelation-related, confessionally committed scholarly endeavor, namely, the field that studies Christian religious experience as such in an interdisciplinary way."[15] While recognizing the intimate relation of theology to spirituality, Schneiders here rejects spirituality's subordination to systematic or dogmatic theology and outlines their lines of division as academic disciplines.

The academic discipline of spirituality is thus *the field of study which attempts to investigate in an interdisciplinary way spiritual experience as such.*"[16] She concludes that the "emerging discipline" of spirituality has certain characteristics. First, it is essentially interdisciplinary; second, it is descriptive-critical rather than prescriptive; third, it is ecumenical, interreligious, and cross-cultural; and fourth, it is a holistic discipline in that its inquiry into human spiritual experience is not limited to exploration of the explicitly religious, that is, the so called interior life.[17] In the final pages of this discussion she notes that spirituality does not prize pure objectivity but is rather self-involving. While the discipline seeks to provide knowledge of texts and of comparative materials, "it is also intended for most students to assist them in their own spiritual lives and enable them to foster the spiritual lives of others," so that it is "not much different from the objective of the study of psychology or art."[18]

In one of the most recent explorations of the shape of the discipline, Schneiders begins by noting the general acceptance of spirituality as an appropriate designation for a new discipline.[19] The "subject matter" or "material object" is "the experience of conscious involvement in the project of life-integration through self-transcendence."[20] This essay spells out in suggestive detail the relation of spirituality to other disciplines—primarily theology and biblical studies—that will provide the main segue to the purpose of the present essay.

Schneiders describes the discipline as "teaching and learning, including research and writing, on subjects specified by the material and formal objects of Christian spirituality in the context of the academy."[21] She develops her notion of spirituality as interdisciplinary by distinguishing between *constitutive* disciplines and *problematic* disciplines. The former are disciplines "which necessarily function in relation to the subject matter precisely because they supply the positive data of Christian religious experience as well as its norm and hermeneutical context, namely Scripture and the history of Christianity." The latter or second layer of interdisciplinarity is termed problematic because these disciplines "are called into play and integrated into the methodology of a particular study because of the problematic of the phenomenon being studied." These problematic disciplines can include psychology, sociology, literature, and science. Furthermore, at times, the constitutive disciplines can be problematic if they are the leading discipline used to understand the phenomenon's problematic. The *constitutive* disciplines come into play "because the experience being studied is *Christian*," and the *problematic* disciplines "because the object of study is *experience as such*."[22]

Scripture "mediates the foundational and normative access of the Christian to revelation" with the result that "the scholar of Christian spirituality, therefore, needs a functional knowledge of the Christian Scriptures, that is, a deep familiarity with the content and dynamics of that literature and a methodological competence that will allow her or him to handle biblical material responsibly."[23] In the final sections of this study, Schneiders returns to her earlier concern, the relation of theology to spirituality, with a desire again to affirm both the independence of spirituality from theology and their intimate relationship.

She speaks of the three *personae* of theology.[24] The first affirms that spirituality is the living out of theology, so that spirituality means mediating theological truth into religious practice. Here theology is prescriptive and normative of spirituality, which is not considered a research discipline in its own right. Under the ethos of the second *persona*, theology studies experience by means of theological methods and through theological categories. Here spirituality can disappear into such categories. For example, the spiritualities of John of the Cross and Hildegard of Bingen might appear the same when analyzed under the theological category of grace. But their spiritual experiences are really very different when seen through other categories like gender,

77

experiential background, and historical setting.[25] The third case or *persona* is when "spirituality is understood as the experienced multi-faceted living of faith, and theology as critical reflection on faith, theology and spirituality are equal partners in the academy."[26] Schneiders offers a helpful example: "Theology might ask what theory of grace would best explain Teresa of Avila's mystical prayer, while spirituality is asking about the mystical experience of Teresa from psychological, psychosomatic, artistic, cultural and literary, as well as theological angles."[27] There exists, then, a dialectical and dynamic relationship between spirituality as experience and spirituality as an academic discipline. Experience funds critical research and reflection, yet experience is always historically conditioned, so that new religious experiences (such as a realization of full equality of women) lead to new avenues of research.

THE QUEST FOR ACADEMIC BIBLICAL SPIRITUALITY

Interest in and study of the Bible has characterized the whole career of Sandra Schneiders, with a profound engagement with the Gospel of John. Her doctoral dissertation was entitled "The Johannine Resurrection Narrative: An Exegetical and Theological Study of John 20 as a Synthesis of Johannine Spirituality," and over the past decades she has written often on problems of biblical interpretation along with studies of particular texts and motifs.[28] In 2003 she returned to the Johannine resurrection narrative in an exceptional paper given at a conference in tribute to her longtime friend and colleague Raymond E. Brown.[29] She has devoted two major books to biblical topics, one to biblical interpretation and the other to the Gospel of John, as well as recent articles.[30]

The Context of the Quest

Prof. Schneiders is a member of that fortunate generation who followed academic vocations in the wake of the Second

Vatican Council. Though the council did not contain an explicit document on scripture, the *Dogmatic Constitution on Divine Revelation (Dei Verbum)* capped the long struggle for acceptance of modern methods of biblical criticism in the church, and the other documents were suffused with biblical motifs and a biblical spirit.[31] Yet, as we will indicate, even the major achievements of the Council concerning biblical studies reflected the progress of biblical studies of a generation ago and have been modified and transformed in the ensuing decades.

One of the major contributions of *Dei Verbum* was a move from "propositional" revelation to a dialogic and interpersonal understanding. After surveying God's work in the Old Testament and in the incarnation, the document concludes, "Through divine revelation, God chose to show forth and communicate Himself and the eternal decisions of His will regarding the salvation of men" (no. 6).[32] Putting to rest, also, the old debate about the "two sources" of revelation (tradition and scripture), the council stressed the primacy of scripture while affirming a dialectical relationship between scripture and tradition:

> Hence, there exists a close connection and communication between sacred tradition and sacred Scripture. For both of them, flowing from the same divine wellspring, in a certain way merge into a unity and tend toward the same end. For sacred Scripture is the Word of God inasmuch as it is consigned to writing under the inspiration of the divine Spirit, while sacred tradition takes the Word of God entrusted by Christ the Lord and the Holy Spirit to the Apostles, and hands it on to their successors. (*DV*, no. 9)

The decree also described concepts such as inspiration and inerrancy in a manner that moved away from quasi-fundamentalist understandings. In a memorable sentence that undergirded much of the approach to scripture by Elisabeth Schüssler Fiorenza,[33] *Dei Verbum* described inerrancy as follows: "Therefore since everything asserted by the inspired authors or sacred writers must be held to be asserted by the Holy Spirit, it follows that the books of

Scripture must be acknowledged as teaching solidly, faithfully and without error that truth which God wanted put into the sacred writings for the *sake of our salvation*" (*DV*, no. 11, emphasis added). This last phrase introduced a critical principle into biblical interpretation, since not everything in the Bible can be "for the sake of our salvation," and conceptions of salvation are historically conditioned. *Dei Verbum* also cautiously authorized modern biblical criticism, approving of methods such as form and redaction criticism, and stated that "the interpreter of sacred Scripture, in order to see clearly what God wanted to communicate to us, should carefully investigate what meaning the sacred writers really intended, and what God wanted to manifest by means of their words" (*DV*, no. 12). Though limitation of interpretation to the intention of the author was seen at the time as liberation from ungrounded allegorical or doctrinal readings of texts, it became one of the goals most challenged by biblical approaches subsequent to the council and by the work of Prof. Schneiders.

One other section of the council document is crucial for the evolution toward biblical spirituality. In a passage often overlooked, *Dei Verbum,* when speaking of the growth of the apostolic tradition in the church, states: "This tradition which comes from the Apostles develops in the Church with the help of the Holy Spirit." Development occurs in a number of ways: by growth in understanding *(perceptio)* of the realities and words handed down, through contemplation and study of believers *(contemplatione et studio),* through the intimate understanding of the spiritual realities they experience *(intima spiritualium... experientia),* and through the preaching *(praeconio,* also translated "proclamation") of those who through episcopal succession have received the sure charism of truth (*DV*, no. 8). Historical exegesis, the work of scholars, the experience of believers, the prayer of the church, and preaching by church leaders all contribute to understanding divine revelation. For the subsequent development of spirituality, most important is the acknowledgment by the council that the religious experience of believers—"treasuring in their hearts," "penetrating understanding of spiritual realities"—is a source for the development of tradition. Spirituality as a source of understanding is explicit later in the same section when speaking of the tradition "whose wealth is poured into the practice and life of the believing and praying Church." In this paragraph, too, the "preaching of those who have received episcopal succession" is put on a parallel with the experience of believers. Yet, later in *Dei Verbum*, the magisterium is given the task "of authentically interpreting the Word of God, whether written or handed on," while simultaneously affirming that the magisterium is "not above the Word of God but its servant" (*DV*, no. 10). Immediately after the council both Catholic and Protestant commentators noted the tension in this view, a tension that still remains with us as questions are raised about how the lived experience of the church challenges magisterial teaching.[34]

The immediate history of post–Vatican II Catholic biblical scholarship, in concert with other theological disciplines, presents a multicolored tapestry. An immediate effect was that a great number of people committed themselves to biblical and theological studies. More and more talented laypeople, especially women scholars, entered the field. Roman Catholic scholars quickly became leaders in the scientific study of the Bible. The biblical renewal became the soul of bilateral ecumenical dialogues, as groups turned to the scriptural roots of disputed issues only to find that a historical-critical reading of the scriptures challenged positions once thought to be set in concrete.[35] Theologians such as Edward Schillebeeckx, Walter Kasper, and Roger Haight all wrote significant studies of Jesus solidly informed by biblical scholarship.[36] Redaction criticism helped to recognize the theological creativity and literary achievement of the Evangelists and disclosed a multicolored pluralism in the New Testament itself. Fresh translations, such as the Bible of Jerusalem and the New American Bible, were produced, and Catholics participated in the production of commentaries no longer divided along confessional lines. Creative theological movements such as feminist theology and liberation theology wrestled critically with the biblical texts as a source of their insights. Literally thousands of clergy, laypeople, and members of religious orders flocked to summer institutes and workshops sustained by the joyful discovery of the manner in which the Bible touched their lives.

Roman Catholicism was becoming a Bible-reading, Bible-praying, and Bible-studying community. The first great generation of presenters, such as John L. McKenzie, R. A. F. Mackenzie, Raymond E. Brown, Roland E. Murphy, Joseph A. Fitzmyer, Katherine Sullivan, and Carroll Stuhlmueller (to name but a few), was, in effect, communicating a biblical spirituality, though some would have blanched at the term.[37] People's faith lives were nurtured and changed as the unknown terrain of the Bible was opened to them.

Defining Biblical Spirituality

Less than a decade after the council new approaches to the Bible began to challenge one of the lynchpins of the conciliar teaching, "the intention of the author," as the foundation of all interpretation. Biblical scholars employed approaches such as narrative criticism and reader-response criticism that focused not on the "world behind" the text, that is, its historical context, but on the "world of the text," its inner dynamics and structure, and "the world in front of the text," how the text invites readers into its world and how every reader in effect creates meaning.[38] Also, especially within the last decade, more and more studies by biblical scholars have appeared with the word *spirituality* in the title.[39] With the exception of the work of Barbara Bowe, most of the works have neither discussed what constitutes biblical spirituality nor outlined a method for pursuing it.[40] Much of the work of Prof. Schneiders over the last three decades has been to propose a reading of the Bible that is both responsible to contemporary canons of interpretation and productive of a true biblical spirituality.

Schneiders distinguishes three meanings of the term *biblical spirituality:* (1) spiritualities that come to expression in the Bible; (2) a pattern of Christian life deeply imbued with the spirituality(ies) of the Bible, and (3) a transformative process of personal and communal engagement with the biblical text.[41] Though the third meaning has been the major focus of her writing over the last decade, she states that "such an approach, rooted in faith, cannot bypass historical-critical exegesis and literary analysis" and that the text must be understood "on its own terms," so that readers may be "interrogated by that which is 'other,' by that which challenges us to fidelity in living of our Christian vocation."[42] This brief but important article summarizes much previous reflection that has been collected in *The Revelatory Text* and *Written That You May Believe,* which provide the substance of the following discussion.[43]

Put somewhat simplistically, Schneiders's efforts in limning a biblical theology operates between two poles: (1) a reading of the biblical text that is faithful to its historical and literary context, and (2) a realization that this is a sacred text, which leads to human transformation. Overemphasis on the first pole leads to a distanced historicism that enables us to plumb the ideals and even experiences of those who first read or produced a text without affecting the reader, while sole attention to the contemporary religious and transformative meaning could result in an ungrounded piety. To accomplish her task, Schneiders employs not only careful methods of exegesis but turns to two leaders in contemporary hermeneutic theory, Georg Gadamer and Paul Ricoeur. I will first summarize briefly Schneiders's guidelines for a faithful reading of the text in its original context and then turn to her use of Ricoeur and Gadamer, leading to appropriation and transformation.[44]

One of the lingering criticisms of spirituality by dyed-in-the wool historical criticism is that it is arbitrary and bordering on "eisegesis." Schneiders suggests guidelines that counter such a charge: respect for the text as it stands; an interpretation, consistent with itself, that elucidates the whole text; an interpretation that explains anomalies; one that uses proper methods; and one that its compatible with what is known from other sources (for example, the destruction of the Jerusalem Temple in AD 70). Another important guideline is "fruitfulness" of interpretation. A laborious interpretation that comes up with an obvious meaning is fruitless, as is one that results in banal religious truth. So too, I might add, are interpretations that are downright destructive of the divine human encounter and human relationships.

These criteria are part and parcel of the process of appropriation proposed by Ricoeur and adapted by Schneiders. Ricoeur argues that, "as readers, we begin to read a text naively, opening ourselves to its dynamic in the same way that children listen to stories; this first movement is a 'naive grasping of the meaning of the text as a whole.'"[45] Often, especially for Catholics not nurtured on the biblical tradition, this involves simple exposure to biblical texts as a prerequisite to any significant use of these texts. Subsequent explanation and exegesis may simultaneously challenge and enrich this initial engagement, but always as a preparation for an appropriation that leads to individual and social transformation.

The next movement involves explanation of the text: "The reader steps back from the text and engages in the kind of research necessary for a deeper comprehension at a number of levels. Here the historical-critical method and related tools of biblical study play their part."[46] This movement also involves "distanciation" as the reader moves beyond initial and naive interpretations that arise from an initial engagement, culminating in a "second naiveté," which enables an informed explanation of the text.[47] During this process the normal methods of historical-critical exegesis are at work. Thus, "criticism" involves a double distancing, first from the text itself so that its independence and intrinsic power can be recognized, and second, from the world view of the authors.

Ricoeur's insights also lead to the concept of the semantic autonomy of a text: its meaning is not *limited to* the "intention" of an original author, yet this autonomy does not imply that "authorial meaning has lost all significance"; there will always be a dialectical relationship between authorial intention and subsequent meaning.[48] The "semantic autonomy" of texts opens them to interpretations beyond their original context. Allied to this autonomy are the observations of biblical scholars about the development of traditions.[49] Texts engender traditions of interpretation that involve genres and settings quite different from the originating discourse. For example, the Exodus is celebrated perhaps originally by the hymns at the sea (Exod 15:20–21, 1–18) and in psalms (Pss 78, 105), then in narrative form of the Exodus itself, which is replayed in the sagas of the "taking of the land" in Joshua and Judges (Josh 3:14–17). The return from Exile in Isaiah is seen as a second Exodus from oppression to liberation,[50] and the Exodus motif shapes much of New Testament theology.[51] The "effective history" *(Wirkungsgeschichte)* of texts and traditions continues beyond the canonical scriptures and can continue to influence the interpretation and appropriation of the originating narratives.

In a seminal essay Ricoeur states, "Interpretation concerns essentially the power of the work to disclose a world,"[52] and "interpretation" overcomes distantiation and "actualizes the meaning of the text for the present reader."[53] He then notes that "appropriation is the concept which is suitable for the actualization of meaning as addressed to someone," and "as appropriation, interpretation becomes an event."[54] Ricoeur understands *appropriation* in the sense of the German *Aneigen,* which conveys the sense of "making one's own" what was initially "alien."[55] Appropriation involves both dispossession and a new possession. It involves moving beyond both sedimented meanings of texts and the myth of subjectivity, where the person "subjects" meaning to intention. Appropriation follows the "arrow of meaning" in a text and engenders a new self-understanding.[56] The cryptic phrase "arrow of meaning" is important, since, throughout his works on biblical interpretation, Ricoeur speaks of the "surplus of meaning" of biblical texts and following the direction of the text itself rather than literally reproducing its original meaning.

In appropriating carefully the methods of Ricoeur and Gadamer, Sandra Schneiders describes the process of appropriation primarily as the "fusion of horizons," whereby "the world horizon of the reader fuses with the horizon of the world projected by the text."[57] She then states:

> Appropriation of the meaning of a text, the transformative achievement of interpretation, is neither mastery of the text by the reader (an extraction of its meaning by the application of method) nor mastery of a reader by the text (a blind submission to what the text says) but an ongoing dialogue with the text about its subject matter.[58]

Appropriation, as described by Schneiders, is the prerequisite to her goal of biblical spirituality, transformation. I feel, however, that the term *transformation,* needs more development.[59]

Appropriation of a biblical text, while necessary for transformation, may not be adequate to the total process of transformation that extends over a long period of time. Schneiders herself notes ways in which transformative readings of scripture take place communally through response to the preached word, liturgy, faith-sharing groups, and communal commitments to transformative action.[60]

CONCLUDING REFLECTIONS

Clearly the work of Sandra Schneiders provides thoughtful, consistent, and cogent directions for biblical spirituality. By way of continuing conversation, though, I would like to supplement her program with some exploratory observations of my own, which are probably implicit in her work.

First. While Schneiders's efforts over more than two decades to claim spirituality as an independent field of academic inquiry is clearly of major importance, certain concerns emerge. Success creates its own set of problems. Edward Farley, who chronicled theological education for decades, warned that academic disciplines have evolved into a collection of "specialty fields."[61] Farley contrasts a specialty field to a discipline, which is described as "a pedagogical area that exists in a teaching and learning situation in which the teaching and learning are facilitated by the pursuit of scientific, scholarly inquiry."[62] In contrast, a specialty field is described as "an area of cognitive undertaking which has assumed certain features of professionalization and which is focused on a sufficiently restricted set of problems to be able to generate published research in a short time."[63] Biblical studies, with its proliferation of *posts*—post-structuralist, postmodern, post-colonial, post-feminist—seems already to have fulfilled Farley's fears; it is to be hoped that biblical spirituality will not devolve into such a specialty field. Also, various descriptions of postmodernity stress that clear lines of division no longer hold in art, literature, and the scholarly disciplines. Because of spirituality's rich scope, neither an exclusive definition as lived experience nor a distinct understanding of its academic home will ever be possible. The overlapping between experience and practice creates a certain "messiness" but gives spirituality a dynamic quality and prevents it from being conceptually frozen.

Second. Amid the various specializations within biblical studies, certain approaches are more promising than others for those in spirituality, who wish also to engage the Bible as a constitutive partner. Approaches that respect the final form of texts, such as narrative criticism, canonical criticism, and intertextual readings, as well as those that assess the effect of a text on readers, such as reader response criticism, are most helpful. When joined to critical readings of those texts that have been oppressive throughout history, these methods become a vital part of spirituality.

Third. Schneiders carefully distinguished constitutive and problematic disciplines as part of Christian spirituality, with scripture and history as constitutive, while theology can function as either constitutive or problematic, depending upon the research project. I propose that Christian ethics or moral theology now be assessed as also constitutive. Hesitancy arose in the past because spirituality was often subsumed under moral theology. Now, however, moral theology itself has changed radically. Following the lead of Vatican II, which said that "Scripture...ought to be the soul of all theology,"[64] many important Catholic moral theologians, such as Lisa Sowle Cahill, William Spohn, and James Bretzke, have responded to this challenge and now propose a Christian ethics of discipleship in which spirituality is a constitutive factor.[65] Equally important Catholic moralists have followed James Gustafson, who argued that "comprehensive and coherent theological ethics must be adequate with reference to the four following sources": (1) the Bible and Christian tradition; (2) philosophical methods, insights, and principles; (3) scientific information and methods that are relevant; and (4) human experience, broadly conceived.[66] Clearly, spirituality, biblical spirituality, and moral theology must be dialogue partners lest spirituality continue to be considered something added to the demands of Christian existence and moral theology be divorced from religious experience.

Fourth. Understandably, Schneiders has centered her work on the New Testament and mainly on John's Gospel. An adequate biblical spirituality must be open to the whole Bible and especially to the Old Testament and to those texts there that might at first seem least suited—such as "the texts of terror" discussed by Phyllis Trible, the lament and even the "cursing" psalms, legal material, and the sobering reflections of much wisdom literature.[67] In dealing with material from the Old Testament, Christian scholars also must respect the autonomy and fruitfulness of Jewish readings of their scriptures and become familiar with trends in Jewish interpretation, however daunting the task.

A corollary is that, since biblical interpretation has itself become so complex, spirituality and its constitutive partner, biblical spirituality, being interdisciplinary, must involve "communities of interpretation."[68] In describing biblical spirituality Schneiders notes ways in which transformative readings of scripture take place communally through response to the preached word, liturgy, faith-sharing groups, and communal commitments to transformative action.[69] Pheme Perkins has likewise called for communities of interpretation.[70] An academic counterpart to faith communities of shared interpretation would be shared cross-disciplinary and cross-cultural explorations of problematic areas, for example, mysticism. I present here more of a challenge to biblical scholars than to those working in spirituality.

Fifth. In discussing biblical spirituality the focus has necessarily been on descriptive studies of the biblical texts themselves, issues of hermeneutics and appropriation, and history of interpretation. This perspective gives the enterprise a certain "logocentric" character. Three decades ago William E. Lynch, a pioneer in integrating theology, literature, and art, wrote: "Faith is a life of the imagination; it is particularly a life of the ironic imagination....Let theology, among the many things that it is, become a set of images of faith and a life of the imagination. Let the poet, always the image-er, become also the thinker without limit."[71] Throughout Christian history, when literacy was not widespread, and even today when we have a surfeit of words, art in its widest sense, comprising the visual arts and drama, can touch the depth of the human spirit and convey the most profound message of the Bible. Art is the "text" of the imagination, and the language of the Bible is primarily a language saturated with vibrant images.[72]

Finally, and most obviously, continued effort will be needed to forge spirituality as both practice and academic discipline. A number of years ago Francis Moloney, now Katharine Drexel Professor of New Testament at Catholic University of America, and former member of the Vatican Theological Commission, wrote, "There is every indication that the golden era of biblical enthusiasm in the Catholic Church is on the wane."[73] Cardinal Carlo Martini, who packed the Milan Cathedral on Sunday evenings by offering reflective *lectio divina* on biblical passages, has said that there is a need to renew the renewal.[74] Seminaries often require only two courses in each Testament as part of priestly formation, and these are now overwhelmed by an avalanche of magisterial statements with an emphasis on doctrinal conformity. Homilies frequently are geared to support moral and doctrinal pronouncements or to chart the most recent liturgical directives. Yet there is a prodigious hunger for a vibrant biblical spirituality among God's people. The goals and practice of biblical spirituality so elegantly forged by Prof. Sandra Schneiders over the last decades are a sign of hope and a mandate for the future.

Notes

1. The bibliography in Part III of this volume contains Schneiders's most important works.

2. I presume that most readers of this essay will be familiar with Schneiders's extensive writings on spirituality. Her important work on interpretation, *The Revelatory Text,* is equally crucial to this project (2nd ed. [Collegeville, MN: Liturgical Press, 1990]).

3. All these references are from the web edition of the *Oxford English Dictionary,* s.v. "spirituality."

4. Walter Principe, "Toward Defining Spirituality," *Studies in Religion/Sciences Religieuses* 12, no. 2 (Spring 1983): 127–41; see also the important essay by Henri de Lubac, "Spiritual Understanding," in *The Theological Interpretation of Scripture,* ed. Stephen E. Fowl, 3–25, Blackwell Readings in Modern Theology (Oxford: Blackwell, 1998).

5. Principe, "Toward Defining Spirituality," 130. No summary can do justice to the importance of "spirit" in Pauline theology nor to the vast literature written on it. Some helpful

resources are Joseph A. Fitzmyer, "Pauline Theology," in *New Jerome Biblical Commentary*, eds. Raymond E. Brown, Joseph A. Fitzmyer, and Roland E. Murphy, §81–137 (Englewood Cliffs, NJ: 1992); and Gordon Fee, *God's Empowering Presence: The Holy Spirit in the Letters of Paul* (Peabody, MA: Hendrickson Publishers, 1994). See also the helpful summary in Sandra Schneiders, "Theology and Spirituality: Strangers, Rivals, or Partners?" *Horizons* 13 (Fall 1986): 257–58.

6. Schneiders, "Theology and Spirituality," 259. In this brief overview I am summarizing Schneiders's presentation here and in other articles.

7. Ibid. See also Sandra Schneiders, "Biblical Spirituality: Life, Literature and Learning," in *Doors of Understanding: Conversations in Global Spirituality in Honor of Ewert Cousins*, ed. Steven Chase (Quincy, IL: Franciscan Press, 1999), 51–76, esp. 56–57; and idem, "Spirituality in the Academy," *Theological Studies* 50 (1989): 676–97.

8. Schneiders, "Theology and Spirituality," 259–62, referencing Adolphe Tanquerey, *The Spiritual Life: A Treatise on Ascetical and Mystical Theology*, 2nd rev. ed., trans. H. Banderis (Tournai: Desclee, 1930); and Pierre Pourrat, *Christian Spirituality*, 4 vols., trans. W. H. Mitchell and S. P. Jacques (Westminster, MD: Newman, 1953–55; original in French, 1927).

9. Principe, "Toward Defining Spirituality," 133.

10. Ibid., 135–37.

11. Schneiders, "Theology and Spirituality," 253–57.

12. Ibid., 264–65.

13. Ibid., 266.

14. Ibid., 271–72.

15. Ibid., 272.

16. Schneiders, "Spirituality in the Academy," 692.

17. Ibid., 693. In commenting on this latter point she stresses the affinity between spirituality and feminism.

18. Ibid., 695.

19. Schneiders, "The Study of Christian Spirituality: Contours and Dynamics of a Discipline," *Christian Spirituality Bulletin* 6, no. 1 (Spring 1998): 2.

20. Ibid., 2–3.

21. Ibid., 3.

22. Ibid., 4.

23. Ibid. The second part of this presentation will, in effect, unpack this statement.

24. Schneiders's own writing is so clear and concise that my comments here closely paraphrase or embody her statements, even when not directly quoted. The term *persona* is not explained. It seems to describe roles or functions much like a *persona* in classical drama.

25. Schneiders, "Study of Christian Spirituality," 5.

26. Ibid., 5–6.

27. Ibid., 6.

28. STD from Pontifical Gregorian University, 1975, excerpt published by Gregorian University Press, 1975, now available in 2 volumes from Ann Arbor, MI: University Microfilms International, 1982.

29. "The Resurrection (of the Body) in the Fourth Gospel: A Key to Johannine Spirituality," paper presented at St. Mary's Seminary and University in Baltimore, Maryland, October 16–18, 2003. The address appears in *Life in Abundance: Studies in John's Gospel Given in Tribute to Raymond E. Brown,* ed. John R. Donahue (Collegeville, MN: Liturgical Press, 2005), 168–98.

30. Sandra Schneiders, *Written That You May Believe: Encountering Jesus in the Fourth Gospel,* 2nd ed., rev. and exp. (New York: Crossroad, 2003); and idem, *The Revelatory Text: Interpreting the New Testament as Sacred Scripture,* 2nd ed. (Collegeville, MN: Liturgical Press, 1999). See also Sandra Schneiders, "Biblical Spirituality: Life, Literature, and Learning," and "Biblical Spirituality," *Interpretation* 56 (April 2002): 133–42. See the bibliography in Part III for multiple titles dealing with biblical interpretation. An adequate dialogue with Schneiders's understanding of a spirituality informed by biblical scholarship would require engagement with her significant studies of Catholic religious life: *Finding the Treasure: Locating Catholic Religious Life in a New Cultural and Ecclesial Context,* vol. 1 of *Religious Life in a New Millennium* (Mahwah, NJ: Paulist Press, 2000); *Selling All: Commitment, Consecrated Celibacy, and Community in Catholic Religious Life,* vol. 2 of

Religious Life in a New Millennium (Mahwah, NJ: Paulist Press, 2001). A third volume is forthcoming.

31. For surveys of the events leading up to *Dei Verbum* and its contributions, see John R. Donahue, "Scripture: A Roman Catholic Perspective," *Review and Expositor* 79 (April 1982): 231–44; and idem, "Between Jerusalem and Athens: The Changing Shape of Catholic Biblical Scholarship," in *Hermes and Athena: Biblical Exegesis and Philosophical Theology,* ed. Eleonore Stump and Thomas P. Finn, 285–313 (Notre Dame, IN: University of Notre Dame Press, 1993).

32. *Dei Verbum,* in *The Documents of Vatican II,* ed. Walter M. Abbott, SJ (New York: America Press, 1966). Henceforth, *DV.*

33. This perspective is most fully stated in Elisabeth Schüssler Fiorenza, *Bread Not Stone: The Challenge of Feminist Biblical Interpretation* (Boston: Beacon Press, 1984).

34. This tension of perspectives was perceived during the conciliar debates by Cardinal Emile Léger of Montreal, who felt that the council did not submit tradition strongly enough to the authority of the word, and noted shortly after the council by Abbot Christopher Butler, OSB, who wrote: "It is all very well for us to say and believe that the magisterium is subject to holy Scripture. But is there anybody who is in a position to tell the magisterium: Look you are not practicing your subjection to Scripture in your teaching?" See J. J. Miller, ed., *Vatican II: An Interfaith Appraisal* (Notre Dame, IN: University of Notre Dame Press, 1966), 89.

35. See R. E. Brown, "Historical Biblical Criticism and Ecumenical Discussion," in *Biblical Interpretation in Crisis: The Ratzinger Conference on Bible and the Church,* ed. Richard J. Neuhaus (Grand Rapids, MI: Eerdmans, 1989), 24–49.

36. Edward Schillebeeckx, *Christ: The Experience of Jesus as Lord,* trans. J. Bowden (New York: Crossroad, 1980); Walter Kasper, *Jesus the Christ,* trans. V. Green (New York: Paulist Press, 1976); and Roger Haight, *Jesus, Symbol of God* (Maryknoll, NY: Orbis Books, 1999).

37. Virtually all of the pre– and immediately post–Vatican II generation of scripture scholars were male religious or priests; gifted women scholars who combine exegesis and spirituality now

characterize subsequent generations, e.g., Schneiders herself, Diane Bergant, Barbara Reid, Bonnie Thurston, Kathleen O'Connor, again to name but a few.

38. For an excellent survey of the different methods, see Joel B. Green, ed., *Hearing the New Testament: Strategies for Interpretation* (Grand Rapids, MI: Eerdmans, 1995); and Mark Alan Powell, with Cecile Gray, *The Bible and Modern Literary Criticism: A Critical Assessment and Annotated Bibliography* (Westport, CT: Greenwood, 1992).

39. Represented by Barbara E. Bowe, *Biblical Foundations of Spirituality: Touching a Finger to the Flame* (Lanham, MD: Rowman and Littlefield, 2003); Walter Brueggemann, *Spirituality of the Psalms,* ed. Patrick D. Miller (Minneapolis: Fortress Press, 2002); Michael Gorman, *Cruciformity: Paul's Narrative Theology of the Cross* (Grand Rapids, MI: Eerdmans, 2001); Wilfrid J. Harrington, *Seeking Spiritual Growth through the Bible* (Ramsey, NJ: Paulist Press, 2002); Carroll Stuhlmueller, *The Spirituality of the Psalms,* foreword Donald Senior, eds. Carol J. Dempsey and Timothy Lenchak (Collegeville, MN: Liturgical Press, 2002).

40. Bowe offers a brief but most helpful discussion of spirituality and theology along with a description of biblical spirituality: "*Biblical spirituality,* moreover, defines our lived faith experience that draws on the special biblical treasure-house of stories, images, prophetic challenges, and prayers and on the ultimate example of the life and death of Jesus for its understanding of God and for its convictions about the meaning of human existence" (*Biblical Foundations of Spirituality,* 19). The similarity with the understanding proposed by Schneiders will be evident below. Bowe offers a wide-ranging engagement with multiple biblical texts and themes, which makes her work an ideal classroom text.

41. Schneiders, "Biblical Spirituality," 135–36.

42. Ibid., 136.

43. In addition to *The Revelatory Text* itself, see also the "Review Symposium" on the book published in *Horizons* 19 (Fall 1992): 284–309, with comments by William Thompson, Susan A. Ross, John Koenig, and Mary Gerhardt. Schneiders enters into

dialogue with these essays in the preface to the revised edition of *The Revelatory Text.*

44. I have been guided also in my adaptation of Ricoeur by Dorothy Lee, *Flesh and Glory: Symbolism, Gender and Theology in the Gospel of John* (New York: Crossroad, 2002), esp. 5–7.

45. Paul Ricoeur, *Interpretation Theory: Discourse and the Surplus of Meaning* (Fort Worth: Texas Christian University Press, 1976), 24, cited in Lee, *Flesh and Glory,* 6.

46. Lee, *Flesh and Glory,* 6

47. Schneiders, *The Revelatory Text,* 169–70.

48. Ricoeur, *Interpretation Theory,* 30.

49. On semantic autonomy, see Schneiders, *The Revelatory Text,* 142–44; on developing traditions, see Michael Fishbane, *Biblical Interpretation in Ancient Israel* (New York: Oxford University Press, 1985).

50. Carroll Stuhlmueller calls Exodus the "controlling theme" of Second Isaiah ("Deutero-Isaiah and Trito-Isaiah," *New Jerome Biblical Commentary,* Article 21, §5).

51. Willard M. Swartley, *Israel's Scripture Traditions and the Synoptic Gospels: Story Shaping Story* (Peabody, MA: Hendrickson Publishers, 1994).

52. Paul Ricoeur, *Hermeneutics and the Human Sciences: Essays on Language, Action and Interpretation,* ed. and trans. John S. Thompson (Cambridge: Cambridge University Press; Paris: Éditions de la Maison des Sciences de l'Homme, 1981), 182.

53. Ibid., 185.

54. Ibid. He further notes here that in texts "revelation or disclosure" takes the place of ostensive reference in the dialogical situation.

55. Ibid.

56. Ibid., 192–93.

57. Schneiders, *The Revelatory Text,* 172.

58. Ibid., 177.

59. Among the Vatican dicasteries, the Pontifical Biblical Commission continues to issue the most helpful documents. In its 1993 document *Biblical Interpretation in the Church,* in addition to offering an approving survey of contemporary methods, the commission spoke of the need for the "actualization" of bib-

lical texts, without, however, explaining in depth its meaning. See J. A. Fitzmyer, *The Biblical Commission's Document, "The Interpretation of the Bible in the Church": Text and Commentary,* Subsidia Biblica 18 (Rome: Biblical Institute Press, 1995), published also in *Origins* 23 (January 6, 1994). The work of Professor Schneiders offers a solid grounding for such actualization.

60. See Schneiders, "Biblical Spirituality," 137–41. Limitations of space, unfortunately, do not allow a full exposition of how Schneiders's program for biblical spirituality has informed her engagement with a major biblical text, the Gospel of John, in *Written That You May Believe* and her two volumes on religious life (see the bibliography in Part III of this volume).

61. Edward Farley, *The Fragility of Knowledge: Theological Education in the Church and the University* (Philadelphia: Fortress Press, 1988).

62. Ibid., 35.

63. Ibid., 42.

64. Vatican II, *Decree on Priestly Formation (Optatum Totius),* no. 16.

65. For a survey of this shift, see John R. Donahue, "The Challenge of the Biblical Renewal to Moral Theology," in *Riding Time Like a River: The Catholic Moral Tradition since Vatican II,* ed. William J. O'Brien, 59–80 (Georgetown: Georgetown University Press, 1993); see also Lisa Sowle Cahill, "Sexual Ethics: A Feminist Biblical Perspective," *Interpretation* 49 (1995): 5–16; William Spohn, "Scripture, Use of in Catholic Social Ethics," *New Dictionary of Catholic Social Thought,* ed. Judith Dwyer (Collegeville, MN: Liturgical Press, 1994), 861–74; idem, *Go and Do Likewise: Jesus and Ethics* (New York: Continuum, 1999); James T. Bretzke, *Bibliography on Scripture and Christian Ethics* (Lewiston, NY: Mellen, 1997); and idem, "Scripture and Ethics: Core, Context and Coherence," in *Moral Theology: Fundamental Issues and New Directions, Festschrift for James Hanigan,* ed. James Keating (New York: Paulist Press, 2003).

66. James Gustafson, *Protestant and Roman Catholic Ethics: Prospects for Rapprochement* (Chicago: University of Chicago Press, 1978), 142. Lisa Sowle Cahill has developed these

in *Foundations for a Christian Ethics of Sexuality* (Philadelphia: Fortress Press; Ramsey, NJ: Paulist Press, 1985), esp. 1–13. People have noted that these reference points have their origin in the Methodist "quadrilateral" of scripture, tradition, reason, and experience.

67. I have used the term *Old Testament* rather than *Hebrew Bible* or *Jewish writings*, not only because certain Jewish scholars think that Christians should continue to use this term, but also because there is a literary and theological claim in these terms. What Christians call the Old Testament, and Jews the *Tanak*, exists as a fountain from which flow two great streams of interpretation. Christians *do not* read the Hebrew Bible, mainly because most do not know Hebrew and, most important, do not follow the Jewish post-biblical tradition of interpretation. On texts often neglected, see Gina Hens-Piazza, *Nameless, Blameless, and without Shame: Two Cannibal Mothers before a King* (Collegeville, MN: Liturgical Press, 2003), which integrates modern methods with spiritual sensitivity; Phyllis Trible, *Texts of Terror: Literary Feminist Readings of Biblical Narratives* (Philadelphia: Fortress Press, 1984); Tod Linafelt, *Surviving Lamentations: Catastrophe, Lament, and Protest in the Afterlife of a Biblical Book* (Chicago: University of Chicago, 2000); Claus Westermann, *Praise and Lament in the Psalms* (Atlanta, GA: John Knox, 1981); Erich Zenger, *A God of Vengeance? Understanding the Psalms of Divine Wrath,* trans. Linda Maloney (Louisville, KY: Westminster/John Knox, 1994).

68. Paul Ricoeur speaks of "a community of reading and of interpretation." He states, "It is in interpreting the Scriptures in question, that the community interprets itself" (Andre LaCocque and Paul Ricoeur, *Thinking Biblically: Exegetical and Hermeneutical Studies* [Chicago: University of Chicago Press, 1998], xvi).

69. Schneiders, "Biblical Spirituality," 137–41.

70. Pheme Perkins, "Paul and Ethics," *Interpretation* 28 (1984): 268–80.

71. William E. Lynch, SJ, *Images of Faith: An Exploration of the Ironic Imagination* (Notre Dame, IN: University of Notre Dame Press, 1973), ix–x. In one of his earliest and most impor-

tant writings, *Christ and Apollo* (New York: Sheed and Ward, 1960), Lynch used the phrase "analogous imagination," a concept now current through the work of David Tracy.

72. Art history should be integrated with history as a "constitutive" discipline for the academic study of spirituality. For a wonderful resource, see Elena Curti, "Every Picture Tells a Story," *The Tablet* (London) (June 25, 2004), 8–9. Curti reports on the work of Dee Dyas of the Christianity and Culture Project of York University (England), which has produced a superb CD of medieval art with explanations of the symbolism and context entitled "Images of Salvation: The Story of the Bible through Medieval Art." Evidence for the importance of art in the practice of spirituality is shown by the increased appreciation of spiritual guides using icons and other images. See, for example, Neil MacGregor with Erika Langmuir, *Seeing Salvation: Images of Christ in Art* (New Haven, CT: Yale University Press, 2000); Rowan Williams, *Ponder These Things: Praying with Icons of the Virgin* (Norwich: Canterbury, 2002); and idem, *The Dwelling of the Light: Praying with Icons of Christ* (Grand Rapids, MI: Eerdmans, 2003).

73. Francis Moloney, "Whither Catholic Biblical Studies," *Australian Catholic Record* 66 (January 1989): 84.

74. See "A Pastor's Vision: Cardinal Carlo Martini: Interview with Gerard O'Connell," *The Tablet* (London), July 10, 1993, 876–78.

5

THE GENRE OF GENDER
Gender and the Academic Study of Christian Spirituality

Lisa E. Dahill

In Jeffrey Eugenides's Pulitzer-Prize winning novel *Middlesex,* the main character is born with a rare genetic mutation. Categorized as female at birth, Calliope (or Callie) grows up a "normal" Greek American girl in Detroit, until at puberty her body starts developing differently from her friends'. She disguises her difference as long as she can, but an observant doctor finally notices something amiss. Sent off to a New York clinic specializing in gender ambiguities, Callie undergoes an intensive series of physical examinations, interviews, and psychological tests to determine her "real" gender and place in the world. Then, while her parents are meeting with the doctor to find out her medical fate, Callie spends a morning in the New York Public Library and decides to research some of the terminology she has overheard the doctor using about her. Moving to the huge Webster's Dictionary, she begins with *hypospadias* ("an abnormality of the penis"), then traces its synonyms to *eunuch* and eventually to *hermaphrodite.* There in Webster's she reads:

> *Hermaphrodite–1.* One having the sex organs and many of the secondary sex characteristics of both male and female. **2.** Anything comprised of a combination of diverse or contradictory elements. See synonyms at MONSTER.

The novel continues:

> There it was, *monster,* in black and white, in a battered dictionary in a great city library....*Monster.* Still there. It had not moved. And she wasn't reading this word on the wall of her old bathroom stall....The synonym was official, authoritative; it was the verdict that the culture gave on a person like her. *Monster.* That was what she was. That was what Dr. Luce and his colleagues had been saying. It explained so much, really. It explained her mother crying in the next room. It explained the false cheer in Milton's [her father's] voice....It explained the photographs, too. What did people do when they came upon Bigfoot or the Loch Ness Monster? They tried to get a picture. For a second Callie saw herself that way. As a lumbering, shaggy creature pausing at the edge of woods. As a humped convolvulus rearing its dragon's head from an icy lake. Her eyes were filling now, making the print swim, and she turned away and hurried out of the library. But the synonym pursued her. All the way out the door and down the steps between the stone lions, Webster's Dictionary kept calling after her, *Monster, Monster!*[1]

INTRODUCTION

Much work in the area of gender and spirituality has already been done. Recent decades have seen an incredible outpouring of research in areas never before conceived, exploring complex connections within particular historical contexts among gender, biological sex, sexuality, spiritual experience, culture, and God.[2] Yet when we look for studies specifically of gender and methodology within the field of Christian spirituality, many fewer come to light.[3] This essay takes its place in the latter category as an attempt to reflect methodologically on the significance of gender for the academic study of Christian spirituality—or more precisely, for the study of a given person's or community's spirituality within the rubrics of the field of Christian spirituality. The essay proceeds as follows. I first suggest commonality between analysis of *gender* and that of *genre* in literary studies, arguing that in both cases categories often viewed simplistically as merely classificatory are better understood as hermeneutical. Given the centrality of hermeneutics for Sandra Schneiders's approach to the study of Christian spirituality—indeed, her casting of the discipline itself *as* essentially hermeneutical—this view of gender allows for fruitful exploration in Christian spirituality.[4] Next I develop seven "levels" in relation to which one may explore the significance of gender for a particular person or community, particularly as these begin to open up the person's experience of divine presence. The levels are arranged in broadly ascending order as to their potential significance for the study of spirituality per se; yet what is perhaps most significant in exploring particular human experience on these levels is careful attention to holy or unholy "gaps" *between* them, places where others' perceptions of a person fail to correspond to the person's own self-perception, or where one's sense of God's vision of oneself transforms an inherited bias. The third section of the essay then briefly traces features of the necessary relationships among all three major "actors" in the scholarly exploration of gender and spirituality: the scholar, the person(s) being studied, and the God (however understood) perceived in the experience of the person(s) studied. In the final section of the essay I point to key implications emerging from examination of gender for the study and practice of Christian spirituality in contemporary US contexts.

TERMINOLOGY: THE GENRE OF GENDER

Callie's experience with Webster's Dictionary helps frame important questions around the study of gender and spirituality. Specifically, the episode cited, in which Callie discovers her "official" classification to be that of *monster,* lays bare the nearly irresistible human tendency toward conceiving of gender as a fixed, binary opposition. Human beings are assumed to be male *or* female, one or the other, and most cultures, churches, religions, and families around the world and throughout history have had very clear ideas about what a boy or girl, woman or man is supposed to do, feel, think, say, and so on. Those who don't fit within the binary mode in such a fundamental human classification as gender can, like Callie, only be conceived of as monsters.[5]

As a move toward a more helpful understanding of gender for the study of spirituality, I find it fruitful to compare the examination of gender with what goes on in literary studies around conceptions of *genre*. One sees this connection in the very roots of the words themselves: as literary scholar Mary Gerhart notes, "When we locate the term *genre* etymologically in a family of meanings across several disciplines, we find that the family of resemblances to which *genre* belongs includes such words as general, *gender*, genes, genus, generic, generation, generative" (emphasis added).[6] Genre is a category often thought to function in merely prescriptive or normative ways (such as in regulating poetic forms like sonnets); in this view genre is a timeless taskmaster functioning somehow from on high to restrict creativity into certain preset boxes. This static understanding corresponds to views of gender that are similarly rigid and binary. In reality, however, the function of genre is a much more fluid, back-and-forth process of meaning making between traditions of literature and present-day creativity and reception, all of which affect both the author's shaping and the reader's or audience's perception of a given work (think of the difference it makes to approach a play thinking it is a tragedy, only to realize mid-production it is actually a satire). Fundamentally, genre channels meaning—as much by innovative breaches or deviations from the expected norm as by conformations to them—even as each new instance stretches the genre itself.

As with genre in literature, then, gender in human culture and identity functions broadly to *locate* given phenomena (here, human beings rather than texts) within some standard framework of reference. Like other cultural markers such as race, class, generation, tribe, family/gang/cohort, and so on, categories of gender simplify otherwise impossibly complex human perception, allowing us to place one another instantly—usually subconsciously—within an interpretive category that determines how we will relate to this other person. Studies have shown that perception of gender difference arises very early among human children, and children take great care in learning, exploring, and testing what exactly these differences mean. Similarly, the experience of those who cross-dress, or otherwise do not seem to conform to predominant gender expectations in terms of demeanor or general appearance, can testify to the extraordinary degree of disorientation such "gender bending" can elicit in those who realize they don't immediately know where to place—and thus how to relate to—this person. In cultures where language itself contains explicitly gender-based coding, it might in fact be linguistically impossible to address such a person; and in nearly all human cultures, these persons often arouse the startled or horrified confusion Callie felt directed at her through the use of terms like *monster* or *freak*.[7]

We need classificatory frameworks in order to negotiate our way through an otherwise overwhelmingly complex world. Yet, as Callie's story illustrates, the schemata that are so helpful in simplifying the infinite particularity of human diversity, allowing us to relate coherently even with strangers, and giving us overarching frameworks of identity to which to aspire (or from which to deviate), also oversimplify reality—at times very painfully. Persons whose biological genitalia do not place them clearly within either gender, like Cal/Callie,[8] are rare. But their experience is all the more important in making clear the extent to which we each, though necessarily gendered in some way, are also simultaneously much more than any fixed binary conception can ever contain. For, of course, in reality Callie, transfixed at the New York Public Library Webster's Dictionary, is not a monster at all; she is a real, living human child, loved by her parents, successful in school, and undergoing an adolescence in which the "usual" teenage questions of personal identity, sexuality, individuation, and relationality are playing out, albeit in forms outside most others' experience.

For the academic study of Christian spirituality, then, which looks at data beyond the biological in its passion for the heart of human experience, questions of gender both include and go beyond often more binary-oriented explorations of feminist (or masculinist) spirituality-per-se, or even gay/lesbian or transgender spirituality and the like. Because feminist and other gender-oriented spiritualities tend to be formulated in more general[9] categories, while the study of spirituality typically prefers the particular, one might conclude that lenses like gender are not fine-grained enough to be of much direct use in the field. Yet that conclusion would miss the significance of gender studies in unmasking even greater generalizations, as when feminist analysis challenges male-biased voices purporting to speak for all of humanity. To ignore gender as a primary category of human experience also obscures the ways each person's experience is constructed through appropriation of these basic dimensions of selfhood,[10] and the ways social reality both forms and "de-forms" people along lines of power shaped by gender and other generic categories. At the same time, however, because such spiritualities are indeed oriented to *the* experience of, for instance, women (or smaller groupings of women or men around age, class, culture, race, sexual orientation, and so on), they can provide at best only coarse-grained levels of insight into the experience of any *particular* human being. To explore in greater complexity the actual contours of a given person's spiritual experience, rich and vast and mysterious as that is, requires additional forms of analysis.

SEVEN LEVELS OF GENDER

For the purpose of initial exploration, then, let us differentiate seven levels on which we might speak of gender in relation to the study of Christian spirituality. I illustrate each briefly by returning to the example of Cal/Callie in *Middlesex*.

1. Chromosomal: the sex coded into a person's genes, generally either female (XX) or male (XY). Occasionally mutations occur as well (XXY or XYY). *Cal/Callie is a chromosomal male.*

2. Medical/biological: the sex a person "presents as" at birth and beyond, according to genitalia and post-pubescent secondary sexual characteristics. This level includes, in addition to the usual forms of female and male physical-

ity, the appearance also of unusual genital forms, as in Cal/Callie's case as she matured. *Despite his chromosomal type, a genetic mutation caused Cal/Callie to look female and be so identified at birth.*

3. Socially/culturally/politically perceived: how a given individual is "read" according to gender norms by the person's culture or society within complex, widely shared coding systems outlining and, to a greater or lesser measure, attempting to prescribe core dimensions of identity according to medical/biological gender. This level describes the sex a person "presents as" socially.[11] *Cal/Callie is understood as female until puberty, at which point her gender becomes increasingly murky, especially in sexual explorations. After a fluid liminal period of being socially identified specifically as ambiguous, he moves into adulthood coded as male: Cal.*

4. Church perceived (if different from social/cultural perception): the ways the church perceives a person, which can be *positively* different from social perceptions as well as negatively so. *For Cal/Callie, church perception of her gender mirrors that of society, though key moments in the novel's narrative are captured through ecclesial ritual. The baby's baptism provides a sort of foreshadowing of future penile capacity, and a powerful image at the close of the novel shows Cal, returned home in his newly adopted male identity for his father's funeral, taking his place in a traditional Greek Orthodox male role in the leave-taking ritual.*

5. Other perceived: by close friends and family. *For Cal/Callie, family perception of his or her gender began even before birth. As the novel opens, Grandmother Desdemona is enacting her traditional ritual of predicting the gender of the unborn child. Having predicted a male, she is chastened (and her power in the family diminished) when Cal/Callie is born—apparently—female. The novel thus traces this level of other-perception from beginning to end and shows the ways various levels of perception fold over on one another. Predicted male, born and raised*

*female, Cal/Callie must negotiate a difficult family transi-
tion in the move into male adulthood—a move that, as it
turns out, Desdemona is uniquely positioned to receive.*

6. Self-perceived: the ways a person experiences himself or
herself as a gendered and sexual human being. Of course,
this is sometimes different from the person's biological sex
or the ways in which culture, society, church, and/or family and friends perceive the person. *Cal/Callie, in distinction from what many transsexuals describe, experiences
herself as female from birth. Only as male hormones
begin to reshape her body and emotions at puberty does
Cal/Callie move into a self-perception that eventually
draws him into adulthood; even here, however, strongly
masculine secondary characteristics cover a still ambiguous self-perception and relationality.*

7. God-perceived: what one might call the ultimate level of
gender identity. Of course, this could be debated. To what
extent do we imagine our ultimate identity is (or is not)
affected by our gender? How do the people we study sense
how God "sees" them as female, male, sexual, relational,
embodied, unique, precious? as communal and connective
and encultured? as Christian men, women, and other?
Does a given person's core God-experience include a gendered dimension (of God or oneself), or does it seem not
to? Does the way people experience God relating to them
confirm, deepen, or transform their sense of gendered
self?

The distinctiveness of the study of spirituality is found in its
desire to include this ultimate level within the academic exploration of Christian experience, here around questions of gender.
Yet our study can also and often must take place in relation to
other levels as well—except perhaps the chromosomal, since,
although very real, this does not involve direct human experience
(also, interestingly, it is the most overwhelmingly binary dimension
of gender).[12] All the other levels on which gender can be located
and traced are far from binary, as we each learn to negotiate the
overlapping, conflicting, confusing, or liberating ways in which we

experience ourselves on each level or are perceived by others. How, for example, does a girl's self-perception as female shape her emerging spirituality? How does her culture's or church's expectations of her as female shape her? How does her sense of God's relation to her as female affect her? What if this girl is a chromosomal male like Callie? What if a person's biological sex and self-perception are female, but in ways that challenge her culture's notions of female behavior, like Hildegard of Bingen?[13] Or what if (like Perpetua in her dream), a woman finds God treating her as a male, even as her breasts drip with milk for her newborn baby?[14] The texts of Christian mystics through the ages are replete with gender-expanding or gender-inverting images, and the complexity is hardly less in studies of contemporary figures. Clearly, in order to understand a given person's *actual* experience in its fullness, as that includes gender, we must look carefully at how the person seems to perceive herself or himself at these levels, how certain levels of perceptions may seem to contradict or illumine others, and how each may contribute to a fuller appreciation of that person's spirituality in all its complexity and particularity.[15]

Let me conclude this section with a summary observation. Given this complexity of dimensions shaping the significance of gender in any given project in the study of Christian spirituality, I suggest that scholars in this field claim gender as a primarily *hermeneutical* rather than *classificatory* framework. That is, because the understanding of gender in a given text, community, or human life is necessarily inductive and particular, grounded in the experience (in all its richness and texture) of the person(s) in question, the significance of gender for the person(s) under study cannot be assumed a priori. Rather, the ways in which the scholar can trace the seven levels of "gendered" experience delineated above, as those juxtapose in the experience of the person(s) being studied, must be explored to a greater or lesser extent anew for each new project. As is well known in the case of *genre,* so too in *gender* study: each new instance, whether outwardly conforming to the canons of its type or not, subtly or radically changes the meaning of the genre to which it apparently belongs.[16] A woman who does "unwomanly" things not only risks drawing fire from those most invested in her culture's gender norms; but she also in unmistakable ways changes the very meaning, or the perceived range of potential identity, role, and actions, of female humanity itself for those who know (of) her. And even persons who have no interest in challenging gender norms, simply by their very existence and the choices they make within a given personal, familial, social, or religious milieu, are incarnating the category of woman or man in contexts never before experienced—so here too the *meaning* of their gender must always be explored and can never be assumed.[17] Like genre, gender is a hermeneutical tool, not a classificatory one.

THREEFOLD INTERRELATION OF GENDERS

Yet these reflections are not yet adequate, for they focus to this point solely on the (perceived) meaning of gender for the *person(s) being studied*. Because of the self-implicating nature of the study of Christian spirituality, and the inherently relational quality of the subject matter itself—that is, a person's experience of God, whether or not divine reality is understood in personal terms—there are two further dimensions of gender important to note here. First, in reference to the *scholar* engaging in a given project, clearly his or her conscious or unconscious experience of gender shapes the very questions perceived and pursued, as well as methodology, analysis, and so on. As with many other dimensions of self-implication, each scholar approaches the study of gender in spirituality as both insider and outsider; the careful recognition of both commonality and difference in relation to the subject(s) of one's study is necessary for that blend of empathy and detachment conducive to insightful critical scholarship.[18] To some extent, an "insider" position of scholar to subject(s), for example, within the same gender, can be helpful. And scholarship in this field always presumes some level of "insider" connection between the scholar and the person(s) under study: sometimes gender or culture, sometimes denomination or spiritual tradition, and, if nothing else, simply the assumption of shared Christian faith. Yet, of course, gender norms of dominant US academic circles in the early twenty-first century—to say nothing of the scholar's own particularities of roles, identity, and faith experience—shape even those of the same gender as their subjects in ways that can make them as much an outsider as an insider to the experience of the person they are studying. Scholars' awareness of the seven levels of gender delineated above, as these shape *our own* experience of femaleness or maleness and condition us (often unconsciously) in our approach to the men or women we are studying, can make possible more conscious awareness of difference as well as similarity and fewer instances of blatant distortion of the other. So, a scholar studying Cal/Callie's (fictional) experience would do well to pay close attention to the ways one's own perceptions of identity, role, and so forth have been shaped not only by gender but by encounter with persons who blur gender boundaries, in order to do justice to Cal/Callie's experience as *human* and *particular* rather than simply as "monster" (or an idealized version of the same category of "freak"). Our gender as scholars and our experience of that gender on some level shapes our lenses of analysis, and we do well to pay attention.

In addition to the person(s) being studied, and the scholar doing the study, both of whom are human and therefore gendered, scholarship in this field has also to do necessarily with perceptions of *God*, to whom in Christian history a great deal of energy has also been invested around questions of gender. Who *is* this G*D perceived to be active (or absent or indeterminate) in the experience of the subject?[19] And how is S/He understood to be gendered, if at all? Needless to say, any adequate notion of God transcends—and shatters—idolatries of divine gender as exclusive or ontological categories of the divine being. Yet despite consistent biblical prohibitions on graven images, humans seem perennially unable to resist casting our experience of the utterly Transcendent into human and thus necessarily gendered names, perceptions, and metaphors. The Christian Trinity, named Father, Son, and Holy Spirit, seems to give (at least in Latin and its derivative languages) a normative maleness to all three Persons. And, of course, Jesus' male humanity makes unavoidable these questions of gender in relation to God, even as Jesus himself takes on various female or maternal forms in mystical literature from very early on in Christian tradition. Given all this gender floating around even in relation to the One supposedly transcending all human categories, to what extent do internalized notions of gender unconsciously frame God-experience into the terms a given person "expects" of a male or female Other: stern, caring, friendly, tender, passionate? Or, in the other direction, to what extent does a person's *actual* God-experience subvert or recast the individual's internalized sense of gendered relationality, through, for example, experience with Jesus as Mother, or surprises like homoerotic God-experience among heterosexual pray-ers? One hears in spiritual direction or finds in mystical texts unending varieties of bodily and "gender-y" plasticity and surprise in God-relationship, making impossible again any predetermined understandings of what an experience of God "as" male or female might *mean* (to a given person), or how experiences of the "gender" of G*D might reinforce, challenge, or entirely deconstruct internalized or enacted sexism, homophobia, personal/sexual self-image, and so on. Once again, for study of Christian *spirituality*, not only the scholar and the subject's experience of gender but the significance of the (perceived) gender of God as well is primarily a hermeneutical datum. It is of interest for its meaning *to the person* experiencing God in a particular way, rather than in attempts to state a priori that a given image is, by definition, problematic for certain categories of persons. Ultimately, projects exploring spirituality and gender look at questions like, Who is G*D for the person(s) being studied, and how, if at all, does this God-experience support or recast or transform their understanding of their own humanity or others' humanity, *as* gendered? Finally, that is, God is the ultimate hermeneut potentially opening human perceptions of gender beyond self-imposed or other-imposed limits. Thus again, it is with level seven on the chart above that the study of spirituality is distinctively concerned.

We have identified three "actors" whose perceived gender, understanding of gender, or experience of gender may affect any given project in the study of Christian spirituality: the scholar, the subject of scholarship, and the G*D perceived in the experience being studied. All three of these actors may relate in surprising ways in these questions; as scholars we may find our God-experience being stretched in the encounter with the subject(s) of study, or we may discover that our own gender presuppositions need recasting through the One our explorations reveal. The question, Who is God for Julian, or Ignatius, or Thérèse, or Bonhoeffer, as female/male? may turn out to become the question, Who is God for me as female/male? And the stretching these encounters make possible can, in turn, open up unexpected space for insight into Julian's, Ignatius's, Thérèse's, or Bonhoeffer's gendered and utterly human God-experience as well.

SUMMARY AND IMPLICATIONS

To this point we have been exploring the significance of gender in the academic study of Christian spirituality as that study engages scholars with subjects, that is, persons, in all their particularity and in all the fullness of their experience our methodological and historical limits may permit us to glimpse. While I assume a feminist stance throughout this essay, I have refrained here from focusing primarily on feminist (or other) spiritualities because the circle of experience they encompass is typically so large (here, some subset of all women's experience) as to be far removed from the concrete, textured, and unpredictable lived experience our discipline desires to trace. Thus, I have been attempting instead to set forth space within which the *meaning* of gender as a hermeneutical category might unfold in a given project, within a project's particular confluence of scholar, subject(s), and God as these (appear to) relate to gender. For both scholar and subject the implicit and explicit meaning of their own and others' genders are conditioned, I have asserted, by the complex interplay between seven levels of perception and reality regarding gender, ranging from the chromosomal to the broadly social to the personal, and finally to the most intimate mystery of God's own vision of a person. I am interested in how, within these interrelations, a given scholar might consciously frame and pursue a given research project involving a given subject and attend responsibly to the significance of that subject's gender—as well as how the scholar's own explicit or implicit experience of gender and God necessarily shapes these person-forming encounters in all their personal particularity.

Yet, even within an essay devoted to the particular, I nevertheless wish to make some concluding comments oriented to *general* potential dimensions of gender as well. For, of course, individuals, even in all their unpredictable and unrepeatable particularity, exist within social systems as well, and spiritual experience unfolds in ways essentially formed—or deformed—by these. I find four primary constellations around which questions of gender take especially urgent form in the study and practice of Christian spirituality today: (1) gender, embodiment, sexuality, and intimacy; (2) gender, anger, sexism, and homophobia in church and society; (3) gender and violence; and (4) gender, identity, self-love, and self-transcendence. The first two find important treatment in a nearly endless, and endlessly important, series of studies exploring topics around questions of justice and fullness of life for all, especially in repressive church structures.[20] The third of these constellations is increasingly finding resonance in a variety of texts oriented toward ministry with those who suffer sexual trauma of many kinds.[21] In a sense, the first two—body/sexuality and sexism/homophobia, both considered in light of Christian spirituality—lay the groundwork for consideration of this third constellation of themes, namely, gender and violence. That is, one needs (1) a healthy, vibrant, and life-giving Christian view of the body, gender, and sexuality in order to perceive (2) how demonically sexism and other forms of sexual oppression violate God's intention for the created flourishing of all persons, precisely as gendered—particularly in the church as those invited into loving communion with God's own *imago* in Jesus Christ. And these foundations make possible then the further exploration into (3) the experience of violence itself, since ultimately sexism and sexual oppression, like racism and other forms of systemic dehumanization, are simultaneously manifestations and justifications of debilitating violence against human beings. The experience of trauma (particularly when sustained over time, as in domestic violence or other forms of imprisonment and torture, but also in shorter-term violence such as rape or combat) strips a person of coherence, core security, and essential facets of identity—indeed, as many survivors attest, ultimately of the connection to their essential humanity itself, and to God.[22] Because gender so often factors into violence; because violence in subtle, systemic, verbal, sexual, or physical forms represents the antithesis of divine intention for human experience; and because in Jesus Christ God joins us in gendered, physical, bodily vulnerability to torture and trauma, and provides a way out, ending the dominion of terror—for all these reasons, our own explorations of gender and spirituality do well to take seriously the effects of trauma and our participation in God's endless and tender healing of all those caught in its hell and hopelessness.

Finally, this progression leads to consideration of connections among (4) gender, identity, self-love, and self-transcendence as well. Embraced in our gendered bodily fragility, redeemed from the endless infliction of violence, we begin to experience ourselves in reality as the selves we are created to be in that same *imago Dei,* Jesus Christ. Self-love has had a very bad name in Christian history, used more often than not as an unthinking synonym for sin. Yet in reality, of course, the capacity for authentic self-love—of the sort that opens out in freedom and trust to God and other persons, and in self-offering of one's gifts to the world—is a fruit not of hell but of heaven itself. For those whose core identities, their gendered body-selves, are marked by shame or abuse, the self is abhorred, suffocated, regarded as filthy.[23] And often, learning to love *this very self* proves the most difficult, and the most liberating, part of a person's spiritual healing and growth; that is, learning to live entirely, physically, soul and heart and spirit, into that radical and astonishing mercy of God permeating and transforming all things—even the most despised. For many people, self-love is *itself* an essential part of that radical reformation of heart in Christ they desire and fear. Spiritualities, therefore, that teach children or adults to disregard themselves, that speak too glibly of self-love as sinful or of selflessness as holy, risk unwittingly reinforcing the self-hatred at the core of those invisibly traumatized persons who fill our churches' pews and our seminaries' classrooms—and thwarting the Holy Spirit's own stirrings toward the birth of an authentic and life-giving self-love. Similarly, the language of self-transcendence can be beautiful and holy, moving us to visions of God and vocations of service beyond the limits of ego, opening us to communion with others and that awesome Other sweeter than any self-serving greed can imagine.[24] Yet to those struggling even to imagine God and self in the same breath, images of self-transcendence can seem to promise premature escape from precisely that messy, hated, shadowy self God longs to embrace. To flee the self God treasures, "transcending" it for the sake of a holiness more ethereal than incarnate, could mean fleeing the very place God is waiting.

On the seven levels of gender explored earlier, I included reference to the character of Cal/Callie at every level except the final one. Despite occasional clues, the novel does not provide direct insight into how its central character may have experienced God, let alone how Cal/Callie may have sensed God's relation to him (or her) as gendered. Yet the place the novel ends, so to speak, is where our discipline steps in. In relation to persons for whom we do have texts, ministries, words, actions, art works, or other artifacts embodying more clearly—though always incompletely—lived experience of God, we can begin the fascinating exploration of how gender and spirituality come together in actual, particular human lives. We can explore with great respect and with playful creativity that mysterious and fundamental human genre of gender.

Notes

1. Jeffrey Eugenides, *Middlesex* (New York: Picador/Farrar Straus Giroux, 2002), 430–32.

2. Many of these studies of interest for Christian spirituality are oriented historically, attempting to shed light on the role of gender, or the experience of women in particular, in specific historical and spiritual contexts. For instance, for studies specifically oriented to historical questions of spirituality and gender, see Carolyn Walker Bynum, *Fragmentation and Redemption: Essays on Gender and the Human Body in Medieval Religion* (Cambridge, MA: MIT Press, 1991); Grace M. Jantzen, *Power, Gender, and Christian Mysticism* (Cambridge: Cambridge University Press, 1995); and Amy Hollywood, *Sensible Ecstasy: Mysticism, Sexual Difference, and the Demands of History*

(Chicago: University of Chicago Press, 2002). For theological overviews of contemporary gender studies, see, for instance, Elaine L. Graham, *Making the Difference: Gender, Personhood, and Theology* (Minneapolis: Fortress Press, 1995); and Anne-Louise Eriksson, *The Meaning of Gender in Theology: Problems and Possibilities* (Uppsala: Acta Universitatis Uppsaliensis, 1995).

3. A promising analysis of feminist spiritualities, specifically around themes of power, is found in Sarah Coakley, *Powers and Submissions: Spirituality, Philosophy, and Gender* (Oxford: Blackwell Press, 2002). Yet, despite including *spirituality* in its title, this study is actually oriented more to theology and philosophy. My own work on Dietrich Bonhoeffer's spirituality provides a gender-based analysis but does not attempt the more methodologically oriented work on gender and spirituality of the present essay (see Lisa E. Dahill, "Reading from the Underside of Selfhood: Bonhoeffer and Spiritual Formation," in *Minding the Spirit: The Study of Christian Spirituality*, ed. Elizabeth A. Dreyer and Mark S. Burrows [Baltimore: Johns Hopkins Press, 2005], 249–66).

4. Sandra Schneiders, "A Hermeneutical Approach to the Study of Christian Spirituality," in Dreyer and Burrows, *Minding the Spirit*, 49–60.

5. Only very recently have understandings of gender as a spectrum of sorts, rather than clear and ontologically binding binary categories, become even thinkable. For an overview of major shifts in Western conceptions of gender beginning with Plato, see Elaine Graham, "What Is Gender?" in Graham, *Making the Difference*, 11–34. However, for millennia at least, possibly as a result of such apparently rigid classifications, human beings have been fascinated by the play possible between gender roles and identities. In ritual dramas and jesters' personae, costume balls and fairy tales, trickster stories and dreams, legends of magic and adventure, children and adults have loved to vicariously "try on" gendered possibilities closed to them in their ordinary lives. Certainly the play of imagination across otherwise tightly enforced boundaries shows the extent to which *humanity* far transcends gender stereotypes.

6. Mary Gerhart, "The Dilemma of the Text: How to 'Belong' to a Genre," *Poetics* 18 (1989): 367.

7. Some cultures view persons of ambiguous gender, like Cal/Callie, as a "third sex," to which may be attributed special spiritual powers of insight, discernment, or prophecy. See, for example, Gilbert Herdt, ed., *Third Sex, Third Gender: Beyond Sexual Dimorphism in Culture and History* (New York: Zone; Cambridge, MA: MIT Press, 1993). For a sensitive medical-sociological study of the experience of "intersexual" persons, see Sharon E. Preves, *Intersex and Identity: The Contested Self* (New Brunswick, NJ: Rutgers University Press, 2003).

8. The present-day narrating male is called Cal and the remembered childhood female, Callie.

9. Note the etymological connection again between *gender* and *general;* to speak of gender *is* to speak in general, of (once again) the genre/generic, at least to the extent one attempts to speak for all representatives of a given gender.

10. In *Landscapes of the Soul: The Loss of Moral Meaning in American Life* (Oxford: Oxford University Press, 2001), 30ff., Douglas Porpora uses the sociological language of "master statuses" to explore the significance of gender as well as culture and sexual orientation in providing core framing structures of human identity.

11. Though often thought of as rigidly binary, in reality these norms function in more fluid ways. We see this in matters of genre as well as gender. In literature, for instance, some texts may seem to embody a given genre more paradigmatically than others, as in biology robins or eagles or retrievers seem somehow more inherently "bird-y" or "doggy" than, say, ostriches, penguins, or Chihuahuas. So too, even though all males and females are chromosomally equivalent, the social "genre of gender" in a given culture perceives some women or men as more paradigmatically "womanly" or "manly" than others.

12. Note the etymological connection here again; only on the level of *genes* can we typically speak of *gender* as binary. The above levels show a progression from more to less fixed binary character, or simultaneously from less to more potential fluidity.

13. See, for instance, Sabina Flanagan, *Hildegard of Bingen: A Visionary Life* (London: Routledge, 1998); and Barbara Newman, *Sister of Wisdom: St. Hildegard's Theology of the*

Feminine (Berkeley and Los Angeles: University of California Press, 1997).

14. On the martyrdom, visions, and dreams of Saint Perpetua, see *The Acts of the Christian Martyrs,* trans. and intro. Herbert Musurillo (Oxford: Clarendon Press, 1972).

15. A recent analysis by Elizabeth A. Dreyer ably traces these complexities with regard to female medieval mystics, drawing implications for the study of Christian spirituality. See "Whose Story Is It?—The Appropriation of Medieval Mysticism," *Spiritus* 4, no. 2 (Fall 2004): 151–72.

16. Alastair Fowler notes in *Kinds of Literature: An Introduction to the Theory of Genres and Modes* (Cambridge: Harvard University Press, 1982), 22: "To have any artistic significance, to mean anything distinctive in a literary way, a work must modulate or vary or depart from its generic conventions, and consequently alter them for the future....However a work relates to existing genre—by conformity, variation, innovation, or antagonism—it will tend, if it becomes known, to bring about new states of these genres." The same is true, if apparently imperceptibly in most cases, for *gender* as well in the lived/embodied experience of each new person.

17. I am not asserting this to be a process of simplistic clarity. Mary Gerhart describes three primary frameworks for understanding genre, and, by my own analogy, gender: (1) traditional: how each new instance is understood within, and does not transcend, its given categories; (2) ideological: constructions of gender as "systematically biased" and unavoidably political (356); and (3) deconstructive: each new instance of gender not only subtly or dramatically recasting the whole genre but destroying it outright. That is, just as "written texts control writers and readers" (365), so too each new personal enactment of gender has the potential to reframe it in ways neither individuals nor culture itself control.

18. See Dreyer and Burrows, *Minding the Spirit,* 61–151. This section deals with self-implication in the study of Christian spirituality; see also the works cited on this topic in that volume's bibliography.

19. I use *G*D* here to highlight the essentially unknowable nature of another's experience of the Divine—indeed, of our own

as well. When *God* is used too glibly it can at times seem to imply that we know exactly what we mean by this word and by others' use of it. The unusual spelling provides an occasional reminder (like the Jewish refusal to speak or even spell out the holy Name) of divine transcendence—God's own inherent genre-breaking capacities, if you will.

20. Sandra Schneiders's work has included work on this level, taking on institutional forms of sexism in her own Roman Catholic Church. See for instance, *With Oil in Their Lamps: Faith, Feminism, and the Future* (New York: Paulist Press, 2000).

21. Key texts for those interested in pursuing questions of gender and violence specifically around implications for spirituality include Pamela Cooper-White, *The Cry of Tamar: Violence against Women and the Church's Response* (Minneapolis: Fortress Press, 1995); Mary Jo Barrett, "Healing from Trauma: The Quest for Spirituality," in *Spiritual Resources in Family Therapy,* ed. Froma Walsh (New York: Guilford Press, 1999), 193–208; and Flora A. Keshgegian, *Redeeming Memories: A Theology of Healing and Transformation* (Nashville, TN: Abingdon Press, 2000).

22. See the psychiatrist Judith Herman's *Trauma and Recovery: The Aftermath of Violence—From Domestic Abuse to Political Terror* (New York: Basic Books, 1992), for a devastating comprehensive examination of the effects of trauma on the human psyche. Herman highlights *as parallel* traumas typically associated with men (combat, torture) and with women (rape, domestic violence), treating as well the compounding horror of trauma begun in childhood (child physical and sexual abuse). Her exploration of recovery from trauma in the later sections of the book is an essential resource for those in ministry as well as all who work with persons exposed to violence in any form.

23. On themes of self-silencing or the suffocation of the self precisely as gendered/female, see, among others, Dana Crowley Jack, *Silencing the Self: Women and Depression* (Cambridge, MA: Harvard University Press, 1991); Janet L. Jacobs, "The Endangered Female Self and the Search for Identity," in *The Endangered Self,* ed. Richard K. Fenn and Donald Capps (Princeton, NJ: Center for Religion, Self, and Society, 1992),

37–46; and Bernice Martin, "Whose Soul Is It Anyway? Domestic Tyranny and the Suffocated Soul," in *On Losing the Soul: Essays in the Social Psychology of Religion,* ed. Richard K. Fenn and Donald Capps (Albany, NY: SUNY Press, 1995), 69–96.

24. See, for instance, Walter E. Conn, *The Desiring Self: Rooting Pastoral Counseling and Spiritual Direction in Self-Transcendence* (New York: Paulist Press, 1998).

6

THE CONTRIBUTIONS OF THE NATURAL SCIENCES TO THE ACADEMIC DISCIPLINE OF CHRISTIAN SPIRITUALITY

Robert John Russell

> The study of spirituality as experience requires us to bring into play not only theology and historical studies but...the natural sciences.
>
> —Sandra Schneiders

WORKING DEFINITION OF CHRISTIAN SPIRITUALITY AS AN ACADEMIC DISCIPLINE

In her 1997 presidential address to the Society for the Study of Christian Spirituality, Sandra M. Schneiders offered a pivotal definition of the subject matter of *spirituality as an academic discipline.* Spirituality is "the experience of conscious involvement in the project of life-integration through self-transcendence toward the ultimate value one perceives." For Christians, the ultimate value is "the triune God revealed in Jesus Christ" as lived in the context of the church community and mediated by the Holy

I want to thank Nancy Wiens for her extensive, careful, and insightful suggestions during the editing of the final version and of her corrections to Figure 6–1.

Spirit. By living within this context, "one relates in a particular way to all of reality and it is this relationship to the whole of reality as a Christian which constitutes Christian spirituality."[1] In short, Christian spirituality in the academy is the study of "the experience of the Christian spiritual life."[2]

Crucial to this definition is a twofold understanding of the term *spiritual*. (1) Anthropological: the term reminds us that the discipline of Christian spirituality is concerned with "the radical capacity of the human subject for self-transcendence." This focus on the human subject means that anthropology, psychology, and related disciplines play an essential role in relation to Christian spirituality as an academic discipline. (2) Theological: The term *spiritual* also reminds us that Christian spirituality is "concerned with the divine Spirit with which the human spirit is engaged." Theology then plays an essential role in critically reflecting on the meaning of spirit and in naming it as the Spirit of God. Equally crucial to Schneiders's definition is the term *experience*. It distinguishes Christian spirituality as an academic discipline from theology, historical studies, and religious studies, since it both includes and transcends them.[3] Finally, the term *life* points beyond isolated moments or episodes to the whole sweep of integration involving what Schneiders calls "the life project." In fact, such integration extends even further beyond us for, as Schneiders so eloquently writes, we live within the horizon of ultimacy, and Christian spirituality is constituted by the particular way we relate to *the whole of reality* within this horizon of ultimacy.[4] Let us turn to a more careful, though all too brief, discussion of further details in Schneiders's treatment of the object and method before discussing the role of the natural sciences in relation to Christian spirituality.[5]

TWO LAYERS OF DISCIPLINES WITHIN CHRISTIAN SPIRITUALITY

Schneiders asserts that the discipline of Christian spirituality requires a hermeneutical methodology that is "intrinsically and irreducibly interdisciplinary" because "the object it studies, transformative Christian experience as such, is multi-faceted." This interdisciplinarity consists in two layers of intertwined method-ologies:[6] (1) The first layer consists of two "constitutive" disci-plines and their methodologies: the study of scripture and the study of the history of Christianity, or "divine self-revelation" and "lived human response to revelation." (2) The second layer involves the "problematic" disciplines that offer crucial perspec-tives on the experiential aspect of Christian spirituality. Here Schneiders explicitly includes science along with psychology, soci-ology, literature, and so on. In sum, "as Scripture and history of Christianity come into play because the experience being studied is *Christian,* the problematic disciplines come into play because the object of study is *experience as such.*"[7]

What about theology? Schneiders sees it as belonging to both layers. It functions as a constitutive discipline when, through critical reflection on scripture and the history of Christian experi-ence, it sets out the Christian character of such experience. Still, it remains within the scope of the *problematic* disciplines because, while offering critical reflection on experience, it can never sup-ply the actual data of Christian spiritual experience.

FOUR WAYS IN WHICH THE NATURAL SCIENCES ENTER INTO THE ACADEMIC STUDY OF CHRISTIAN SPIRITUALITY

[Many topics] demand an interdisciplinary approach in which the problematic discipline(s) are often much more central to the research than the constitutive disciplines which function as a background or frame of reference.[8]

The spirituality of many Christians is deeply influenced by the effect on their God-image of developments in the natural sciences.[9]

Given Schneiders's discussion about the academic study of Christian spirituality, what are the ways in which the natural sciences enter into this study? Schneiders has already given us several important suggestions.

First, as the first of the two quotations above suggests, Schneiders holds that the natural sciences function as one of the problematic disciplines when they offer crucial perspectives on Christian spiritual experience *qua* experience. Drawing on an example Schneiders offers, suppose we are studying the spirituality of Teresa of Avila (1515–82). If, as Schneiders points out, we wanted to study Teresa's self-esteem, it would be appropriate, even necessary, to employ psychology. In a similar fashion, I suggest, if we wished to study Teresa's experience of being creaturely, that is, of dependence on food, water, and air, and of being finite and mortal, it would be appropriate to discuss her understanding of the natural world and her place in it. In the sixteenth century two traditional cosmologies were operative: a biblical view of a three-storied universe, and an Aristotelian/Ptolemaic cosmology of nested spheres surrounding the Earth with God in the highest realm above the stars. (Both were to be displaced by the new Copernican heliocentric cosmology.) These cosmologies would to some extent affect Teresa's experience of God as both transcendent, the majestic creator of heaven and earth, and as the immanent divine presence in her innermost self. Finally, we might explore the ways in which Teresa's spirituality can be reclaimed today by seeking to reframe it in the context of Big Bang cosmology, biological evolution, and contemporary scientific anthropology.[10]

A second way the natural sciences enter into the academic study of Christian spirituality is as a shaping—often even a defining—factor in contemporary culture. Here I need to question Schneiders's limitation of the constitutive disciplines to scripture and the history of Christianity. Although I would place culture as a third-order source following on scripture as foundational and the history of Christianity as secondary, without the explicit inclusion of culture I am concerned that we might isolate Christian spirituality within the confines of sacred text and tradition.[11]

If we include culture as a third source for Christian spirituality, then it follows that science influences Christian spirituality through its role in culture. Clearly, there are innumerable ways in which science explicitly shapes contemporary culture through such discoveries as the origin of the universe thirteen billion years ago in the Big Bang, the 3.5 billion year evolution of life on earth, and the myriad connections among all living species through the four-letter genetic code. This wondrous knowledge is the common inheritance of our age and the framework that shapes every dimension of culture from education to the media, from international space programs to modern medicine, communications, and travel. Just as the prevailing cosmologies, anthropologies, and natural histories shaped the culture in which scripture was formulated and historical Christianity unfolded, so too is contemporary culture contoured by the discoveries and horizons of science. In sum, science, transmitted through culture, impinges profusely on Christian spiritual experience.[12]

Third, Schneiders also stresses the "horizon of ultimacy" within which our lives transpire, and it is through this horizon that Christian spirituality relates constitutively to the *whole of reality.* Along with the more explicit ways we have just seen that science influences Christian spirituality, I believe that the natural sciences have a profound, if often implicit, effect on Christian spirituality by the way they shape our intuitive understanding and lived experience of ourselves in relation to the "whole of reality." Of course, science offers us moving images of the "denizens" of this whole: galaxies strewn like candles across the inky black night of inter-galactic space, molecules dazzling in endless dance within every grain of sand on every beach on earth, the future of the universe stretching out forever in endless expansion. Even while these are only created portions of the "whole of reality," they offer analogies and mirrors and images of that truly ultimate horizon of divine life in which our Christian spirituality is constituted and toward and through which it lives in hope. But science might also be able to shed some light, at least, on what we might mean by the "whole of reality." In 1915, Albert Einstein's general theory of relativity led to a scientific perspective on that "whole" in terms of Big Bang cosmology. Here space and time merge into a single, four-dimensional framework, spacetime, and the universe is depicted as a three-dimensional sphere or saddle expanding in time from its "absolute beginning" some thirteen billion years ago. Using Big Bang cosmology, many scholars in theology and science talk about God as the transcendent Creator *ex nihilo* of the "universe-as-a-whole," to use Arthur Peacocke's phrase.[13] Others, however, such as William Stoeger, argue that the concept of the "universe as a whole" is a philosophical concept that embraces but extends beyond what science can ever adequately describe.[14]

This leads to a crucial insight into the unique role of Christian spirituality as an academic discipline: It may well be that the "whole of reality," even the "whole of physical reality" or the "whole of the physical dimension of reality," will continue to transcend science. In that case it would serve as a philosophical limit question that points to theology and spirituality for its ultimate expression. Hence I suggest that with Christian spirituality, the conceptual goal of scientific cosmology, that of addressing the universe as a whole, meets an academic discipline capable of interpreting the "whole of reality" based on the lived experience of the God who transcends that whole and yet is immanent to every part of it.

Fourth and finally, the natural sciences enter into the academic study of Christian spirituality through the relations theology has to spirituality and in light of the many ways science and theology interact. Theology, according to Schneiders, can be both a constitutive discipline and a problematic discipline of spirituality. When "theology" refers to those specific programs in which theology and science are in dialogue and, more so, interaction, it seems reasonable that this interaction in turn makes science, even if indirectly, a constitutive and a problematic discipline of spirituality. We will explore this approach in the rest of this essay.

FOCUSING ON "THEOLOGY AND SCIENCE" AND ITS RELATION TO CHRISTIAN SPIRITUALITY

Barbour's Typology in Relation to Christian Spirituality

There is an exponentially growing wealth of literature on "theology and science" at both introductory and research levels.[15] One very helpful way to sort through this literature is to start with the many ways science and theology can be related, using the very illuminating typology offered by the pioneer of the field, physicist-theologian Ian G. Barbour.[16] This scheme includes four broad types of relations: conflict, independence, dialogue and integration. Each of these types carries with it important implications for Christian spirituality, as we shall see.

CONFLICT

The *conflict* model is common in Western culture, where the triumph of scientific theories too often leads to the hegemony of the scientific world view. Atheistic scientists (Jacques Monod, Richard Dawkins, Stephen Weinberg, and others) interpret science through the lens of philosophical reductionism, claiming that scientific knowledge is the only valid form of knowledge (epistemological reductionism), that only physical causes can affect the world's future (causal reductionism), and that only science describes reality (ontological reductionism, materialism). Since God is necessarily left out of scientific theories, the conclusion they draw is that there is no God, yielding metaphysical naturalism or scientifically based atheism. Needless to say, the implications of this *interpretation* of science for Christian spirituality, if left unchallenged, would be devastating. If scientific materialists were correct in their interpretation of science, Christian spirituality would be reduced to the study of psychological neuroses at best!

Fortunately, a growing number of scholars over the past half century have developed a variety of careful and convincing responses to this interpretation, responses that undercut arguments for reductionism and make room for a constructive approach to religion in light of science. For example, although science does not invoke God in its explanations, that does not mean that God does not exist. As the saying goes, absence of evidence is not evidence of absence. It is true that religious fundamentalists all too often fall victim to such atheistic interpretations of science by attacking science instead of attacking atheism; a classic example is the 1920s Scopes trial. I believe, however, that we should liberate science from its atheistic imprisonment and give it a robust theological interpretation, one that informs and enlivens our Christian spiritual experience of the astonishing universe that God is creating.

INDEPENDENCE

Many scholars walk away from the conflict by insisting that science and religion are totally *independent* of each other. If this were true, conflict, in principle, would be irrational. This approach is often rooted in the philosophy of the eighteenth-century Enlightenment, Protestant liberal theology in the nineteenth century, and twentieth-century existentialist and neo-orthodox theologies, all of which tend to keep science and religion in separate "watertight compartments."

Granted, the independence model can relieve some of the tension generated by the conflict model, and many seek it for this reason. Still, the cost to Christian spirituality in both its academic and lived forms is a treasured opportunity lost. Imagine the *spiritual* impoverishment of not being able to gaze at the stars at night and recognize our home in the universe, or not being able to ponder the profound implications of human genetics and our indelible link with all of life on earth. In sum, the independence model divorces our spiritual experience of nature from our scientific understanding of nature—and this divorce is unnecessary since there are creative ways to engage science without wholesale conflict or glacial isolation.

DIALOGUE

Barbour's pioneering scholarship takes us beyond the fruitless and costly "conflict or independence" options into a rich new world of shimmering vistas. Following the path of *dialogue,* he reminds us that, historically, Christian theology contributed to the intellectual climate in which the natural sciences arose. Its distinctive claim that the world is created *ex nihilo* by God means that the world is both contingent and rational. *Contingency* means that the universe need not exist, that its sheer existence is its most profound mystery. Contingent existence cries out for an explanation, and for theists, that explanation is God the Creator. Being contingent also means that genuine knowledge about nature can only come from empirical methods and not from purely deductive reason. The *rationality* of the universe means that nature is knowable to reason and our rational knowledge can be represented in mathematics, as Thomas Torrance[17] and John Polkinghorne[18] have stressed.

These features—contingency and rationality—have tremendous implications for Christian spirituality. The *contingency* of the universe and all that is within it—including us—means that we are all creatures. There is no Gnostic "divine spark" within our mortal bodies, nor is the material universe a strategy by which God saves immortal souls from an endless fall into oblivion (Origin). Instead, God's ongoing gift to us is our sheer existence, just as it is to all creatures and to "all that is," our universe. The spiritual significance here is that our very being as a living creature—that which is presupposed as a condition for the possibility of experience and thus of spiritual experience—is a continuous gift of God who is more immanent to us than we are to ourselves. The significance for Christian spirituality of the *rationality* of the universe is that this rationality is grounded in the Logos/Word of God through which all things are created and redeemed and which is present to us in our capacity to understand the universe through science.[19]

The model of dialogue points to the limit questions (or what David Tracy calls "limit-situations") that science raises but that science cannot explain, such as why the universe exists per se or why it is intelligible. For Christian spirituality, limit questions like these, which start with science and point beyond science, resonate with our experience of being creatures called by God to the life-long project of integration through self-transcendence.

Perhaps the most important result of dialogue, as Barbour's careful analysis shows us, is the *analogy* between the way theories are constructed, deployed, and evaluated in science and in theology (here, read "doctrine" for "theory"), although there are important differences as well. This analogy provides a *bridge* between theology and science. Thus paradigms, with their metaphysical and aesthetic elements, shape both science and theology. In both fields it is the theories that tell us how to interpret data. As Norwood Hanson puts it, "All data are theory-laden." In both fields imagination plays a key role in the construction of models and theories. In both fields theories are tested by their fruitfulness in interpreting new kinds of data and in their practical consequences for life. Both can be given a critical-realist interpretation where knowledge is referential although partial and revisable. Both science and theology rely on metaphorical language to express their truth-claims: the "expanding universe," the "genetic code," the ecological "web."

The bridge these arguments offer between theology and science can be extended to include Christian spirituality when we consider the analogies between the rationality deployed in Christian spirituality as an academic discipline and the rationality of the natural sciences. Paradigms of spiritual practice shape the way historical communities grow and deepen, and they include metaphysical views of nature and aesthetic views of what is truly beautiful. The practice of discernment is, at bottom, an openness to the influence of the Spirit as to what "data" count and how to integrate this data within our life project drawn from scripture, tradition, personal experience, and the experience of one's community. Imagination is crucial in the spiritual move toward virtue and hope. The test of fruitfulness is central to Christian spirituality, whose commitment is to the "fruits of the spirit." Metaphors drawn from science can provide rich resources for Christian spirituality, as beautifully illustrated by Sallie McFague's metaphor of the universe as the body of God.[20] Finally, Christian spirituality, in its references to God, presupposes that "God" is taken in a critical-realist fashion to refer to what it attempts to name, even given the inherent mystery of such reference and naming. Thus, my first suggestion is that the methodology of Christian spirituality as an academic discipline is *analogous* in many ways to the methodology of science.

The model of dialogue between theology and science has also been developed in key ways by Arthur Peacocke[21] and, more recently, by Nancey Murphy and George Ellis.[22] They view the sciences and humanities as layered in an epistemic hierarchy starting with physics at the bottom level and working upward through chemistry, biology, neurophysiology, psychology, linguistics, economics, the arts, ethics, and theology. In this approach the lower levels place epistemic constraints on the upper levels; yet there are genuinely new and irreducible properties and processes that emerge at the upper levels. Thus biology cannot contradict physics, but it also cannot be reduced to physics. This approach means that theology must take seriously all the knowledge of the other disciplines, including the natural sciences, even while it deals with realities, such as divine grace and the *imago Dei,* which cannot be reduced to and explained away by these other disciplines.

Following their argument, we could propose that spirituality as an academic discipline, in its interaction with theology, must allow all the disciplines that theology deals with, including the natural sciences, to place *constraints* on its epistemology. At the same time, the fruits of lived Christian spirituality include genuinely *emergent* new domains of knowledge and experience that can never be reduced away from the academic study of spirituality in its dialogue with theology and the other disciplines including science.

If we take these suggestions regarding analogy, constraints, and emergence together, we can propose that *Christian spirituality, as an academic discipline, can learn enormously from the sciences while retaining its irreducible character as an academic discipline.*

INTERACTION

With this in place, we can proceed to explore the *interaction*[23] of theology and science, and its importance for Christian spirituality. Interaction presupposes dialogue but goes further in opening up the possibility of genuine and mutual two-way exchange and fruitful growth in our theological and scientific understanding of the universe and humanity. Barbour lists three distinctive ways that theology can be affected by science: natural theology, a theology of nature, and systematic synthesis as modes of interaction.

Natural theology. The cosmological and teleological arguments of classical natural theology continue to be discussed in contemporary reflections on cosmology and biological evolution. Physicists including Freeman Dyson, John Barrow, Frank Tipler, and George Ellis, and philosophical theologians such as Nancey Murphy and Philip Clayton, write that the universe is "fine-tuned" for the possibility of life. For Christian spirituality, the renewed interest in natural theology in light of science can encourage an intuition for moving from our grounded experience of the world around us toward the divine source of all that is.

Theology of nature (constructive reformulation). A wide variety of scholars, including Philip Clayton, Jürgen Moltmann, Nancey Murphy, Wolfhart Pannenberg, Arthur Peacocke, Ted Peters, John Polkinghorne, Rosemary Radford Ruether, and Keith Ward are engaged in projects ranging from reformulating specific doctrines to radically reconstructing the whole of theology in light of contemporary natural science. They view the universe as dynamic, indeterministic, and open-ended, and thus open to God's non-interventionist divine action in all levels of nature. They stress God's continuous creation through the processes of biological evolution, and depict the universe as filled with creativity, novelty, and genuine emergence. Here there are enormous resources and opportunities for Christian spirituality: to integrate our experience of being connected genetically and ecologically to all life on Earth into our own journey and pilgrimage; to be open to the stunning implications for human spirituality if (and when) life is discovered elsewhere in the universe (project SETI) and we can look into the "face" of the truly "other" as "sibling"; to recognize through the "eyes of faith" God's intimate and continuous action in weaving together of the fabric of life in the evolutionary processes; to experience what it means to truly be "just creatures among creatures"; to contemplate God's presence in the beauty of a coral reef, the astonishment of a child's birth, the tranquility of a full moon rising; to be spiritually sensitized in order to identify with the suffering of all life on earth, with its tortuous predator-prey cycle; to proclaim the suffering of God not only with all of humanity but with the history of life on earth and the victory of the resurrection of Jesus as pointing to an eschatological and universal new creation that embraces all life.

Systematic synthesis. A systematic synthesis offers the possibility of bringing all disciplines of knowledge in an integrated whole to the project of Christian spirituality. Scholars attempting to synthesize science and theology most often turn to metaphysics to provide a complete set of concepts and categories by which all our knowledge of reality can be organized. Contemporary neo-Thomists, such as Ernan McMullin and William Stoeger, work in the modified tradition of Aquinas's use of Aristotle, while process scholars such as Charles Birch and John Cobb, Jr., explore the philosophy of Alfred North Whitehead for theological purposes. Syntheses like these invite scholars in Christian spirituality to engage with an encompassing philosophy of nature based largely on contemporary natural science, one in which religious experience and scientific knowledge can be brought together in mutual edification. At the same time, we must acknowledge that new discoveries in science and new insights into spirituality might not fit within the existing categories of philosophies of nature that were developed within the context of earlier cosmologies—even those of the early twentieth century—leading us to adjust these philosophies or abandon them for newer constructions, or perhaps work with a less articulated philosophy of nature. Scholars following the latter approach include John Haught, who combines insights from Teilhard de Chardin, process philosophy, and Roman Catholic theology, and Denis Edwards, who is developing an ontology of relationality drawn both from evolutionary biology and from patristic and contemporary trinitarian theology, Karl Rahner's evolutionary Christology, and biblical Wisdom literature.

Extending Barbour's Typology to Include Genuine Interaction among Science, Theology, and Christian Spirituality

In recent work, I have extended Barbour's approach to include ways in which theology has played, and can continue to play, a positive role both in inspiring new research in theoretical science and as offering a criterion of theory choice between competing research programs in theoretical science. These new ways can be brought together with the preceding discussion to form an overall pattern of the multiple interactions between theology and science, as suggested by Figure 6–1.

Figure 6–1: Methodology of Creative Mutual Interaction

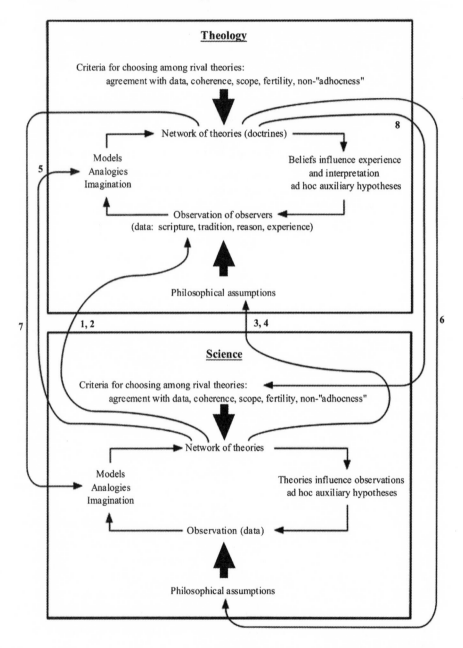

In Figure 6–1, arrows within the domain labeled *science* are meant to suggest the ways empirical data are brought through a process of modeling into the construction of theories, and the ways these theories are then tested against an ever-expanding domain of data. Here, aesthetic and metaphysical, as well as empiricist, criteria of theory choice function in the construction of and choice between competing scientific theories. Similar arrows in the domain labeled *theology* suggest the analogy Barbour proposed between theological and scientific methodology. Following Peacocke's and Murphy's suggestions for the ordering of epistemologies between different disciplines, I have placed science below theology to make it clear that (a) science constrains and informs theology, but (b) theology remains irreducible to science. With this in place, we can now indicate the various "paths" between science and theology.

From Physics to Theology: Implications for Christian Spirituality

As Figure 6–1 suggests, there are at least five paths by which the natural sciences can affect constructive theology. For brevity, I focus here on physics and cosmology for specificity, but examples can easily be found from the whole range of the natural sciences. In the first four, theories in physics can act as *data for theology* both in a direct sense—(1) and (2)—and indirectly through philosophy—(3) and (4).

(1) Theories in physics can act directly as data that place constraints on theology. For an example, consider God's temporal relation to nature. This relation, typically referred to as the question of time and eternity, has been formulated in a variety of ways throughout the twentieth century: (a) trinitarian theology views the eternity of God not as timeless or as unending time but as "supra temporal," the fully temporal source of creaturely temporality; (b) process theologians interpret God's "consequent nature" as God's temporal experience of the present moment; (c) scholars pursuing natural theology typically stress God's immanence in the ongoing processes of the world while maintaining God's transcendence of the world; (d) those interested in special

divine action argue that God acts in specific events in nature; and (e) needless to say, our working definition of Christian spirituality presupposes that the experience of God's self-revelation to us takes place in time even if it points to eternity. Now these attempts at formulating God's temporal relation to nature, despite their theological diversity, all make a fundamental assumption about time, namely, that a unique, flowing, global present divides the universal past from the universal future. The moment in which an event occurs is the same moment everywhere in the universe; my "now" is everyone else's "now," regardless of how we set our clocks or time zones.

The problem is that, according to Einstein's special theory of relativity (1905), there is no physical basis for a universal present moment. Instead, the present is starkly different for persons in relative motion, breaking the universal "now" into countless relative "presents." How, then, should we reformulate our concept of God's temporal relation to nature to take special relativity into account while maintaining the integrity, significance, and power of the concept of God as experiencing the world and our individual lives in time? And what would this new formulation entail for our understanding of Christian spirituality as fully temporal and lived experiences of God?

(2) Theories in physics can act directly as data to be "explained" theologically. For example, standard Big Bang cosmology (1940s–1960s) suggests that there was an absolute beginning of the universe, an event labeled t=0. Yet Big Bang cosmology on its own cannot explain t=0; instead, it is left as an unexplained fact. Now, if we embed Big Bang cosmology in a theology of creation *ex nihilo*, we may be able to give it a fruitful theological explanation as the effect of God's creative act. Then, by looking at t=0 through the lens of Christian spirituality, we can experience the wonder and beauty of the creation of the universe as deepening our relationship to God its/our Creator. We should keep clearly in mind, however, that the theological explanation is not a scientific explanation but a way of relating the more general, philosophical meaning of a theological doctrine, here that the universe is contingent (it need not exist), to a specific model

in science (in standard Big Bang cosmology, t=0 represents the contingency of nature as temporal origin).

We should also remember that scientific theories and theological formulations will change, and thus we will need to find ways to build change into the ongoing relationship between them. For example, inflationary Big Bang and quantum cosmology, developed over the past three decades, includes the possibility of a prior "mega-universe" from which ours arose. Our task, then, is to embed these cosmologies in a theology of creation *ex nihilo* and explore the implications once again. Still, since any scientific cosmology will leave the existence of the universe (that is, "all that is," all "mega-universes," and so on) as a contingent fact, the *ex nihilo* tradition will always view this fact as leading to God as the ultimate source of existence. Christian spirituality can help us make a connection between the experience of the undeniable contingency of our own life with the universe, which, as revealed by science, we can even more profoundly experience as a contingent gift of our Creator God.

(3) Theories in physics, after philosophical analysis, can act indirectly as data in theology. For example, quantum mechanics can be interpreted philosophically as indicating that nature is ontologically indeterministic: there simply is not an efficient cause for all subatomic processes such as radioactive decay. Now an indeterministic interpretation of quantum mechanics can function within theological anthropology as providing a precondition at the level of physics for an incompatibilist view of free will, namely, that our actions are the product, at least in part, of our choices and decisions and not totally determined by impersonal physical forces. The mechanistic world of Newtonian physics challenged such a view of free will, but quantum indeterminism makes this idea intelligible once again. The implications for Christian spirituality go to the underlying assumptions about lived experience and human agency as a free and enacted response to God's grace. Now we can relate these assumptions to the open character of even the most basic physical processes of nature that make the enactment of such a response possible.

(4) Theories in science can also serve indirectly as the data for theology when they are first used as a basis for the construction of

a complex philosophy of nature. A traditional example is Thomistic theology's appropriation of an Aristotelian philosophy of nature. Contemporary examples include Whiteheadian philosophy and its adoption by process theology, ecological philosophies of nature and eco-feminist theology, and relational views of nature and the human person and trinitarian theology. By appropriating a scientifically informed philosophy of nature in these various ways, we can explore new forms of Christian spirituality based on an appreciation and celebration of nature through the lens of science and philosophy as interconnected, holistic, and dynamic.

Finally, (5) theories in physics can function heuristically in our "theological imagination," leading us to renewed conceptions of God's relation to the universe and a deeper awareness of God's presence in our lives. Cosmology, as we have seen, can expand our experience of God as our Creator. Quantum mechanics can inspire us to take with renewed seriousness the claim that God acts in the world. This, in turn, can encourage our practice of spiritual discernment, since it is a presupposition of discernment that God acts in and among us and in nature. The aesthetic beauty of mathematical physics can lead us to a deeper experience of the inexhaustible beauty of God as Logos.

From Theology to Physics: The Potential Contributions of Christian Spirituality

To see the genuinely interactive, but asymmetrical, nature of the relations I am proposing, I suggest at least three paths by which theology, and in turn Christian spirituality, can influence the assumptions underlying science as well as the directions that scientists take in their research.[24] (6): As mentioned above, theological theories provide some of the philosophical assumptions that underlie scientific methodology. For example, we have already seen that the doctrine of creation *ex nihilo* combined the Greek assumption of the rationality of the world with the theological assumption that the world is contingent. Together they gave rise to the empirical methods and mathematical tools of science. Similarly, Christian spirituality presupposes that nature is contingent and rational since our lived experience of our dependence on nature is taken as leading us to our absolute dependence on God its source, and since our ability to explore this experience presupposes reason as well as intuition. However, other assumptions grounded in the *ex nihilo* tradition, such as the goodness and purpose of creation, were not carried over into the scientific conception of nature. It would be interesting to explore whether these assumptions about axiology and teleology in nature could lead to new and fruitful research programs in science. Since Christian spirituality includes our experience of the goodness of nature and the purpose of all God's creatures, it offers further encouragement to explore the fruitfulness of these assumptions in scientific research.

(7) Theological theories can act as sources of inspiration in the construction of new scientific theories. An interesting example can be found in the variety of theologies and philosophies that, to a varying degree, apparently influenced many of the pioneers of quantum theory in the period from 1900 to 1930, including Vedanta for Irwin Schroedinger, Spinoza for Albert Einstein, and Kierkegaard for Niels Bohr. Another example is the subtle way Fred Hoyle's atheistic views influenced his search for a cosmology that could challenge Big Bang cosmology. For Hoyle, the theistic implications of t=0 in Big Bang cosmology were intolerable, leading him and several colleagues to construct a scientifically viable alternative cosmology in the 1940s, the "steady-state cosmology," which depicted the universe as eternally old, bearing no t=0 event in its past. It competed successfully with Big Bang cosmology for over two decades. Given the way theology can function to inspire scientists, I suggest that spirituality, in turn, might function in this way when it is informed by and engaged with research science. For example, scientists in the neurosciences and cognitive sciences who are open to spirituality might be inspired to take much more seriously the irreducible human capacity for spiritual experience.

Finally (8), theological theories can lead to "selection rules" within the criteria of theory choice in physics. If one considers a theological theory as true, then one can delineate what conditions must obtain within physics for the possibility of its being true. These conditions, in turn, can serve as reasons for an individual research scientist or group of colleagues to choose to pursue a particular scientific theory. For example, a frequent assumption within Christian spirituality is that because of the grace of God we are capable not only of discerning but also of responding to God's will in our lives. Thus we might chose to pursue scientific research involving the relationship between genetics and behavior with the goal of showing that while we may be genetically predisposed to certain behaviors we are never genetically predetermined to them. Instead, while our biological inheritance plays a factor in our life's journey, there is always an irreducible role for personal decisions as responses to God's inviting grace.

CONCLUSION

I hope to have shown that Christian spirituality, as an academic discipline, can both learn enormously from the natural sciences while retaining its irreducible character as an academic discipline *and* contribute to fruitful new agendas and research programs in science through its focus on our lived experience of God's grace. With this as one point of departure, I believe that we can begin the project of more fully articulating a genuinely creative mutual partnership among science, theology, and Christian spirituality. I am immensely grateful to my trusted and dear colleague Sandra Schneiders her the pioneering work that frames this research and illuminates its future.

Notes

1. Sandra M. Schneiders, "The Study of Christian Spirituality: The Contours and Dynamics of a Discipline," *Christian Spirituality Bulletin* 6 (Spring 1988): 1, 3–12.

2. Schneiders, "A Hermeneutical Approach to the Study of Christian Spirituality," *Christian Spirituality Bulletin* 2 (Spring 1994): 9.

3. Ibid., 10–11.

4. Schneiders, "The Study of Christian Spirituality," 3.

5. For a more general discussion of science and spirituality, see Robert John Russell, "Natural Sciences," in *The Blackwell*

Companion to Christian Spirituality, ed. Arthur Holder, 325-44 (Oxford: Blackwell Publishers, 2005).

6. Schneiders, "The Study of Christian Spirituality," 6–19.

7. Ibid., 4.

8. Ibid., 14.

9. Schneiders, "A Hermeneutical Approach to the Study of Christian Spirituality," 9–11.

10. Robert John Russell, "Contemplation: A Scientific Context," *Continuum* 2 (Fall 1990). It is interesting to note that while the Reformation and Counter-Reformation were in full array during Teresa's lifetime, a revolution was occurring in astronomy and physics that, in the end, would prove equally—even more profoundly—influential in changing the geocentric and anthropological assumptions that so profoundly and ubiquitously shape our experience of being human, the experience that lies at the core of Christian spirituality as spiritual *experience.*

11. Paul Tillich offers a profound analysis of the relation between culture and religion: "Culture is the form of religion and religion the substance of culture." Paul Tillich, *Systematic Theology: Three Volumes in One* (Chicago: University of Chicago Press; New York: Harper and Row, 1967), 3:158, also 1:149 and 3:95.

12. A growing number of internationally distinguished scientists from all world religions is now bringing to the public at large, through major conferences and extensive writings, their unique experiences of science as a "spiritual quest." See W. Mark Richardson and Gordy Slack, eds., *Faith in Science: Scientists Search for Truth* (London: Routledge, 2001); W. Mark Richardson, Robert John Russell, eds., *Science and the Spiritual Quest: New Essays by Leading Scientists* (London: Routledge, 2002). In the Introduction to this book, Richardson provides a very helpful analysis of the literary genres found in the growing number of writings on science and spirituality. For an example of media coverage, see Sharon Begley, "Science Finds God," *Newsweek,* July 20, 1998.

13. Arthur Peacocke, *Theology for a Scientific Age: Being and Becoming—Natural, Divine and Human,* enl. ed. (Minneapolis: Fortress Press, 1993), esp. chap. 9; see also Ian G. Barbour, *Religion in an Age of Science,* Gifford Lectures, 1989–90 (San

Francisco: Harper and Row, 1990), chap. 5; Ted Peters, "On Creating the Cosmos," in *Physics, Philosophy, and Theology: A Common Quest for Understanding*, ed. Robert J. Russell, William R. Stoeger, SJ, and George V. Coyne, SJ (Vatican City State: Vatican Observatory Publications, 1988), 273–96; Robert John Russell, "Cosmology, Creation, and Contingency," in *Cosmos as Creation: Theology and Science in Consonance*, ed. Ted Peters (Nashville, TN: Abingdon Press, 1989), 177–210.

14. William R. Stoeger, SJ, "What Is the 'Universe' Which Cosmology Studies?" in *Fifty Years in Science and Religion: Ian G. Barbour and His Legacy*, ed. Robert John Russell, *Ashgate Science and Religion Series* (Aldershot, England: Ashgate Publishing Company, 2004).

15. For introductory material on theology and science, see Robert John Russell and Kirk Wegter-McNelly Russell, "Science," in *The Blackwell Companion to Modern Theology*, ed. Gareth Jones (Oxford: Blackwell Publishing, 2004), 512–56; Ian G. Barbour, *When Science Meets Religion* (San Francisco: HarperSanFrancisco, 2000); Ted Peters, "Theology and the Natural Sciences," in *The Modern Theologians: An Introduction to Christian Theology in the Twentieth Century*, 2nd ed., ed. David F. Ford (Cambridge, MA: Blackwell Publishers, 1997), 649–68; John Polkinghorne, *Science and Theology: An Introduction* (London: SPCK; Minneapolis: Fortress Press, 1998); W. Mark Richardson and Wesley J. Wildman, eds., *Religion and Science: History, Method, Dialogue* (New York: Routledge, 1996); Christopher Southgate, et al., eds., *God, Humanity and the Cosmos: A Textbook in Science and Religion* (Harrisburg, PA: Trinity Press International, 1999). For research material see Barbour, *Religion in an Age of Science*; Peacocke, *Theology for a Scientific Age*; John Polkinghorne, *The Faith of a Physicist: Reflections of a Bottom-up Thinker* (Princeton, NJ: Princeton University Press, 1994); and the CTNS/VO five-volume series (1993–2001) subtitled *Scientific Perspectives on Divine Action* (Vatican City State: Vatican Observatory Publications; Berkeley, CA: Center for Theology and the Natural Sciences).

16. Barbour, *Religion in an Age of Science*, chap. 1.

17. Thomas F. Torrance, *Divine and Contingent Order* (Oxford: Oxford University Press, 1981).

18. Polkinghorne, *The Faith of a Physicist,* esp. 74.

19. The Logos tradition dates back to such second-century apologists as Justin Martyr, who used it to bridge Greek philosophy and the Gospel of John.

20. Sallie McFague, *The Body of God: An Ecological Theology* (Minneapolis: Fortress Press, 1993). McFague's development of what she calls metaphorical theology and her creative use of metaphors drawn from science in her theology are rooted in the way metaphor is used by Barbour and others in science and religion. See Sallie McFague, *Metaphorical Theology: Models of God in Religious Language* (Philadelphia: Fortress Press, 1982).

21. See, for example, Peacocke, *Theology for a Scientific Age,* esp. fig. 3, p. 217.

22. Nancey Murphy and George F. Ellis, *On the Moral Nature of the Universe: Theology, Cosmology, and Ethics,* Theology and the Sciences Series (Minneapolis: Fortress Press, 1996), esp. fig. 9.3, p. 204.

23. Barbour usually calls this approach "integration," but I prefer "interaction," for two reasons: it leaves the relative independence of the dialogue partners in place and at the same time it stresses the possibility of mutual, two-way influences between them.

24. First, though I want to stress at the outset that by "influence" I am in no way appealing to or assuming that theologians speak with some special kind of authority, whether based on the Bible, church dogma, magisterial pronouncements, or whatever. Quite the contrary; the overall context should be an open intellectual exchange between scholars based on mutual respect and the fallibility of hypotheses proposed by either side and based on scientific or theological evidence. Instead, the case I wish to make is that such influences have occurred historically and that they continue to occur in contemporary scientific research. It is, first of all, then, a descriptive claim, but it has a mildly prescriptive component as well: I believe a more intentional exploration of such influences could be fruitful for science as it has been for theology, and that it could be particularly fruitful for the "theology and science" interaction.

7

THE WEIGHT OF THE WORLD
The Heaviness of Nature in Spiritual Experience

Douglas Burton-Christie

The name of the world is not world. It is load.
—Kuranko Proverb

If ever my grief were measured
or my sorrow put on a scale,
it would outweigh the sands of the ocean.[1]

Here, in three simple, devastating lines from the Book of Job,
we are brought face to face with one of the oldest human questions: how much grief, sadness, loss can we bear? How much of
the world's weight can we carry? One recognizes immediately that
such questions, arising out of a place of profound struggle and
uncertainty, cannot be answered simply or easily. Indeed, all that
such questions can do, in the midst of an experience of profound
disorientation, is reveal the depth and density of the experience
out of which they arise and invite a compassionate and sensitive
response. What is the source of this grief, this heaviness? Why
does it feel so heavy? In Job's case, simply acknowledging the
extent of his loss already sheds some light on these questions. He
has lost almost everything—his possessions, his family, his
health—everything but his life. And even his life remains only tenuously within his grasp. But merely naming the losses hardly
begins to approach or account for what it feels like to carry them.

142

Nor does it bring us close to what is perhaps the most devastating and haunting loss of all: loss of trust in the world's order, loss of confidence in God.

To get a feeling for this magnitude of loss, we must listen to the howling cry of grief that pours forth from Job once he realizes what has befallen him:

> God damn the day I was born
>> and the night that forced me from the womb.
> On that day—let there be darkness;
>> let it never have been created;
>> let it sink back into the void.[2]

It is difficult to miss the chilling, nihilistic spirit of this cry. Job wishes for the unthinkable: that the day of his birth would somehow be undone. Why? Because, if that day remains, if it is allowed to stand and to be re-created every year, then his existence will continue until death. Whereas if somehow the memory of that day can be extinguished, if every trace of his ever having existed can be erased, then his present agony will disappear. Because *he* will disappear. Job seems to be asking for the day of his birth to be returned to the primordial chaos. But if we consider the entire passage of which this cry forms just one part, we realize that he is asking for even more than this: he wants the cosmic order itself to be returned to the primordial chaos. He wants the world never to have existed.

It is hard to imagine a more harrowing expression of grief and loss. It is not too much to say that it reaches cosmic proportions—the world and one's experience of the world have become too much to bear. There seems to be no way out, no possibility of resolution to such an experience, no hope of redemption. Whether such redemption eventually emerges as part of Job's experience has, of course, long been debated. I offer no judgment on that question here. Rather, I wish only to note the depth of Job's crisis, the astounding sense of how much he has been given to carry, and the difficulty of the questions that emerge from the sheer effort at struggling under such a burden.

This sense of the world's heaviness has long been part of Jewish and Christian spirituality. In the Jewish scriptures such questions surface most sharply in the Wisdom texts, where nature and the cosmos as a whole are often experienced as radically ambiguous and where God's benevolent presence is anything but assured.[3] In the Christian tradition one encounters such questions in the debates with the Manicheans and the Gnostics over the nature of material reality. While Christian writers involved in these debates almost uniformly affirm the goodness of creation and the natural world in light of the doctrine of the incarnation, one also encounters in the Christian tradition a continuous struggle to make sense of the anomalous and seemingly capricious dimensions of material, embodied existence.[4] This struggle has come to form an important part of the Christian theological tradition, especially the part of the tradition that has worked to come to terms with God's justice and God's (possible) participation in the burdens of the world.[5]

Given how deeply embedded and pervasive such questions are within human experience, it is hardly surprising to discover that they are surfacing again in contemporary experience. But it is intriguing to note how and where they are surfacing. It is not only in formal theological discourse that one encounters questions about the presence or absence of God in the natural world, but also in literature and poetry. In the North American context the literary genre known as nature writing, which traces its origins back to the transcendentalist writings of Henry David Thoreau and Ralph Waldo Emerson, has long been occupied with spiritual questions. In the contemporary moment the work of writers such as Annie Dillard, Barry Lopez, Edward Abbey, Leslie Marmon Silko, Linda Hogan, Terry Tempest Williams, Mary Oliver, and many others continues to offer vivid, if varied expressions of spiritual longing. The spirituality expressed in this literature is not easy to describe or categorize. In part, this is because of the oblique relationship many of these writers have to classic religious traditions. While significant elements of Jewish, Christian, Buddhist, and Indigenous religious thought can be found in this writing, often the language and symbols of these traditions are used freely and combined with an insistent eclecticism that makes it difficult to "locate" them as part of a given religious tradition. Still, there is no denying that a real and vibrant spirituality exists here.[6]

Increasingly, scholars of spirituality are coming to recognize that such improvised and oblique expressions of spiritual experience make up an important part of this moment in history.[7] Yet the challenge of locating and interpreting these diverse and varied expressions of spiritual experience is daunting. At the very least, it requires a willingness to engage in an open-ended phenomeno-logical-hermeneutical approach of the kind advocated by Bernard McGinn and Sandra Schneiders.[8] To respond to contemporary experience of the natural world in this way means, first and foremost, attending carefully to the range of experiences described without moving too quickly to impose a theological meaning on them. It also means being prepared to engage in a rigorously interdisciplinary investigation of experience. To understand the spiritual significance of nature as it emerges in contemporary literary texts requires attention not only to spiritual language and symbols, but also to rhetoric, ecology, geography, biology, and any number of other cognate fields that shape a particular writer's understanding of nature. It may be that certain theological patterns will emerge from such an inquiry, but they must be allowed to emerge from the work itself, however unexpected or disturbing such patterns may turn out to be.

One of the patterns that emerges insistently in the contemporary literature of nature concerns the question of God's justice, or, as it is sometimes framed, the question of evil. These are old questions, and their contemporary expressions echo with the same numbing pain and anxiety found in the Book of Job.[9] The questions arise in different ways, depending on the perspective and experience of the writers. But the central questions are surprisingly consistent: when we look out onto the natural world or into our own bodies and find the world to be ambiguous, shifting, and possibly even hostile to our own hopes, how do we respond? How does one learn to live, to feel, and to know the presence of God in such a world? Is it even possible? To consider the way such questions emerge in contemporary literature is to be brought close to the texture and feeling of heaviness that has so often marked the human experience of the natural world. It is also to find ourselves invited to participate in the struggle of making sense of such experience and to consider again one of the oldest and primordial spiritual questions: Can God be trusted?

In this essay I consider the work of two contemporary writers, Mary Karr and Czeslaw Milosz, asking how their struggle with this question sheds light on what it means to seek meaning in a world whose very trustworthiness has been called into question. Their work, though particular to their respective worlds, is representative of the way the sense of the world's heaviness and the question of God's justice often arise in contemporary discourse. To examine such questions, honestly and openly, is, I believe, critical to our efforts to understand contemporary spiritual experience and practice.

"THE BIG BLIND SWIPE OF DEATH"

"I couldn't sit in her silence anymore. It just weighed too much." This is how Mary Karr describes her response as a young girl to her mother's withdrawal into a space of chronic and painful depression. As she sat in the Houston Zoo watching her mother drink stale coffee, she realized that she was losing hold of the emotional and psychological threads that bound her to her mother. Reflecting on the experience years later, she names this moment as a crucial turning point when things simply became too heavy to bear. The memory of this experience forms one of the axis points of her remarkable memoir, *The Liar's Club*.[10] Nature is not the primary subject of this book, at least not if by nature one means plants, animals, the wind and the sun and the stars, understood as distinct elements of existence against which our human lives unfold. The subject of the book, or at least the context in which the subject (the story of a child's felt experience of her life) unfolds, is something larger. It is the cosmos—the entire world of existence. The central questions that emerge as Karr's sense of the cosmos begins to fray and tear concern the very possibility of living with meaning in such a torn, broken world.

As is true of most children, Karr's working cosmology, the sense of how the world works and holds together, is fragile and not fully formed. It depends for its meaning on the stability and reliability of things that are rarely either stable or reliable—persons, relationships, the world itself. When at age seven the world begins to unravel—as the psychological trauma and resulting emotional distance of Karr's mother begins to deepen, when her grandmother dies after a protracted illness, and, finally, when a devastating hurricane blows in off the gulf to rain death upon a nearby community—the young child's sense of the trustworthiness of the world begins to erode. The cumulative effect of many different losses—unexpected, inexplicable, seemingly capricious and random losses—provoke in her questions about whether there is any center, any order to the cosmos. Nor can she comprehend how, in the midst of all this loss and death, there can be a God who cares about her or anyone else.

The idea of nature as an ambiguous, even malevolent reality first began to take hold in her consciousness in response to her grandmother's deepening illness. Karr was scared of her grandmother, a person she experienced as domineering, capricious, and cold. Then, suddenly, her grandmother became ill and had to have the lower part of her leg amputated, after which she came to live with Karr's family. She occupied a room in the house that, to Karr, reeked of death. "Let me take a minute to tell you about the smell in that room," she says. "It stank of snake, specifically water moccasin."

> If you are walking in waders through a marsh, say, on a warm winter morning, scanning sky for mallards riding their jagged V overhead, you can smell a moccasin slithering alongside you long before you see it. It has the odor like something dead just before the rot sets in and the worms in its belly skin set it to jiggling around unnaturally. Often the smell of some rotting carcass—armadillo or nutria rat or bird—has stopped me in my tracks and gotten me to turn my eyes expecting to find on the ground the triangular, near–black head of a cottonmouth, which is related to both cobra and pit viper

and the most vicious snake on this continent....On land, it gives off a musk easily as strong as a skunk....It's not just the smell of death, but the smell of something thriving on death, a smell you link up to maggots, or those bacteria that eat of corpses one cell at a time.[11]

Here, nature manifests itself as threatening, awful, and repulsive, death insinuating itself into the presence of the living. The fact that Karr feared and hated her grandmother no doubt influenced her perception of her grandmother's condition and the smell in that room; her grandmother was a malevolent presence in her life. But, in the decaying flesh of her grandmother's body, she encounters the brutal and unavoidable fact of death as irresistible, faceless, and ravenous. Even though she will welcome (though not without serious guilt) her grandmother's eventual death, the stench of the body's slow decay stunned and frightened Karr.

Her grandmother's slow descent toward death coincided with the gathering threat of Hurricane Carla, roaring in off the Gulf of Mexico and heading straight for Leechfield, the oil town in East Texas where Karr and her family lived. The families in their neighborhood began fleeing for safety, while Karr and her family inexplicably did not (her mother sat in the house staring into a roaring fire, unable or unwilling to move in the face of the oncoming storm). Looking out the window of her house, Karr noticed that their neighbors, the Sharps, were leaving. The Karrs were the last ones left. In that moment she recalled what her friend Carol Sharp's father had said about the hurricane—what it really meant:

Carol described how the Four Horsemen of the Apocalypse would come riding down out of the clouds with their black caps flapping behind them, and how the burning pit would open up in the earth for sinners like me, and how Jesus would lead her family up a golden stair to heaven....*What if old Mr. Sharp's right about God and Jesus?* I must have said out loud. Or maybe I suggested we pray just in case—I don't remember. What's dead clear now is how Mother lifted her middle finger to the ceiling and said, *Oh, f**k that God!* Between that and the tornado sirens and the black sky that had slid over all our windows...I began to think we'd be washed out to sea for all our sins at any minute.[12]

They were not washed out to sea. But her mother's gesture of defiance—at the notion of a capricious, apocalyptic God who would save some and damn others based on some inscrutable process of selection—lodged itself in her consciousness. Later on, when the hurricane had done its worst and Carol Sharp offered her assessment on the school playground of why those who had died had died and why those who lived had been saved (God had saved the Baptists and left the Catholics to die), Karr herself was defiant: "I was screaming to Carol Sharp that her Jesus was a mewling dips**t." This outburst got her pulled off the playground by her teacher, who gave her a box of crayons and instructed her to "make something pretty." Instead, she wore down the black crayons to a nub, "making a sky full of funnel clouds....On a green hill in the background, I drew grave mounds in brown and topped them off with white crosses, each penciled with 'R.I.P.' That truth—that death came in a big blind swipe—was gradually taking form in my head, picking up force and gaining momentum like its own kind of storm."[13]

It would be tempting to dismiss all of this as nothing more or less than a young child's inability to hold in her consciousness the radical ambiguity of experience. Yet, to do so would be to underestimate drastically the power of such experience to shape and form a young person's sense of the world. It would also be to miss the fact that these reflections are those of a grown woman reflecting back upon her experience after many years and, struggling to make sense of her own past experience, finding that such feelings of cosmic dislocation still stir her. This is why Karr's account of what finally drove her to the edge of herself, to a place where the world began to crumple in upon itself, is so telling and significant. Here we gain access to that moment when the sense of the world's order and meaning begins to evaporate.

She was sitting in the middle of her parents' bed with a steaming plate of beans and biscuits on her lap watching TV. The news footage was from Cameron, Louisiana, not Leechfield. The hurricane had inexplicably, and at the last possible moment, veered off course and crashed into Cameron, which had been completely unprepared for the storm. This weird, random turn of events, and the sight of all those victims and the ones left behind grieving over them, provoked in Karr what she called a metaphysical crisis. "Why was everybody so fired up about nature all the time, and God?" Karr wondered. The fact was "that the ocean had decided for no good reason to dislodge itself on top of hundreds of people across the river in Louisiana. Our bodies could have been the ones people saw on TV newsreels after school." She watched as

> families...went from one child-sized body bag to another—the bags having been lined up in rows across some movie-theatre parking lot. The sheriff would unzip the bag's top a little bit, and the daddy would peer in, then shake his head no. Then he'd step back while the sheriff rezipped before going on to the next bag. This happened over and over till the sheriff finally unzipped the face the family was looking for—little Junior or baby Jackie, blue-skinned and bloated, tongue black and sticking out.[14]

What really frightened her in all of this was

> the news footage of some daddy folding in on himself once he'd recognized a kid's face....You could tell by the moans and bellows those grown men let out that their grief had absolutely nowhere to go. I watched from the middle of my parents' bed...while one grown man after another buckled in the middle like everything inside him was going soft all at once, and I knew that the dead child's face would stay on each daddy's eyeballs forever. I stopped trusting the world partly from seeing how

those meaty-faced men bellowed under the shadowy
bills of their tractor caps or cowboy hats.[15]

In the shadow of this dawning awareness Karr gradually grew
more and more isolated from her classmates, descending into a
solitude that was necessary but painful. "They still saw the world
as some playground smiled over by God. I couldn't and their
innocence rankled me to the point of fury....Why would God set
Death loose among us like some wind-up destroyer if he loved us
so much?...I keenly felt the loss of my own trust in the world's
order."[16]

It should not be imagined that *The Liar's Club* is nothing
more than a catalogue of disasters, or that Karr is insensitive to
the beauty and grace that coursed through her life continuously.
She gives careful attention to these moments and recognizes them
for what they are: gifts woven into the crazy-quilt fabric of her
life. But it is the effect of the blows she absorbed that interests me
most here, and her struggle to carry everything she has been given
to carry. It was too much for the child to carry. As one reads the
narrative of the grown woman reflecting on that child's experience, it is difficult to tell whether it is still too much to carry. The
weight remains, even in memory.

But how much weight remains? And how heavy is it? How
complete is the loss of trust? It is difficult to know, of course. The
fact of the memoir itself suggests part of a response, or at least a
way of asking the question. It suggests something about the creative power of art to help heal what might otherwise remain unre-
solved trauma. Can the work of constructing a narrative in which
such experience is expressed in all its sharp-edged horror, held
and honored and not explained away, help in the subtle and challenging process of living into one's life, a life that has so long
seemed bereft of shape or hope that one had almost stopped
believing it possible to live any other way? Can the work of constructing a memoir help in redeeming one's experience of the
world? Any response to such questions would have to arise from
a reading of the entire work. And it may be that this response is
not possible for the readers of the memoir but only for the author.
Still, the work itself stands as a testament to the deep need for

expressing the precise shape of loss—in this case the loss of confidence in the world itself—as part of the larger process of rekindling hope.

THE LAW OF NECESSITY AND
THE BEAUTY OF THE EARTH

Czeslaw Milosz's memoir *Native Realm,* published in 1968, carries the subtitle *A Search for Self-Definition.*[17] In this, Milosz signals his self-conscious awareness that in depicting the events of his life up until that point, he is in truth seeking to discover and construct a self. But Milosz, unlike Karr, understands this process to involve not only the realm of the personal and familial, but also the events of history, within which every human life is caught up, whether consciously or not. In this sense Milosz's account reflects his origins as a European whose life, like the lives of so many of his fellow Europeans, was changed forever by the events of World War II and their aftermath. A further difference concerns Milosz's self-conscious awareness of the philosophical and theological influences that shaped his thinking about history and nature. Whereas Karr arrives at her questions about the meaning of nature mostly through the impact of her experiences, which provoke a level of self-reflection that is both naive and probing, Milosz is provided from early on with an intellectual framework for confronting the radical ambiguity of his experience in the world. It may well be for him, as it is for many of us, that the crucial ideas that came to define his sense of the world simply corresponded to and confirmed aspects of his own temperament and orientation, helping him to understand and make sense of what he had already begun to determine from his own experience. But these ideas did shape and frame his experience. Crucial to his emerging sense of the world was a sense of the intractability of both nature and history. A deep pessimism pervades his sense of the world, something he claims he learned from the Manicheans and Gnostics as well as from his own observations. At the same time, he never denies the fundamental beauty of the world or the capacity of that beauty to fill us with joy. It is within the space of this paradox—"How to cope with beauty and at the same time with the mathematical cruelty of the universe?"[18]—that Milosz struggles to find his way.[19]

In 1918, with Europe still reeling from the shock of war, Milosz returned with his family to his native Lithuania. There, he says, "I found an earthly paradise....I entered into a stunning greenness, into choruses of birds, into orchards bent low with the weight of fruit, into the enchantment of my native river."[20] Nature was, initially anyway, a gift, simple and beautiful, to be cherished. His early education did nothing to change this fundamentally sacramental outlook. "The lakes and forests that surrounded the town gave one a sense of being constantly in touch with nature....So I was initiated early into the habits of animals and birds, into the species of trees and plants, and as a supplement I had my textbooks on ornithology and botany."[21] Milosz became part of a circle of nature lovers, and delivered his first talk on Darwin and natural selection, settling confidently on his future profession as a naturalist. However, he notes that it was at just this time that his religious crisis began.

The crisis had its roots in a growing awareness of an inherent tension between the world known to science and that known to faith:

> If nature's law is murder, if the strong survive and the weak perish, and it has been this way for millions and millions of years, where is there room for God's goodness? Why must man, suspended on a tiny star in the void, no more significant than the microbes under a microscope, isolate his own suffering as though it were different from that of a bird with a wounded wing or a rabbit devoured by a fox?...Such questions plunged me, sometimes for weeks, into a state bordering on physical illness.[22]

The growing sense of the "law of necessity" that governed nature led Milosz eventually to embrace certain ideas from the Gnostics, Manicheans, and Albigensians. Milosz notes with some relief that "they at least did not take refuge behind some vague will of God in order to justify cruelty. They called necessity, which rules every-thing that exists in time, the work of an evil Demiurge opposed to God." It was this sense of nature as "an abode of evil" that Milosz believed helped account for his "propensity for Manicheanism." In his 1974 collection of poems, *From the Rising of the Sun*, Milosz writes, reflecting on this propensity:

> Indeed, quite early you were a gnostic, a Marcionite,
> A secret taster of Manichean poisons.
> From our bright homeland cast down to the earth,
> Prisoners delivered to the ruin of our flesh,
> Unto the Archon of Darkness.[23]

This propensity would resurface continuously during Milosz's life and manifest itself in both his prose and his poetry, though an equally strong propensity, to see the world as beautiful and sweet and source of deepest joy, never left him.

What does it mean to be caught in such a dilemma, to feel one's very being stretched taut between nature's cruel "law of necessity" and the beauty of the earth? For Milosz, this was not an abstract question but a profound and ongoing spiritual chal-lenge. His willingness to open himself to this challenge, to live and work within that radically ambiguous space where necessity and beauty make their respective claims upon us, gives his work a depth and gravity worthy of the stark questions the past century have put before us.

But what is the nature of the challenge precisely? Is it a mat-ter of trying to live with and reconcile two opposing attitudes—optimism and pessimism—arising in response to an ambiguous world? Perhaps this is part of it. However, I think it goes deeper. There are serious theological and religious questions at the heart of Milosz's poetic struggle that have to do with the *experience* of living in such a world. It is this experience that shapes the partic-ular theological questions that emerge in his work, the brute shape of experience for which simple or clear responses seem both inadequate and dishonest. He describes one such moment, in 1939, as Hitler's armies were gathering force and Europe readied itself for the inevitable cataclysm: "My state of mind in those days could be described as the same dream over and over: we want to run but cannot because our legs are made of lead. I had come up against the powerlessness of the individual involved in a mechanism that works independently of his will."[24]

Here one encounters that feeling of heaviness, of being unable to move, that shows up everywhere in Milosz's writing. The source of the heaviness in this instance is the cruel necessity of history, not nature. But one soon begins to realize that the heaviness is one, that the world itself is a heavy place, and that this heaviness is beyond our control. It is perhaps because of this sense that Milosz finds himself drawn into the company of those for whom the sense of the world's heaviness was integral to their spiritual experience: "I felt a certain affinity with these sectarians [of Eastern Christianity] who, from the ruthlessness of nature and human society, drew the conclusion that the world is in the undivided power of Satan."[25]

Is there any redemption in such a world, any resurrection? Or does the cruel law of necessity eventually crush everything, including hope? Milosz addresses this dilemma in personal terms in his memoir: "The classic result of all sudden ruptures and reversals is the rumination on one's own worthlessness and the desire to punish oneself, known as *delectatio morosa*. I would never have been cured of it had it not been for the beauty of the earth...[which] reconciled me with the universe and with myself."[26] The natural world is not simply cruel necessity. The beauty of the earth does have redemptive power. At least in this moment. Milosz never ceases to struggle with the radical ambiguity of existence, with the sense that nature is at once sacrament and harbinger of death. But he stands (however tenuously) within a tradition that is tenacious in trying to discover the ground for an authentic hope in the face of this ambiguous reality. Thus it is not entirely surprising that Milosz should be able make this confession:

> Yet I belong to those who believe in *apokatastasis*.
> That word promises reverse movement,...
> It means restoration. So believed: Gregory of Nyssa,
> Johannes Scotus Erigena, Ruysbroeck, and William Blake.[27]

155

Milosz refers in several places in his work to the ancient Christian idea of *Apokatastasis Panton,* or "the renewal of all things." It is a vision of eschatological hope rooted in the hope that in the end nothing, not even the tiniest fragment of life, will ever be lost, that everything that ever was will be transformed and renewed, will somehow endure. Here among these Christian mystics and poets, Milosz gives expression to a beautiful and hopeful vision of the world, one that contends fiercely with that of the Gnostics' Demiurge, where death and loss have the final word. When will this restoration commence? Perhaps, says Milosz, it already has begun. Perhaps signs of this reversal are already to be found among us.

> Though not for certain, perhaps in some other year.
> It shall come to completion in the sixth millennium, or next Tuesday.
> The demiurge's workshop will suddenly be stilled.
> Unimaginable silence.
> And the form of every single grain will be restored in glory.[28]

CONCLUSION

Whether or not it is possible to believe in such a restoration is, I think, among the most pressing questions in contemporary spirituality. This is not simply a question pertaining to a possible moment in the distant future when all that has been broken or lost may be restored to us. It touches on the possibility of believing in the world as it exists here and now, and in a God who created and sustains it. Not everyone finds the ambiguity of existence such a potent stumbling block. It is a question that afflicts some more than it does others. But for those who do labor under the weight of the world, nothing matters more than being able to find a way to live in the world with hope. Does death come at us in "a big blind swipe?" Is "the mathematical cruelty of the universe" the final word? These are not abstract questions. They arise from the midst of experience and demand a response that is both honest and courageous. If the struggle described in these texts has anything to teach us about contemporary spirituality, and I think it does, it is primarily about what it means to face the ambiguity of our experience honestly and courageously. It is about what it means to find a way, in spite of the heaviness of existence, to live with hope.

Notes

1. *The Book of Job,* trans. Stephen Mitchell (San Francisco: North Point Press, 1987), 21.

2. *The Book of Job,* 13.

3. While these questions surface throughout ancient Wisdom literature, it is in the Book of Job that the full weight of the moral and spiritual challenge they present can be felt most acutely. Three recent studies that probe the questions arising out of Job's predicament with particular depth and clarity are Carol A. Newsom, *The Book of Job: A Contest of Moral Imaginations* (New York: Oxford, 2003); Philippe Nemo, *Job and the Excess of Evil* (Pittsburg: Duquesne University Press, 1998); and Bruce Zuckerman, *Job the Silent: A Study in Historical Counterpoint* (New York: Oxford, 1991).

4. The question of how much influence Manichean thought has had on Christian spirituality has been much debated. There is little question that it had an enormous influence upon Augustine's thinking and through Augustine on much of the subsequent Christian spiritual tradition. The sense of the heaviness of material existence pervades much of Augustine's thinking about the meaning of sin. For Augustine, sin is often imagined as an experience of being "weighed down," unable to move. This is utterly consistent with the Manichean understanding of embodied existence and the Manicheans' insistent attention on what one scholar has described as the "battle for the body," which was believed to be antagonistic to good congenitally. For a probing discussion of the Manichean understanding of human physiology, see Jason BeDuhn, "The Metabolism of Salvation: Manichaean Concepts of Human Physiology," in *The Light and the Darkness: Studies in Manichaeism and Its World,* eds. Paul Mirecki and Jason BeDuhn, 3–37 (Leiden: E. J. Brill, 2001).

The issue of how much or little Christianity has been shaped by Manichean or Gnostic thought impinges on a wider set of questions concerning whether the Christian tradition has fully embraced the doctrine of the incarnation and its insistence on the inherent and enduring value of material reality. For a trenchant examination of this question, see Wendell Berry, "Christianity and the Survival of Creation," in *Sex, Economy, Freedom, and Community* (New York: Pantheon, 1993), 93–116.

5. For a recent and particularly lucid study on the old question of whether God can be known and trusted amid a world that seems not at all trustworthy, see John G. Stackhouse, *Can God Be Trusted?: Faith and the Challenge of Evil* (New York: Oxford, 1998).

6. For examples of this project of interpreting nature writing as an expression of contemporary spirituality, see Catherine Albanese, *Nature Religion in America from the Algonkian Indians to the New Age* (Chicago: University of Chicago Press, 1990); Lynn Ross-Bryant, "Of Nature and Texts: Nature and Religion in American Ecological Literature," *Anglican Theological Review* 73 (Winter 1991): 38–50; idem, "The Land in American Religious Experience," *Journal of the American Academy of Religion* 58 (Fall 1990): 333–55; Douglas Burton-Christie, "'A Feeling for the Natural World': Spirituality and Contemporary Nature Writing," *Continuum* 2, nos. 2–3 (1993): 154–80; idem, "Mapping the Sacred Landscape: Spirituality and the Contemporary Literature of Nature," *Horizons* 21, no. 1 (1994): 22–47; idem, "The Literature of Nature and the Quest for the Sacred," *The Way Supplement* 81 (Autumn 1994), 4–14; and idem, "Nature, Spirit, and Imagination in the Poetry of Mary Oliver," *Cross Currents* (Spring 1996): 77–87.

7. There has been a lively discussion in recent years regarding how to interpret spirituality that is either disengaged from or stands at an oblique angle to traditional religious practice and belief. While there is no consensus about the meaning of such spirituality, there is a growing understanding of its significance within the contemporary cultural context. See Peter H. Van Ness, ed., *Spirituality and the Secular Quest* (New York: Crossroad, 1996); and Sandra M. Schneiders, "Religion *vs.* Spirituality: A Contemporary Conundrum," *Spiritus* 3 (Fall 2003): 163–86.

8. Bernard McGinn, "The Letter and the Spirit: Spirituality as an Academic Discipline," *Christian Spirituality Bulletin* 1, no. 2 (Fall 1993): 1, 3–10; Sandra Schneiders, "A Hermeneutical Approach to the Study of Christian Spirituality," *Christian Spirituality Bulletin* 2, no. 1 (Spring, 1994): 9–14.

9. A growing number of works within contemporary literature grapple seriously with the ambiguity of the human experience in the natural world; several of these works articulate these questions in theological or religious terms. Among the most significant are Annie Dillard, *Pilgrim at Tinker Creek* (New York: Harper and Row, 1974); idem, *For the Time Being* (New York: Knopf, 1999); Norman Maclean, *A River Runs Through It* (Chicago: University of Chicago Press, 1976); Pattiann Rogers, *Firekeeper* (Minneapolis: Milkweed, 1994); D. J. Waldie, *Holy Land* (New York: St. Martin's Press, 1996); and Terry Tempest Williams, *Refuge: An Unnatural History of Family and Place* (New York: Pantheon, 1991). For a probing analysis of this question, with a particular focus on Annie Dillard's *Pilgrim at Tinker Creek,* see Lynn Ross-Bryant, "The Silence of Nature," *Religion and Literature* 22, no. 1 (Spring 1990): 79–94.

Two impressive examples of recent scholarship that grapple with the ambiguity of nature in human experience within a theological or religious context are Lisa H. Sideris, *Environmental Ethics, Ecological Theology, and Natural Selection* (New York: Columbia University Press, 2003); and Shierry Weber Nicholson, *The Love of Nature and the End of the World: The Unspoken Dimensions of Environmental Concern* (Cambridge, MA: MIT Press, 2002).

10. Mary Karr, *The Liar's Club: A Memoir* (New York: Viking Penguin, 1995).

11. Ibid., 76–77.

12. Ibid., 85.

13. Ibid., 105.

14. Ibid., 103–4.

15. Ibid., 104.

16. Ibid., 105–6.

17. Czeslaw Milosz, *Native Realm: A Search for Self-Definition* (New York: Doubleday, 1968; Berkeley and Los Angeles: University of California Press, 1981).

18. Ibid., 86.

19. For a more extensive discussion of this paradox in Milosz's work, see Douglas Burton-Christie, "The Immense Call of the Particular: Czeslaw Milosz on Nature, History and Hope," *Interdisciplinary Studies in Literature and Environment* 7, no.1 (Winter 2000): 115–29.

20. Milosz, *Native Realm*, 47.

21. Ibid., 64.

22. Ibid., 77.

23. Czeslaw Milosz, *The Collected Poems* (New York: Ecco, 1988), 303.

24. Milosz, *Native Realm*, 120.

25. Ibid., 143.

26. Ibid., 293.

27. Milosz, *The Collected Poems*, 310.

28. Ibid., 314.

8

JUDAISM
Christianity's Partner in Waiting and Working for the Full Redemption of the World

Mary C. Boys, SNJM

Some years ago Sandra Schneiders and I had a conversation about the possibility of my writing a book that would make her biblical scholarship more widely accessible. That aspiration returns each time I read her articles and books or hear her lecture. Schneiders's learned insights hold many implications beyond the borders of academe. I've yet to begin this project, however, in part because of the press of other responsibilities, but more because I've been drawn into a realm of research and reflection that has me in its grasp: Christianity's relationship with Judaism. Thus, my essay for this volume will consider some of our shared interests through the lens of Jewish-Christian dialogue.

Obviously, this relationship between church and synagogue is more than tangential to Schneiders. As a New Testament scholar with a particular expertise in the Fourth Gospel, she is cognizant of the problems associated with its portrayal of "the Jews."[1] Her explorations of the revelatory process, moreover, make the interpretation of such problematic texts essential to exegesis:

> The reason that critical exegesis is insufficient as a total approach to the text and that interpretation in the full sense of the term must terminate in appropriation is pre-

cisely that the ultimate question is not simply, What does the text say? but, What is the meaning of the text for the believing community? Part of that meaning may be that some of the beliefs held and positions taken by the community in the course of its history are untrue or immoral, a judgment based precisely on what the community has discerned through its formation by this text.[2]

Further, in her work on Roman Catholic Religious Life, she identifies interreligious encounter as one of three involvements of Religious Life that illustrate its prophetic character. While speaking appreciatively of ecumenical dialogue, Schneiders notes that interreligious encounter is fundamentally different insofar as it "involves an encounter not between separated siblings but between virtually total strangers."[3] In the ensuing discussion she gives pride of place to the dialogue among monastics. Christians involved in this dialogue are not engaged in a mere experiment, caught up in the latest religious fad. Rather, they reveal a profound commitment to a transformative spiritual experience outside their own tradition, even as it is potentially subversive of their own faith commitments. Monastics and Religious are able to sustain these "ventures into the liminal region between non-Christian religious traditions and Christian faith" because their "final and absolute loyalty…is [to] God, who is not the possession or under the control of any institution or its personnel, or encompassed within any doctrinal synthesis."[4] Although a satisfactory theology of religions has yet to be achieved, the meeting of hearts and minds evident in the monastic dialogue witnesses to the potential of interreligious encounter to heal the divisions that scar humankind.

Thus, we see across the range of Schneiders's work—exegesis, hermeneutical theory, feminism, spirituality, theology of Religious Life—both sensitivity to the way Christian texts have functioned to exclude or denigrate others and appreciation for the power of interreligious encounter.[5]

I propose to enlarge and expand her sensitivity and appreciation by arguing that Christian spirituality must take our relationship with Judaism seriously, that is, as a *partner* in working and waiting for creation's full redemption. In so doing I first sketch the general contours of developments in Jewish-Christian relations. Then I focus in greater detail on two aspects of Jewish life that bear significant implications for the spirituality of Christians: observance of Shabbat and post-Holocaust theology. A concluding section returns to Schneiders's remarks on interreligious encounter.

FROM RIVAL AND ENEMY TO PARTNER

Regarding Judaism as a genuine partner rather than an inferior predecessor requires a major turning—a *teshuvah*—in Christian understanding and attitudes. Indeed, Jews and Christians *are* separated siblings, born out of biblical Israel, contending with each other initially as rivals, and, as the church grew more powerful, as disputants and enemies. Thus, the interreligious encounter with Judaism is *sui generis,* both because of our common origins and because of the long, mostly bitter history between our traditions.[6] Any exploration of Judaism for Christian spirituality must take history into account. We are neither strangers nor friends. Rather, our history vis-à-vis Jews is, as the bishops of France have said, "the heavy inheritance we still bear." It has left us with "open wounds."[7]

For most of the last two millennia the church has, at best, denigrated Judaism, depicting it as a religion of legalism superseded by Jesus' law of love. Much Christian self-understanding was formulated—and remains—"over against" Judaism. Seeing Jesus as the fulfillment of God's promises to Israel and the community of his followers as *verus Israel,* Christians typically understood Judaism to have no further reason for existence.[8] The church, therefore, never developed a theology adequate to explain itself in light of the enduring character of Judaism.

Further, after the late fourth century, the church had power in many places to advance its own growth while placing restrictions on Judaism. Many of these restrictions were "canonical," that is, norms of church life. In some times and places the state sanctioned these canons and/or engaged in anti-Jewish legislation.

By the High Middle Ages, Christian society in Europe had so divorced itself from its origins in Judaism that Jews were regarded as an "other" threatening the stability of the social order. While the Jews were not the only alien "other," the centuries-long theological vilification of Judaism provided a strong ideological basis for such treatment.

The harshness that had evolved over the centuries is evident in "The Decree of the Copts" from the Council of Florence in 1422. According to this council, those who observe Jewish practice have no hope of salvation:

[The Holy Roman church] firmly believes, professes and teaches that the legal [statutes] of the Old Testament or Mosaic Law, divided into ceremonies, holy sacrifices and sacraments, were instituted to signify something to come, and therefore, although in that age they were fitting for divine worship, they have ceased with the advent of our Lord Jesus Christ, whom they signified. [With him] the sacraments of the New Testament have begun. Whoever puts one's hope in these legal [statutes] even after the passion [of Christ] and submits to them as though faith in Christ was unable to save without them, sins mortally. Yet [the church] does not deny that between the passion of Christ and the promulgation of the Gospel *(usque ad promulgatum evangelium)* they could be observed, provided one in no way believed that they were necessary for salvation. But she asserts that after the promulgation of the Gospel *(post promulgatum evangelium)* they cannot be observed without the loss of eternal salvation. Therefore, she denounces as foreign to the faith of Christ all those who after that time observe circumcision, the Sabbath and other laws, and she asserts that they can in no way be sharers of eternal salvation, unless they sometime turn away from their errors. She therefore commands to all who glory themselves in the Christian name that they must, sometime or other, give up circumcision fully, either before or after baptism, because, whether one puts one's hope in

164

it or not, it cannot in any way be observed without the loss of eternal salvation.[9]

In vivid contrast, a 2001 Vatican document asserts that "an attitude of respect, esteem, and love for the Jewish people is the only truly Christian attitude."[10] The dramatic turn in the relation between Christianity and Judaism begun in 1965 with the promulgation of *Nostra Aetate* at Vatican II and continuing in many Christian denominations could scarcely be imagined by our respective ancestors in faith. It is indeed a new thing to acknowledge that Israel's covenantal relationship endures, that Jews remain in covenant with God. Theologically, this means that everything premised on the previous argument—Judaism is superseded—must be rethought.

Yet the notion that Christianity has made Judaism obsolete is deeply embedded, particularly in the church's liturgical life. Paul van Buren accuses the church of "Israel forgetfulness" in, for example, the failure of the Eucharistic Prayer to acknowledge Israel's covenant:

> Generally, it appears that the church does not think it need give thanks for the long history of God's dealing with Israel, or of Israel's life with God prior to the coming of Christ. It seems to be content with creation and "the fall," apparently not thinking that the story of what God then did about the situation by calling Abraham and his heirs, and in calling Moses and giving the Torah, is a matter that should concern the church.[11]

Similarly, R. Kendall Soulen speaks of "structural supersessionism" in the way the church portrays Israel's history as "nothing more than the *economy of redemption in prefigurative form.*" He continues:

> So construed, Israel's story contributes little or nothing to understanding how God's consummating and redemptive purposes engage human creation in universal and enduring ways. Indeed, the background can be completely omitted from an account of Christian faith

without thereby disturbing the overarching logic of salvation history. This omission is reflected in virtually every historic confession of Christian faith from the Creeds of Nicea and Constantinople to the Augsburg Confession and beyond.[12]

Both our history with Jews and the changing character of our relationship with them matter for Christian spirituality. History mirrors an arrogance and triumphalism that have distorted our spirituality. Too few of us seem to wrestle with the fact that *in the name of Christ* and *under the sign of the cross* our ancestors in faith burned Talmuds, segregated Jews in ghettos, and accused them of ritual murder and blood libel—charges, by the way, that have now resurfaced in Arab and Muslim countries. Christians who engage in the study of spirituality today must grapple with the fact that we live in the wake of the Shoah and that Christianity is implicated in it. Unsettling questions arise, however, when we face this history. "With such a catastrophe at my back," Johann Baptist Metz asks, "is there a God to whom one can pray? Can any theology worthy of its name simply continue to speak, continue to speak of God and human beings, as if in the face of such a catastrophe one must not scrutinize the assumed innocence of our human words?"[13]

Christians have so consistently caricatured Judaism that it is we who have been blind, thereby depriving ourselves of its vision. The church that so long imaged Judaism as a blind woman, vanquished by Christ, is beginning to awaken to the beauty and depth of its sibling. Yet the encounter with Judaism in our time necessarily will differ from dialogue with religions of the East, or even with Islam. And it requires a continual reassessment of longstanding theological claims in light of more authentic understandings of Judaism. Like the blind man whom Jesus cured who could see people, "but they look like trees walking" (Mark 8:24), Christian understanding of Judaism remains shadowy, in need of further correction, as the following case illustrates.

Mary C. Boys, SNJM

SHABBAT: RESISTANCE TO THE "WORSHIP OF DOING AND MAKING"

On a sweltering August night several years ago I joined my neighbors, whom I will call Nathan and Deborah Katz, for Shabbat dinner. A frequent guest on Friday evenings, I had come to treasure their invitations. The evenings promised a splendid meal enveloped by the rituals of Sabbath and, typically, intense conversations with the Katz's and their other guests that lasted late into the night.

This night, however, was different. It had been a tough couple of months. Complications had turned Nathan's relatively minor surgery into an ordeal. Worry about her mother's increasing dementia had dominated Deborah's summer. Earlier that week she had moved her mother—a Holocaust survivor—from her Pennsylvania apartment to a New York care center. The uprooting had been traumatic. The Katz's approached this Friday night emotionally spent and physically exhausted.

So it was a simpler meal all around. In concession to fatigue, our meal was not Nathan's usual sumptuous fare but takeout kosher chicken from the store around the corner. I was the lone guest. The candle lighting took place well beyond the appointed time. The sweltering weather dictated casual dress and persuaded me not to bake my usual contribution to our meal, the two loaves of *challah,* the braided bread for the Sabbath.

After *Kiddush*—the blessing that consecrates the Sabbath over wine and bread—I remarked how much their invitation moved me. After such difficult days I would understand if they wanted simply to stare at the walls. Yes, they acknowledged, it had been a dreadful week in a hard summer. They were weary and frazzled, bone tired. "Still," Deborah said, "it is Shabbat."

Some years ago Deborah had remarked to me that the Sabbath had saved their family. She and Nathan, both academics then in major administrative positions, worked long hours in stressful positions. Their two children were also busy with many activities. In the Katz household, however, the weekly ritual of Sabbath gathers them, acting as a centripetal force in their lives.

167

Judaism, with its rich traditions about the sacredness of time, provides an alternative to what Arthur Waskow calls the "worship of Doing and Making."[14] By setting aside one day in seven in which work is laid aside, Jews have a counterpoint to "pathologies of power and work":

> Through Shabbat, Jewish tradition proposes a dialectical movement: to put aside the acts of creation and the products of work and to refocus on the sacredness of the human being. This is achieved by spending the entire day of Shabbat on being, not doing. It is a proclamation, "I am, not I do."...By giving special texture to time, by emancipating human beings, by transforming perspective on life, by enriching human activities, Shabbat brings out life's capacity for holiness.[15]

Yet, demeaning Jewish observance of the Sabbath has been a subtle, if persistent, dimension of the church's argument that it has superseded Judaism. The *Letter of Barnabas* in the early second century claimed that God had abandoned the Jews because of their wickedness. So God abolished their rites and practices—including Sabbath—and established instead a covenant with the followers of Jesus. The Synod of Laodicea, in a clear matter of oppositional identity formation, legislated in 364 that "Christians must not judaize by resting on the Sabbath, but must work on that day" (Canon 29).

Saint John Chrysostom (347–407) intensified these harsher tones in his virulent sermons against the Judaizers. In these eight homilies he confronted Christians still attracted to Jewish traditions: "If the ceremonies of the Jews move you to admiration, what do you have in common with us? If the Jewish ceremonies are venerable and great, ours are lies. But if ours are true, as they are true, theirs are filled with deceit."[16] Saint John of Damascus (ca. 675–749) contended in *The Exposition of the Orthodox Faith* that God gave Israel the Sabbath to offset their "grossness and sensuality...and their absolute propensity for material things." That the Jews observed Sabbath was of no merit to him, since even an ox must rest. Jews, unlike Christians, "do not consecrate their entire lives to God nor with longing serve the Lord as Father." They are like "unfeeling servants" who, "if ever they do allot some short and very small part of their lives to God, do so from fear of the punishment." Yes, the Sabbath allowed Jews to devote at least minimal time to the sacred. Christians, in contrast, "no longer give the Lord just partial service out of fear....We are bound to dedicate the whole space of our life to Him."

Contemporary sensibilities avoid such crass contrasts. Nonetheless, the exposition of Sunday in the *Catechism of the Catholic Church* implicitly disparages Jewish practice. For Christians, the ceremonial observance of Sunday "replaces" that of the Sabbath. "In Christ's Passover, Sunday fulfills the spiritual truth of the Jewish Sabbath and announces man's eternal rest in God. For worship under the Law prepared for the mystery of Christ, and what was done there prefigured some aspects of Christ" (no. 2175).[17] Readers unfamiliar with Judaism—the vast majority of the world's one billion Catholics—would reasonably conclude that Sunday had entirely eclipsed Sabbath. The light of Christ eclipses Judaism's rituals and practices.

While avoiding the virulence of previous centuries, most significant ecclesial documents fail to acknowledge Jewish tradition as a source of wisdom—unless the documents explicitly concern the church's relationship with Jews and Judaism. A recent apostolic letter of Pope John Paul II, *Dies Domini* (1998), provides a case in point. The letter is replete with insight about what more intense observance of Sunday might mean for Christian life. Yet even this letter exalts Sunday at the expense of Shabbat: Christians have a duty, the pope says, to remember that the underlying reasons for keeping "the Lord's Day" holy remain valid, *"although the practices of the Jewish Sabbath are gone."* These practices have been *"surpassed by the 'fulfillment' which Sunday brings"* (no. 62, emphasis added).

Were we Christians to restrain our tendency to present our tradition by means of comparison and contrast with Judaism— and always as the superior way—we might instead discover an embarrassment of riches in Jewish understanding and practice of keeping the Sabbath holy. While the Christian turn to religions of the East has not been without its critics, most notably in the 2000 Vatican declaration *Dominus Iesus,* the constant disparagement, even effacing, of Judaism makes it more difficult for us Christians to open ourselves to learn from Jewish practice.[18] And history makes it more difficult for Jews to trust that Christians will learn from their practices rather than appropriating them, as we have done in celebrating a "Christian Seder." Christians are called neither to imitate nor to appropriate their practices but rather to be guests at the table of Jewish life. As we take our leave and return to our home tradition, we must be attentive to what happened and what it means for Christian self-understanding.

Fortunately, some among us have begun to reclaim the Sabbath for Christian life, most notably Dorothy Bass, but also Wayne Muller and Marva Dawn.[19] Abraham Joshua Heschel's classic monograph *The Sabbath* has rightly enriched Christian reflection, but students of spirituality will find an abundance of sources, particularly in Greenberg's *The Jewish Way,* which also has a seven-section, annotated bibliography on Shabbat.[20]

IS OUR FAITH A "MOMENTARY STAY AGAINST CONFUSION"?

The more one explores, in literature and especially in the practice of living communities of Jews, the more one realizes the profundity of Judaism and the way in which it offers a truly holy way of life. Concomitantly, the more one risks contemplating the shadows cast by the Shoah, the more one realizes the challenge to form Christians so that faith and justice are inextricable. The Holocaust reveals too few examples of a "faith that does justice."

The narrow sort of spirituality that has characterized too many Christians may be seen in the extraordinary first novel of Martha Cooley, *The Archivist,* which portrays a couple in which Christian and Jewish identities play a complicated role. Matthias Lane (named after the disciple who replaced Judas Iscariot) is an archivist at a university library where he oversees rare books and manuscripts of prominent writers, such as T. S. Eliot. His wife, Judith Rudin, is a poet who works as a legal secretary.

Judith, a Jew, is an intense woman who suffers a nervous breakdown; eventually, Matthias—Matt—hospitalizes her. She is haunted by the stories emerging from the camps of Europe, but Matt fails to recognize the ironclad grip these reports have on her. Nor can he deal with the God in whom she believes:

> I shouldn't have tried to take her God from her—the passionate, demanding God of the Old Testament, the God who spoke to the desert tribes as if they were his children or his lovers, capable of wounding him as much as he could hurt them. I found this God unacceptably proximate. The One I had known all my life was believable in direct proportion to the distance he took from all the particulars of my life; His force as well as my faith lay in this remove.[21]

Matt had an excellent memory for his work, yet for him the postwar years were a blur. "I went to school, graduated, worked, read books. I didn't pray or attend church, although I persisted in a belief—unarticulated, unquestioned—that Christ's intercession would govern the course of my days. I did not wish to know how, or why" (57).

In contrast, Judith became obsessed with theodicy, seeking "proof of a beneficent God" (58), poring over Kabbalistic literature, which awakens in Matt memories of "my mother's urgent, alienating faith" (59). A gap opens between them, "a rift in feeling, experience, perception." Once institutionalized, Judith scrutinizes the back issues of the *New York Times* her Uncle Len brings her; she becomes an archivist of the Shoah. Meanwhile, Matt, thinking to protect her, destroys all her files.

Matt's inability truly to understand Judith, whom he loves in his removed sort of way, seems to symbolize Christianity's removal from the agony of facing history. Judith longs for Matt to reveal a "certain kind of hunger. To know what happened and at least ask why. Because the *tikkun* [repair or healing] can't start until everyone asks what happened—not just the Jews but everybody" (118).

In contrast, Matt thinks that Jews ask too many questions and take doubt too far (28); they focus too much on their exile, which "seems arrogant to me." (144). Judith sees Christianity as taking grace too far (28) and as "a lie of consolation" (60). Yes, Matt does feel her suffering, she tells Dr. Clay, her therapist. "But he does nothing. It's all in Christ's hands" (202). She writes in her journal: "Matt's been terribly afraid all his life, and Christ is a cage for the fear that he knows will escape some day. His faith is like that line in Frost: *a momentary stay against confusion*" (163).

Perhaps Cooley's novel is a harsh indictment, but its demand for Christian spirituality haunts me: to form persons in a faith that is more than a "momentary stay against confusion." The radical evil of the Shoah, in which Christianity is so thoroughly implicated, unsettles—and faith must sustain this disequilibrium, not repress it.

MORE DISEQUILIBRIUM: "QUESTIONS THAT TOUCH ON THE HEART OF OUR FAITH"

In 1977 the bishops of France wrote that Judaism poses questions to Christians that "touch on the heart of our faith."[22] Among the many questions Judaism poses to my faith is this: *If Christians were to regard Judaism as a partner in waiting and working for the world's full redemption, what difference would it make both in our self-understanding and in our understanding of the religious "other"?* Since I have begun to address the implications for Christian self-understanding in an earlier book,[23] let me conclude with some comments about the implications for religious pluralism.

To view Judaism as a partner that offers a way of living a holy life is to stand in awe before the mystery of the Holy One. If we are at long last prepared to acknowledge that Jews remain covenanted with God (and with one another as well), then it follows that there is more than one way to the Divine. And if there are two ways to this God, might there not be, as many argue, more than two? Paul Knitter's *Introducing Theologies of Religion* is a superb—and eminently readable—analysis of approaches to religious pluralism, but it is necessary to pause before the distinctiveness of Christianity's relationship to Judaism.[24] Among the schools of thought Knitter analyzes is that of comparative theology, in which deep resonances among religions are sought with a bracketing of questions about which is truer. Comparative theology is more focused on a learned understanding of the "other" than it is on "solving" pluralism. Yet, we lack a comparative theology of Judaism. In light of the centuries-long Christian disparagement of Judaism, this is tragically ironic.

I end as I began, with a conversation with Sandra Schneiders. In a lengthy e-mail message, she told about a two-week journey she had made to Asia in December 2002 to lecture to Religious in Korea. Visiting Buddhist shrines had inspired thoughts about religious pluralism:

> Is Christianity a "successor" to or "supplanter of" Judaism, or even a sister-religion? Or is monotheism, Judaism's most important religious intuition, appropriated by Christians according to the central structures of incarnation, which cannot be acceptable (totally) to Jews but doesn't have to be? And is Christianity's central intuition of radical divine immanence and eternal life through resurrection to be appropriated by all, but according to their own symbolic structures, which probably cannot be and do not have to be acceptable to Christians? And the same for Buddhism's intuition into the Void, the no-thing of the Ultimate? Anyway, I want to keep thinking about it. We're a long way from a workable approach to the multiplicity of religious/spiritual paths—but I think R.L. [Religious Life] has a special role to play in the project.[25]

The rethinking of Christianity's relationship to Judaism is in its early stages, so how to best devolve implications for relationships with other religions will require much further exploration. It will require all of us to keep thinking about these questions that touch on the heart of our faith. For such challenging thinking, we are grateful for learned and reflective scholars like Sandra Schneiders.

Notes

1. See Sandra M. Schneiders, *Written That You May Believe: Encountering Jesus in the Fourth Gospel* (New York: Crossroad, 1999), 41–45; and idem, "Living Word or Deadly Letter? The Encounter between the New Testament and Contemporary Experience," in *Proceedings of the Catholic Theological Society of America* 47 (1992): 45–60, esp. 47.

2. Sandra M. Schneiders, *The Revelatory Text: Interpreting the New Testament as Sacred Scripture*, 2nd ed. (Collegeville, MN: Liturgical Press, 1999), 177.

3. Sandra M. Schneiders, *Religious Life in a New Millennium: Finding the Treasure*, vol. 1 (Mahwah, NJ: Paulist Press, 2000), 336. I have followed her style of the upper case, so as to distinguish this form of life from other modes of religious living.

4. Ibid., 1:337–39.

5. In this generalization I do not mean to gloss over the extraordinary breadth and depth of Schneiders's scholarship. I simply want to indicate her awareness of anti-Judaism, which has so infected Christian thinking, attitudes, and behaviors as a way of connecting this chapter with her work. Nevertheless, this is not a major theme in her work. I have also taken issue with an aspect of her feminist reading of Jesus in relation to first-century Judaism. See Mary C. Boys, "Patriarchal Judaism, Liberating Jesus: A Feminist Misrepresentation," *Union Theological Seminary Quarterly Review* 56 (no. 3–4) (2003): 48–61.

6. The distinctive character of the relationship with Judaism is evident in the structure of the Roman Catholic Church, in which the Commission on Religious Relations with Jews comes under the ambit of the Pontifical Council for Promoting Christian Unity rather than the Pontifical Council for Interreligious Dialogue.

7. The Bishops of France, "Declaration of Repentance [1997]," in *Catholics Remember the Holocaust* (Washington, DC: United States Catholic Conference, 1998), 34.

8. "The fathers [of the church, e.g., Melito, Augustine, John Chrysostom] thought Judaism was dying, that the victory of the Church signified the demise of Judaism. They created a cari-

cature to meet their expectations and refused to look at Judaism for what it really was. But the problem of Judaism arose as a theological issue because Judaism had not died. It had not come to an end in Jesus, and it was still a force to be reckoned with in the Roman Empire." Robert Wilken, *Judaism and the Early Christian Mind* (New Haven, CT: Yale University Press, 1971), 229.

9. The General Council of Florence, 1442, *Decree for the Copts* ("Jacobites"). See Josef Neuner and Jacques Dupuis, *The Christian Faith in the Doctrinal Documents of the Catholic Church,* rev. ed. (New York: Alba House, 1996), nos. 1003, 1004. Jacques Dupuis sets this decree in historical context in *Toward a Christian Theology of Religious Pluralism* (Maryknoll, NY: Orbis Books, 1997), 84–109.

10. Pontifical Biblical Commission, *The Jewish People and Their Sacred Scriptures in the Christian Bible.* Available online.

11. Paul M. van Buren, *According to the Scriptures: The Origins of the Gospel and of the Church's Old Testament* (Grand Rapids, MI: Eerdmans, 1998), 78.

12. R. Kendall Soulen, *The God of Israel and Christian Theology* (Minneapolis: Fortress Press, 1996), 31–32.

13. Johann Baptist Metz, "Between Remembering and Forgetting: The Shoah in the Era of Cultural Amnesia," in *Good and Evil after Auschwitz: Ethical Implications for Today,* ed. Jack Bemporad, John T. Pawlikowski, and Joseph Sievers (Hoboken, NJ: Ktav, 2000), 21.

14. Arthur Waskow, "Getting Time on Our Side." Available online.

15. Irving Greenberg, *The Jewish Way: Living the Holidays* (New York: Summit Books, 1988), 138, 146.

16. John Chrysostom, *Homily One against the Judaizers,* 6:5. Available online. See also Robert L. Wilken, *John Chrysostom and the Jews: Rhetoric and Reality in the Late Fourth Century* (Berkeley and Los Angeles: University of California Press, 1983).

17. *Catechism of the Catholic Church* (Collegeville, MN: Liturgical Press, 1994), 534.

18. *Dominus Iesus* admits that "the various religious traditions contain and offer religious elements which come from

God," and that "some prayers and rituals of the other religions may assume a role of preparation for the Gospel." Nevertheless, "one cannot attribute to these, however, a divine origin or an *ex opere operato* salvific efficacy, which is proper to the Christian sacraments. Furthermore, it cannot be overlooked that other rituals, insofar as they depend on superstitions or other errors (cf. 1 Cor 10:20–21), constitute an obstacle to salvation....If it is true that the followers of other religions can receive divine grace, it is also certain that *objectively speaking* they are in a gravely deficient situation in comparison with those who, in the Church, have the fullness of the means of salvation" (nos. 21–22). *Dominus Iesus* makes explicit mention of Judaism only once (no. 13). See my analysis in Mary C. Boys, "*Dominus Iesus*: A Panel Discussion," in *Proceedings of the Catholic Theological Society of America* 56 (2001), 111–16.

19. See Dorothy C. Bass, ed., *Practicing Our Faith: A Way of Life for a Searching People* (San Francisco: Jossey-Bass, 1997); idem, *Receiving the Day: Christian Practices for Opening the Gift of Time* (San Francisco: Jossey-Bass, 2000); Wayne Muller, *Sabbath: Finding Rest, Renewal, and Delight in Our Busy Lives* (New York: Bantam Books, 1999); Marva J. Dawn, *Keeping the Sabbath Wholly: Ceasing, Resting, Embracing, Feasting* (Grand Rapids, MI: Eerdmans, 1989).

20. Abraham Joshua Heschel, *The Sabbath: Its Meaning for Modern Man* (New York: Farrar, Straus and Young, 1951); Greenberg, *The Jewish Way*. For an excellent work that has appeared since Rabbi Greenberg's annotated bibliography, see Francine Klagsbrun, *The Fourth Commandment: Remembering the Sabbath Day* (New York: Harmony Books, 2002).

21. Martha Cooley, *The Archivist* (Boston: Little, Brown, and Company, 1998), 22. Further references are in parentheses.

22. "Statement by the French Bishops' Committee for Relations with Jews," in *Stepping Stones to Further Jewish-Christian Relations: An Unabridged Collection of Christian Documents,* comp. Helga Croner (London: Stimulus Books, 1977), 61.

23. See Mary C. Boys, *Has God Only One Blessing?: Judaism as a Source of Christian Self-Understanding* (Mahwah, NJ: Paulist Press, 2000).

24. Paul Knitter, *Introducing Theologies of Religions* (Maryknoll, NY: Orbis Books, 2002).

25. E-mail from Sandra M. Schneiders to Mary C. Boys, January 7, 2003.

9

INTERFAITH AESTHETICS
Where Theology and
Spirituality Meet

Alejandro García-Rivera

THE PROMISE OF INTERFAITH AESTHETICS

Some time ago, Prof. Ronald Nakasone and I had a lengthy discussion on some of the failings of the interfaith dialogue.[1] We both came to the conclusion that approaches concentrating on written texts (the True) or moral paradigms (the Good) often led to an impasse or mere niceties between members of the dialogue. We wondered if the arts or aesthetics (the Beautiful) could bring some new notions or life into the interfaith project. Perhaps, we thought, the aim of an interfaith dialogue is not to find a common truth or a common paradigm of moral behavior. If we can come to appreciate the beauty of another's faith, perhaps we can also learn how to love the other's faith. Love, then, ought to be the major aim of an interfaith dialogue.

In the background of our conversation lay my deepest admiration for the work of Sandra Schneiders in the field of spirituality. Her demonstration of the border-crossing ability of Christian spiritual traditions gives hope to the possibility of a corresponding border-crossing project among very different faiths.[2] Also in the background was my conversion to the value of spirituality in the field of theology. This conversion came in reading von Balthasar's seminal article "Theology and Sanctity,"[3] in which he argues for a reunion of spirituality and theology. Von Balthasar's

178

article articulated a deep belief that comes from my study of Latin American popular Catholicism, yet in conversations with Prof. Nakasone I came to the conclusion that some important distinctions need to be made in order to understand the proper relationship between spirituality and theology. I believe that the essence of this relationship lies in the distinction between the particularity of religious identity and the expansiveness of lived community. In this essay I propose that an interfaith aesthetics offers this proper relation between theology and spirituality by joining the particularity of religious identity with the expansiveness of a community whose faith has been formed by the love of a Beauty seen and loved through the eyes of the "other."

One further building block is necessary to construct this argument, namely, a way to distinguish yet relate aesthetics and spirituality. In *The Mystical Now* Wendy Beckett distinguishes between religious and spiritual art. An example of religious art is Eastern icons. They are often not great art. Their power lies instead in the faith people bring to them. As Beckett puts it, "For the believer as such, the actual quality of the art is unimportant— the work stands or falls by its ability to raise the mind and heart towards the truths of faith."[4] Such art, however, does not deepen faith; it merely activates it. Spiritual art, on the other hand, finds its power in a non-conceptual way.[5] "It effects what it signifies…but the mind may be aware only of the impact of some mysterious truth. This is the essence of spiritual art. We are taken into a realm that is potentially open to us, we are made more what we are meant to be."[6] Although, as we shall see, Beckett's distinctions between religious and spiritual art can be challenged in an appreciation of Buddhist art, her distinctions are helpful for the purposes of articulating a relationship between aesthetics and spirituality. This relationship is best seen in the very real issues raised by the theological project of an interfaith dialogue.

THE CHALLENGES OF INTERFAITH DIALOGUE

Interfaith dialogue has been something of a double-edged sword for theologians. The very appeal of interfaith dialogue for

Christian theology lies in the possibility that Christian faith has something universal to say to all people. At the same time, however, that universal message is tied to the very particular and concrete system of doctrines about Jesus of Nazareth and the Christ of faith.[7] Such particularity finds primary public expression in theological language. Theological language, however, was formed, in part (but a very influential part), in the crucial but limited struggle to articulate Christian identity within a community of faith. Beckett's distinction of religious art as that which raises minds and hearts to the truths of faith is consonant with this aspect of theological language.

In other words, a primary function of theological language may be seen as articulating an identity of faith rather than forming a community of faith. This is not to pit identity against community, but to make clear what is prior. A community of faith is assumed in theological language, not the other way around. In a world, however, in which community of *faiths* now becomes a crucial element in the identity of Christian faith, the assumption of community must be reexamined. Theology can no longer look at the identity of Christian faith by assuming such identity lies in a single community of faith.

Nostra aetate, the insightful document from Vatican II that deals with interreligious dialogue, makes precisely the point that Christians, "while witnessing to their own faith and way of life, acknowledge, preserve and encourage the spiritual and moral truths found among non-Christians, also their social life and culture" (no. 2).[8] *Nostra aetate* suggests that theological language may not be enough to do interfaith dialogue. Culture, morality, and spirituality must be brought into a dialogue in a world where identity is to be found not simply in a single community but in a community of communities.

Beckett's distinction of the spiritual in art is helpful at this point. The spiritual opens up to us a non-conceptual realm, or rather, a realm beyond the conceptual. This realm allows a sense of unity without the divisiveness of particularities. The spiritual allows a breathtaking openness to all spiritual truth. Because it exists in a pluralism of faiths, the spiritual realm is particularly congenial to the crossing of identities. The spiritual, however, also leads to an impasse in true interfaith dialogue. An example of this kind of impasse is found in the celebrated Trappist monk Thomas Merton's journey to his appreciation of the faith traditions of the East. In *Zen and the Birds of Appetite* Merton warned of the buzzards that hovered around the corpse of that spiritual "enlightenment" that too easily syncretized two spiritual traditions into one. Those who would see spiritual identity across faith traditions might as well claim to see identity between the subjects of mathematics and tennis![9]

In other words, the very openness of spirituality sometimes blinds it to the very real differences that exist across faith traditions. Spirituality unaided by the hardheadedness of theological distinctions falls too easily into a vapid syncretism. Likewise, theology unaided by the openness fostered in spirituality knocks itself senseless on walls of identity erected by its hardheadedness. Beckett's acknowledgment that there exists an aesthetic reality that is both spiritual and religious gives us an alternative between these two extremes. Such reality is the subject of a theological aesthetics. A theological aesthetics takes the sense of beauty as the place where the non-conceptual element in spirituality can be articulated through the hardheadedness of theology. The sense of beauty allows the non-conceptual to be articulated, it allows the unseen to be seen, and it allows the invisible to become visible.

For these reasons a theological aesthetics may be seen as the place where theology and spirituality meet, where theological hardheadedness and spiritual openness fructify and entwine with each other. That is, theological aesthetics takes seriously both the theological task of articulating Christian faith and the spiritual task of living out that faith.

BETWEEN THEOLOGICAL HARDHEADEDNESS AND SPIRITUAL OPENNESS

Beauty, then, is not only an aesthetic experience; it is a religious experience as well. Indeed, the sense of Beauty in both the concreteness and particularity of its physical sensuality and the universality of its depth dimension is at the same time a religious and aesthetic experience. In this sense of Beauty the hardheaded particularity of theological language and the universal openness of spirituality meet. I propose that, in the sense of Beauty, a true interfaith dialogue, the talk of faith, can take place. This was the conclusion at which Prof. Nakasone and I finally arrived. The sense of Beauty in Buddhist and Christian aesthetics and art opens up the acts of speaking and listening across different faiths into an aesthetics not only of appreciating each other's faith but in engendering a love for each other's traditions. This love fostered by the sense of Beauty intimated another sense, the sense of both Buddhist and Christian belonging to a larger whole. Such belonging is experienced as more than either syncretism or fulfillment of potentialities. This belonging, however, is also experienced as less than a unity of shared beliefs or convictions about salvation or the ultimate.

TASTE AND SEE

The time has come, then, to "taste and see" what an interfaith aesthetics promises. I have chosen examples from two very different faith traditions. The first (Figure 9–1) is a Korean tea bowl from the sixteenth century that exemplifies what the great Buddhist scholar of aesthetics Yanagi Sōetsu called *Mingei* or folk aesthetics.

Figure 9-1

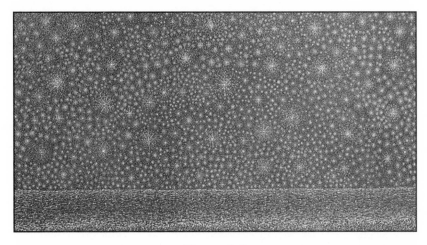

Figure 9-2

The other example (Figure 9–2) is a painting entitled *Starlight* by Camaldolese monk and artist Arthur Poulin of Incarnation Monastery in Berkeley, California.

A COMMON BEAUTY

What do a Western painting and a Korean tea bowl have in common? It is easy, at first, to speak of their differences. These differences can be easily conceptualized. One is a painting, the other a craft. One is two-dimensional, the other three. One emphasizes color, the other mass. One is from the West, the other from the East. Yet, it is surprising to find that it is not easy to say that there is nothing in common between them. Just as the differences between these two works of art are self-evident, it is just as evident that these two works have something in common. The commonality perceived, however, is difficult to articulate. It exists at the non-conceptual level that Beckett speaks of as the spiritual element in art. An interfaith aesthetics seeks to engage these two dimensions, the conceptual and the non-conceptual, the differences and the commonality, the visible and the invisible.

The Korean tea bowl is an example of what Yanagi Sōetsu called *Mingei* aesthetics.[10] Ronald Nakasone summarizes this aesthetics. "The beauty intrinsic to *Mingei* wares mirrors the inner being of unknown craftspersons whose creative effort reflects and is aided by their given craft tradition, historical, and geographical circumstances."[11] Figure 9–1 displays a superb example of *Mingei* aesthetics. This tea bowl was crafted during the Yi dynasty (in the sixteenth century). Its unpretentious form stands in sharp contrast to Western distinctions between crafts and fine arts. More important, its unpretentiousness characterizes values dear to Buddhist thought. The charm of this tea bowl is a presence untroubled by the question of its ugliness or prettiness, of craft or fine art. Indeed, the sense of Beauty that emerges from this bowl has its source in the effortless manner in which such bowls came to be, naturally and inevitably. This effortlessness speaks of a source, as Nakasone puts it, "appearing before the illness of illusion." Or as Yanagi himself says, "[The beauty of Yi pottery] is not that which is attained by eliminating ugliness but rather that which bursts out before the duality even occurs to man. The pottery is not the result of the knowledge of the nature of beauty but is produced before there is any question of knowing or not knowing."[12]

What Nakasone and Yanagi point out is that *Mingei* aesthetics resists Western distinctions because it embodies, at heart, the Buddhist principle of non-duality and the doctrine of no self.[13] We are enslaved to a perpetual cycle of suffering, of birth and death, until we achieve a state of a totally integrated mind in which differentiations and the "self" are dissolved. Beauty marks such enlightenment.

> The sense of beauty is born when the opposition between subject and object has been dissolved, when the subject called "I" and the object called "it" have both vanished into the realm of Non-dual Entirety, when there is no longer anybody to transfer or anything to be transferred. Neither the "I" that faces "it" nor the "it" that faces the "I" can attain reality. A true awareness of beauty is to be found where beauty watches beauty, not where "I" watch "it."[14]

Indeed, the *Mingei* aesthetics of this Korean tea bowl takes the Westerner to religious insights quite different from the elementary distinction from the divinely personal "I" and "Thou" and the doctrine of the soul.

Thus *Mingei* aesthetics resists Beckett's distinction between religious and spiritual art. This bowl is an example where the religiousness of art is the basis of its very spirituality. Moreover, the spirituality of such art does not rely on the refinement of form, but rather on the naturalness and inevitability of such form. Yet Beckett's distinction, though flawed, is still helpful. For this unpretentious tea bowl is also an example of a work of art in which the spiritual and the religious come together *à la* Beckett in a fusion of great aesthetic power.

Fr. Poulin's painting, *Starlight* (Figure 9–2), helps recover the distinction. *Starlight* is unabashedly a painting of spiritual art. *Starlight* is a meditation on God's promise to Abraham: "Your descendants will be as numerous as the grains of sand." There is no iconic element present that would mark this painting as religious in the sense of Beckett's term. It is definitely a work that aims to open up to the beholder a realm of spiritual delight and truth. Indeed, its very method, points of paint layered one upon the other, is the very essence of openness. What is more open than a point?

Many have remarked of Poulin's work that it resembles Pointillism. This comparison is not accurate. Pointillism aims at putting two colors together so that they "vibrate" and create a flat painting. Poulin's points, on the other hand, are brush strokes. They include texture and are many layered. He sums up his technique as "the one makes up the many." It is the potential to be many that lies at the spiritual power of Poulin's point. "You know, Alex," he said to me, "all of life begins with one dot."[15] For Poulin, each brushstroke represents a powerful potential, just like the beginning of a life. Indeed, the "dot" is very special to him, "very powerful." It is the potentiality implied in the "dot," the potential to blossom into a unified whole, that strikes Arthur Poulin as powerful.

I would add to Poulin's self-description of style that such layered points act both to suggest form and to conceal it. Such layered points distinguish forms even as they connect forms with other forms. It is this double play of connecting and distinguishing, of revealing and concealing, that marks the spiritual power of this painting, indeed of much Western spiritual art. Though full of spiritual openness, Poulin's *Starlight* also embodies religious doctrines. The stars in the heavens and the grains of sand bear certain similarities. In color and in shape the stars and the sands are visually connected. As such, *Starlight* speaks of the Christian doctrine of the incarnation. A theme that runs through much of Fr. Poulin's painting, the doctrine of the incarnation connects the human and the divine, the heavens and the earth.

Starlight also embodies another Christian doctrine. Christians form a mystical community as the body of Christ. The many grains of sand interconnect to form one community, a community that is also interconnected with the heavens. As such, this community suggests a heavenly dimension. Given the simultaneous presence of the doctrine of the incarnation, *Starlight* suggests that all of Abraham's children have become a community in the body of Christ. These doctrines, however, appear poles apart from the Buddhist doctrines of non-duality and the no self. Yet, like the Korean tea bowl, *Starlight* combines religious and spiritual dimensions in a work of amazing aesthetic power.

What ought to amaze us is not that these two different works of art embody doctrines that appear to be diametrically opposed. What engenders wonder is that both fill us with a sense of beauty that convinces us that these two works, though quite different, emerge from the same depths. There is a sense of unity that comes with the sense of beauty, even though it is not the unity of shared beliefs. It is the sense of a unity of being connected to a whole, a whole whose depths are the same for the Buddhist as for the Christian. It speaks of a common belonging, if not a shared unity. When the Christian senses beauty in the Korean tea bowl and the Buddhist senses beauty in Poulin's *Starlight,* the theological hardheadedness present in the tea bowl and in the painting now become part of the spiritual openness revealed in their beauty. The Christian can come to appreciate the doctrine of non-duality and of no self, and the Buddhist, the doctrine of the Incarnation and the mystical body of Christ.

Yet the aesthetic experience goes beyond mere appreciation, for the sense of beauty found in both works brings with it a sense of unity that is more felt than articulated. The Christian can sense that the faith journey of the Buddhist belongs to the same whole as the faith journey of his and her own Christianity. I hope I am not misunderstood here. The whole is not the same as a religious end. I am not saying that Buddhist and Christian religions actually envision the same religious end, even an end that is not able to be conceptualized. I am saying that the sense of Beauty is the experience of belonging to a whole that is bigger than an individual or even a community. I am also saying that such experience is also the work of faith. In other words, Beckett's distinction between religious art that activates faith and spiritual art that opens one up to something larger than oneself is helpful not so much in distinguishing one type of art from another but as a way to articulate the unity of all powerful art.

Art that shakes us and grasps us at a fundamental human level is made possible not only through the work of art but also through the work of faith. Such a suggestion means that an interfaith aesthetics needs a more expanded understanding of faith. This understanding of faith must take into account both the particularity of an individual faith community but also be able to elucidate the sense of belonging to a greater whole that the sense of beauty gives.

AN INTERFAITH

Back in the 1930s, John Dewey, the great American naturalist philosopher, put forth a rather provocative thesis. If one separates out the rituals, doctrines, indeed all the particularity that characterizes a religion, one would be left with the experience of the religion, that is, the religious. The religious would be the universal dimension of experience and, as such, would allow for a "common" faith.[16] Dewey's distinction between a religion and the religious roughly corresponds to Beckett's distinction between religious and spiritual art. What is fascinating about these distinctions is that although they come from two very different perspectives, they both attempt an expanded notion of faith. Both identify a limited sense of faith that is concerned with particular customs, habits, and doctrines. They both argue for an expanded sense of faith. This is a faith open to something bigger than itself. This something-bigger-than-itself corresponds to a unity of a whole in Dewey and to a unity in mystery for Beckett. They both agree, however. This unity is an aesthetic unity; it is a unity-in-variety.[17]

The distinction Dewey and Beckett make is valuable in understanding the recent Roman Catholic struggle around the nature of Christian faith. Vatican II wrestled with two important dimensions in a Catholic understanding of faith. Faith involves an extrinsic element. Vatican I affirmed that faith involves submission of the intellect and will to truths that God reveals to men and women. Vatican II, on the other hand, affirms in *Dei Verbum* that it is in Jesus Christ that "the deepest truth about God and the salvation of man is made clear" (no. 2). In other words, faith is also intrinsic. It is rooted in the historical, experiential process culminating in Jesus Christ, who reveals to the human his and her very nature (see *Gaudium et Spes,* no. 22).

The extrinsic and intrinsic dimensions of faith, as identified in recent Roman Catholic understanding, correspond roughly to the two distinctions that Dewey and Beckett make. The extrinsic dimension of faith directs our intellect and will to something bigger than themselves. The intrinsic dimension of faith insists that the extrinsic dimension of faith is to be found in the particularities of the rituals, doctrines, and history of the church.

Dei Verbum leads to an amazing assessment of Christian faith. Other religions can contribute to Christian faith in that their own faith response to the experiential dimension of a reality bigger than their extrinsic selves reveals truths necessary for Christian faith itself. At least, this is my interpretation of that other Vatican II document on religions, *Nostra Aetate.* Both these documents, however, need to be seen in light of a much older theological work from the fifteenth century. Nicholas of Cusa's *De Pace Fidei* amazes by its very contemporary discussion of interfaith dialogue written, in part, as a response to the 1453 Muslim occupation of Constantinople.[18]

De Pace Fidei adds a new element to our ongoing discussion. Contingency marks all expressions of faith, says Cusa.[19] Indeed,

all expressions of faith, such as rites, are signs, and signs are particular, contingent and conditioned. This does not mean that signs
are illusions or empty conceptualizations. Not at all, says Cusa.
Faith is what gives particular expressions, such as rites, their
authenticity, and these particular expressions are signs that give
evidence of belief in an ultimate reality. In this assertion Cusa goes
far beyond the old medieval debates between faith and grace such
as *fides quae creditur* or *fides qua creditor*. Particular expressions
of faith correspond authentically to God's reality because God
wills it, not because God is bound to them. Thus, the crucial religious experience for Cusa is love, not faith. Faith, rather, is *fides
caritate formata* (faith formed by love). Faith alone, that is, faith
unformed, is empty; even the demons have such faith.[20]

Indeed, Cusa tells us, such faith, faith unformed by love, is
responsible for religious conflict.[21] This faith is characterized by
forms divorced from the experience of God's love. As Biechler and
Bond put it, "When religious rite and form assume the place of
religion, dissension and injustice abound; only the common experience of the reality of God by whatever mode of experience is
available to a given people comprises a genuine and reconciling
spirituality."[22] What Cusa proposes, then, is peace among the
nations through an expanded notion of faith. Such peace is not
the harmony of religious practices or even of different faiths, but
a peace worked out through faith, indeed emerging out of the
conditions of faith itself. This peace is worked out, *in actu,* in
heaven because God so desires it, and *in potentia* now on earth as
the nations work out their salvation to a final reunion in some
eschatological Jerusalem.[23]

Cusa's provocative thesis matches Dewey's. Indeed, they are
strikingly similar. Both insist that faith uninformed by religious
experience is empty and succumbs to dissent and, worse, injustice.
Both Cusa and Dewey give accounts of what that experience
ought to be. Cusa tells us that it is the experience of love; Dewey,
the experience of a unity bigger than the experience itself. It is
striking that these two accounts of a reconciling faith are that of
an aesthetic experience.

The reason for putting Cusa, Dewey, Beckett, and Vatican II
in conversation with one another is that together they suggest

another dimension of faith that I would simply call interfaith. *Interfaith* is a term associated with the concrete practice of dialogue between very different religious traditions. In the past the emphasis has been on the term *inter* rather than *faith*. I am suggesting a different nuance to the term *interfaith* in which its components, *inter* and *faith,* are both taken seriously. Dewey's "religious," Beckett's "spiritual," Vatican II's "intrinsic" and Cusa's *fides caritate formata* all speak of an element in faith that is dynamic rather than static, non-propositional rather than propositional, responsive rather than passive; indeed, it is *faith in faith itself.*[24]

Faith in faith itself takes both the contingency and the authenticity of faith seriously. It recognizes both the deep correspondence of faith to an ultimate or divine reality and its contingent particular expression. It recognizes such contingencies not as illusions or constructions of human concepts or desires but as interpretations of an intuition. Faith in faith itself, then, is faith in the formation of faith, faith formed, that is, through the aesthetic experience of love that connects the particular to a greater whole.

Works of art provide one dimension of such an experience and, as works, are exemplary of an interfaith. As works of religious art they indeed work through an experience of faith. As spiritual, they engender and form in others experiences of love that give hope in faith itself. In this way works of art provide an aesthetics that in helping to form faith also helps create an interfaith. I think there is a word for this sort of aesthetics. The North American philosophical tradition, through the work of theologian Jonathan Edwards, calls it the *admirable.* It is a term that combines theological hardheadedness and the openness of the spiritual, that combines sense and sensibility.[25] Indeed, the root meaning of *admirable, ad mirabile,* has both a passive and active interpretation. A passive interpretation might translate *ad* as "at." Thus, the admirable is a passive "looking at." An active interpretation, however, may translate *ad* as "through." Then the admirable is translated as "looking through." Together we have the admirable process that is the key, I believe, to an interfaith "looking at by looking through."

Both the Korean tea bowl and Poulin's *Starlight* help us look at by looking through, help us see by seeing and, in doing so, that which is loved by another becomes ours to love as well. This love, then, becomes, as Cusa observed, the true religious element. It forms a truly sensible faith rather than an empty faith. Such faith coming out of love is no longer *a sola fides,* a faith alone, but a sensible faith, a faith together, in which the admirable can be a true sharing. The Buddhist may not be converted to the Christian doctrine of the incarnation in Poulin's *Starlight,* but he or she might very well come to love what is admirable about it. Likewise, the Christian may not be converted to the Buddhist doctrine of non-duality or the no self in the Korean tea bowl, but he or she may also come to love what is admirable in it.

Such love does not necessarily take us to some shared unity of faith, but it certainly gives us a taste of a certain unity that is real by its very sensibility, even if such taste is only for us at this time a sense of beauty. Interfaith means faith formed in the process of loving that which is admirable for another. The ability of a Christian to appreciate the Korean tea bowl and a Buddhist the Christian *Starlight* is made possible not by bypassing their theological contents. Nor is it possible by studying the abstract elements of their design. Rather, these works invite us to "taste and see," so that in tasting we may also see the admirable, the sense of beauty, the presuppositions of love. Thus, when we detect the particular theological content of each work of art in each tasting, it does not divide or cause dissent; rather, it becomes a revelation of a unity that identifies us as human. Faith in faith itself, indeed, promises, in the end, to make of interfaith dialogue an admirable beauty, the place where theology and spirituality meet, the experience of an interfaith aesthetics.

If theology solely concerns itself with the hardheadedness of articulating the identity of faith and spirituality solely with the formation of a community of faith, then there is little to connect the two. Theological aesthetics, and, in particular, an interfaith aesthetics, suggest a meeting point, however. Identity and community intersect in the admirable sense of beauty. Nowhere is this sense more significant than in the issue of interfaith. Interfaith raises the issue of faith in that it must be seen not in relation to one community but in relation to many communities. Essentially, it raises the question of forming an interfaith community in which a particular faith cannot be the basis for unity. An interfaith aesthetics proposes the admirable sense of Beauty not as a realized ideal but as a place where love can cross identities of faith. Such love emerges out of theological insight into the beautiful forms that are the product of different faith communities. Such insight, in turn, would not be possible without the spiritual openness to beautiful form. Thus, interfaith aesthetics points to a greater unity than is possible with strict identity or a formless openness. An interfaith aesthetics reveals that theology and spirituality meet where spiritual openness is given shape by theological insight into beautiful form.

Paul tells us that there is no river, or mountain, or ocean that can keep us from the love of God. Faith, however, has been used as an exception to this belief. An interfaith aesthetics, however, recovers Paul's insight by showing where theology and spirituality meet. That meeting point is not in the superiority of one faith but in the admirable sense of beauty, the place where spiritual openness given shape by theological insight into beautiful form breaks out into a love that crosses all boundaries. It is, admittedly, a place more felt than visualized. But it is a place where love takes shape in an admirable Beauty that forms and gives hope to our faith. It is the place where faith finds faith in faith itself. It is an interfaith aesthetics where theology and spirituality meet.

Notes

1. Prof. Ronald Nakasone, a Buddhist priest and theologian, is on the faculty of the Center for the Arts and Religion in Education and the Graduate Theological Union in Berkeley, California. The course, HRRA4765 Interfaith Aesthetics, was offered in the fall of 2003.

2. An insightful article that deals with the relationship between theology and spirituality can be found in Sandra Schneiders, IHM, "Theology and Spirituality: Strangers, Rivals, or Partners?" *Horizons* 13, no. 2 (Fall 1986): 253–74.

3. Hans Urs von Balthasar, "Theology and Sanctity," in *The Word Made Flesh* (San Francisco: Ignatius Press, 1989), 88–109.

4. Wendy Beckett, *The Mystical Now: Art and the Sacred* (New York: Universe, 1993), 6.

5. The spiritual role of the non-conceptual in art was most powerfully stated in Modernity by Kandinsky in *Concerning the Spiritual in Art.* Kandisky's notion of the spiritual, however, was ideal or pure form. The spiritual was of the order of an abstract idea, at home more in the mind than in lived practice. Clive Bell, on the other hand, saw the spiritual in art not in abstract form but in significant form. Richard Harries sees three elements as providing the spiritual in art: form, the ability of art to render its subject in all its particularity and uniqueness, and the ability of art to connect that irreducible particularity to a wider meaning and significance. These last two elements correspond closely to what von Balthasar called the "depth" of form. See, for example, Clive Bell, *Art* (New York: F. A. Stokes Co., 1914); Richard Harries, *Art and the Beauty of God: A Christian Understanding* (London: Mowbray, 1993); Wassily Kandinsky, *Concerning the Spiritual in Art* (New York: Dover Publications, 1977).

6. Beckett, *The Mystical Now,* 7. Beckett's distinctions roughly correspond to Hans Belting's thesis that, as Modernity began, the iconic cult of images came to compete with a more sophisticated elite of art. In other words, Belting contrasted the image versus the work of art, the icon versus the artist's idea. See, for example, Hans Belting, *Likeness and Presence: A History of the Image before the Era of Art* (Chicago: University of Chicago Press, 1994).

7. As mentioned above, Richard Harries sees these two elements of particular significance and wider belonging as elements of the spiritual in art.

8. *Nostra aetate,* in *Vatican Council II: The Conciliar and Post Conciliar Documents,* ed. Austin Flannery (Wilmington, DE: Scholarly Resources, 1975).

9. Thomas Merton, quoted in Lawrence Cunningham, *Thomas Merton and the Monastic Vision,* Library of Religious Biography (Grand Rapids, MI: Eerdmans, 1999), 157.

10. Yanagi Sōetsu (1899–1961) was one of the founders of what is known as the *Mingei undō,* or the Folk Craft movement. Yanagi saw embedded in the aesthetics of the common pottery craft made by mostly unknown craftsmen the values and principles of Buddhist faith.

11. Ronald Nakasone, "Yanagi Sōetsu and the Pure Land of Beauty," in *Kitabatake Tensei Kyojè Koki Kinen Ronshu [Essays in Honor of Professor Tensei Kitabatake's 70th Birthday]* (Kyoto: Nagata, 1998), 1.

12. Muneyoshi Yanagi and Bernard Leach, *The Unknown Craftsman: A Japanese Insight into Beauty,* rev. ed. (Tokyo: Kodansha International, 1989), 142.

13. These principles are best explained in books that introduce Buddhist thought to the Westerners. They speak of a deep conviction in Buddhist thought.

14. Yanagi and Leach, *The Unknown Craftsman,* 152.

15. Alex García-Rivera, personal conversation, interview with Arthur Poulin, OSB Cam., Incarnation Monastery, 2001.

16. A concise summary of his thesis can be found in John Dewey, *A Common Faith* (New Haven, CT: Yale University Press, 1991), 84–85.

17. On the history of the tradition of the aesthetic unity-in-variety principle, see Wladyslaw Tatarkiewicz, "The Great Theory of Beauty and Its Decline," *Journal of Aesthetics and Art Criticism* 31, no. 2 (1972): 165–79.

18. Cusa's philosophical theology is crucial for von Balthasar's theological aesthetics. Balthasar sees Cusa's theology as the sword that cuts the "Gordian knot" of the infinite distance between a God that cannot be seen and a beauty that is perceived. See, for example, Louis Dupré, "Hans Urs von Balthasar's Theology of Aesthetic Form," *Theological Studies* 49, no. 2 (1988): 299–318; Hans Urs von Balthasar, "Why We Need Nicholas of Cusa," *Communio* (Winter 2001): 854–59.

19. For an insightful introduction to Cusa's context and thought, see Ernst Cassirer, *The Individual and the Cosmos in Renaissance Philosophy* (New York: Barnes and Noble, 1963).

20. James E. Biechler, and H. Lawrence Bond, *Nicholas of Cusa on Interreligious Harmony: Text, Concordance, and Translation* of *De Pace Fidei* (Lewiston, NY: Edwin Mellen Press, 1991), xlvi–xlvii.

21. Ibid., xxxvii.

22. Ibid., xlvii.

23. Ibid., xxxvii.

24. The inspiration for the notion of faith in faith itself comes from Josiah Royce's notion of loyalty to loyalty found in Josiah Royce, *The Philosophy of Loyalty* (New York: Macmillan, 1928).

25. See, for example, the excellent study on the theological aesthetics of Jonathan Edwards, in Roland André Delatorre, *Beauty and Sensibility in the Thought of Jonathan Edwards: An Essay in Aesthetics and Theological Ethics* (New Haven, CT: Yale University Press, 1968).

10

THE DISCIPLINE OF CHRISTIAN SPIRITUALITY AND CATHOLIC THEOLOGY

Sandra M. Schneiders, IHM

INTRODUCTION

This essay originated in a request from the spirituality seminar of the Catholic Theological Society of America (CTSA) for a paper to focus its 2006 session on the relationship between theology, as it has traditionally been understood in the academy, and Christian spirituality, as it is the specialized interest of some of its members. The request offered me the stimulus to rethink a subject I have addressed more than once in the past thirty years of trying to help this new field of study articulate its identity and clarify its relationship with other disciplines. Responses to my previous attempts by scholars in the field—who have raised questions about my position, amplified it with considerations from other disciplines and diverse classroom experience, or strenuously disagreed with me—have enlightened me and modified my thinking. So this opportunity to "try again" was welcome, as was the request of the editors of this volume to publish the essay, which would bring it to a wider audience than the CTSA participants. Although I am now writing for an audience that includes non-Catholics and perhaps non-academics, traces of the original concern with Catholic theologians and of the oral form of the original presentation will be discernible. I trust my readers can make the necessary adjustments.

I was asked to provide a starting point for the discussion by addressing the questions, What role does theology as a discipline play in studying spirituality from the perspective of a particular religious tradition? Does theology have a unique role or is it only one discipline among many? I want to begin by raising some questions about this implied dichotomy: "unique" or "only one among many." It is somewhat like asking whether the account of creation in Genesis is "historical" or "only a myth," implying that these are the only two choices, that they are necessarily mutually exclusive, and that they involve a choice between hierarchical alternatives. Let us begin by deleting the "only," which implies that being one among many is something negative. I will contend that theology does indeed play a unique role in the discipline of spirituality if by *unique* we mean not hegemonic or superior but *a role that nothing else plays*. The same, however, could be said of some other disciplines that also play a unique but not hegemonic role in the discipline of Christian spirituality: for example, church history, biblical studies, and the human sciences. So, my short answer to the question would be that theology plays a unique role in the discipline of spirituality as one discipline among others within this interdisciplinary field.[1] However, I would prefer to abandon that question altogether, since it does not get us very far in understanding the identity of spirituality as a field of study or the relationship between spirituality and theology, which is the real question with which we are struggling.

Before offering some suggestions on a reformulated question—namely, How are the two disciplines distinct and how are they related?—I need to make some rather extended preliminary observations.

It is crucial to keep in mind that the term *theology* is used today in the academy in two very different ways, both of which have implications for our understanding of spirituality as an academic discipline. One meaning, which might be called "restrictive" or "exclusive," refers only to what has come to be called systematic theology, under which cluster a number of subdisciplines such as trinitarian theology, christology, pneumatology, ecclesiology, moral theology, and so on.[2] Spirituality, as it is understood today among many of its practitioners, myself included, is not among these subdisciplines. In other words, it is not the systematic theology of the spiritual life in the way that trinitarian theology is the systematic theology of the triune God.

The other meaning of the term *theology*, much broader and more inclusive, refers to all confessionally committed religious studies within the Christian tradition. So a theology department at a Catholic or Lutheran university might include not only systematic theology but also biblical studies, church history, pastoral ministry studies, practical theology, world religions, comparative theology, ecumenical theology, theology and aesthetics, and a number of other areas of inquiry. I would suggest that Christian spirituality as an academic discipline, while not a subdiscipline of systematic theology, is a legitimate member of the inclusive household of theology broadly understood as confessionally committed study of reality within a Christian perspective.

A second preliminary remark concerns some hidden or not-so-clandestine misconceptions about the relationship between the disciplines of spirituality and theology, which I hope are disappearing from the horizon but that, for reasons of intellectual hygiene, need to be named and, at least in my view, rejected. It has been suggested, for example, that spirituality is really just "theology done right"; that is, theology done with heart as well as head engaged. Closely related is the suggestion that spirituality is a temporarily useful corrective to a rationalistic and desiccated abstract theology. According to this theory, once theology has relearned to take human experience seriously and has recommitted itself to the ultimately transformative rather than purely academic purpose of theological scholarship, spirituality—like the Communist state—will wither away since it will have done its job. In my opinion these understandings of spirituality as "theology on steroids" or, worse yet, "bad theology in therapy" are neither accurate nor very flattering either to genuine theology (which is neither anemic nor abstractly rationalistic) or to contemporary spirituality. Another theory, equally unflattering, is that spirituality is theology for the intellectually underendowed. A quick perusal of the roster of scholars who today list spirituality as their primary academic location should definitively lay to rest this theory.

While rejecting these hypotheses, which I consider misconceived, we can profit by acknowledging the historical situation to which they indirectly point. Until the High Middle Ages, theology was not equated with dogmatics (the forerunner of systematic theology) and was not divided into subdisciplines such as christology and ecclesiology, nor was it separated from biblical studies or spirituality. All theology was faith seeking understanding; it was also understanding seeking transformation, the transformation of self and world in God through Christ in the power of the Spirit. In other words, theology referred primarily to the global and integrated enterprise of living the spiritual life, and that enterprise was nourished by meditating on the Bible as scripture, thinking clearly and faithfully within and about the tradition, practicing personal prayer, celebrating liturgically within the believing community, and living the life of the Beatitudes that Jesus preached. The theologian was defined as one who prayed truly. Some people, especially bishops and monastics, devoted themselves professionally to this shared Christian enterprise for the sake of their fellow Christians and so were also called, in a more technical sense, theologians. In other words, theology *was* spirituality understood not as an academic discipline but as living faith seeking understanding for the purpose of transformation in Christ. Origen, Antony, Augustine, Gertrude the Great, Hildegard of Bingen, Meister Eckhart, Thomas Aquinas, and Julian of Norwich were theologians in this sense of the word, giants of the spiritual life who were original and articulate teachers and guides of their fellow believers.

There are scholars in both spirituality and theology today who long for the reconstitution in the modern context of this premodern integral approach to theology as theoretically reflective and articulate "lived spirituality." I share their nostalgia for but not their confidence in such a revival. The Enlightenment has happened. Humpty Dumpty, mortarboard and all, has tumbled from the wall and cannot, I am afraid, be put back together again. The multiplication of disciplines defined by distinct material and formal objects and methods of study is a fact of the academy born of, and expressive of, our Western intellectual *Weltanschauung*. I suspect that multi-disciplinarity and inter-disciplinarity are our characteristic and probably only ways of dealing with the excessive fragmentation that is the downside of the critical revolution. A return to an intellectual and academic unity that characterized an earlier time, however desirable, is probably not really possible.

Finally, as my last introductory remark, I would like to say that, just as the term *theology* has both an exclusive meaning and an inclusive meaning, *spirituality* is a also a term used in two quite different ways. The first and inclusive referent of the term *spirituality* is the *lived experience* of the faith.[3] But the referent we are discussing here is spirituality as the *academic discipline* which studies that lived experience. In the description just given of the patristic-medieval unity of theology and spirituality, it was the first meaning of spirituality, the lived experience of the faith, which was functioning. Spirituality as an academic discipline did not arise until some centuries after the breakup of the medieval synthesis, and the emergence of dogmatic theology as an academic discipline with subdivisions. When spirituality did begin to be considered a domain of academic discourse, it was understood as a subdiscipline of dogmatic theology, which, I have already suggested, is not the case today.

It is too cumbersome to keep repeating these distinctions explicitly, but conceptual slippage between the two meanings of each term, *theology* and *spirituality*, subverts the attempt at clear discourse on this topic. In other words, it is simply misleading to talk about the relation between theology and spirituality because the real question is, What is the relationship of *systematic* theology to spirituality *as an academic discipline*? Is spirituality, on the one hand, a subdiscipline of systematic theology or even one way of viewing or approaching systematic theology or, on the other hand, is spirituality a relatively autonomous discipline in the large household of confessionally committed study of reality from a Christian perspective?[4] And if it is the latter, which I think is the case, what role does systematic theology play in the work of this relatively new discipline and, conversely, what role does the discipline of spirituality play in the work of systematic theology?

DISTINGUISHING BETWEEN SYSTEMATIC THEOLOGY AND SPIRITUALITY AS ACADEMIC DISCIPLINES

As philosophy has long known, genuine relationship requires distinction in the service not of separation or alienation but of a union that is neither absorption nor subordination. Appropriate boundaries, including intellectual ones, are both defining limits and points of fruitful contact. So our first order of business is to distinguish between theology in the strict sense and spirituality as an academic discipline. I would like to concentrate on two areas in which the differences between the two are especially important but in different ways: the *object of study of each discipline,* which first distinguishes and then relates them to each other, and the *approach to the study of each object,* which first relates and then distinguishes them.

The Object of Study: Distinctions Which Relate

Theology as a discipline seeks to mediate the faith as it has been formulated in the classical loci—that is, scripture; the creedal, dogmatic, and liturgical traditions; and the history of the Church[5]—into the contemporary religio-cultural situation, which is ever-changing.[6] For example, as post-Newtonian science has revolutionized cosmology, theologians are striving to rethink the traditional understandings of creation, christology, and soteriology. As feminism has challenged the patriarchal construction of intellectual and social reality, theologians are challenged to rethink traditional trinitarian theology, the christological and ministerial implications of the maleness of Jesus, theological anthropology, moral theology, and ecclesiology. Psychology and psychoanalysis have raised similar issues for moral theology. And so on. A privileged tool of theology in its elaboration of the understanding of the faith has, traditionally, been philosophy.[7] As modern and postmodern philosophies have multiplied, and as linguistic-literary modes of reflection have gained a certain ascendancy in the academy, the ways in which theologians interrogate and interpret the faith tradition have also diversified. But the object of the-

201

ology—faith as the thematically formulated response to revelation that has been transmitted in the Church, in relation to faith as it is currently being lived in particular contexts—remains constant.

Spirituality as an academic discipline has a different, though related, object. Spirituality's primary object is not the *formulated tradition* as it illuminates and is illuminated by the lived experience of the faith, but the *lived experience* of the faith itself. I and others in the field have sometimes expressed this as a concern with religious experience *as* experience, a formulation which has sometimes given rise to the misunderstanding of the discipline of spirituality as the attempt to discern what constitutes religious experience; to analyze the nature, structure, and dynamics of religious experience as such; and/or to develop criteria of validity for religious experience. Perhaps it would help to clarify the object if, instead of speaking of studying experience, we use Paul Ricoeur's expression and call spirituality the study of the religious particular or of "the individual."[8] By individual or quasi-individual, Ricoeur goes beyond a particular human subject, like Teresa of Avila. His usage would include distinct religious movements such as the sixteenth-century Carmelite reform in Spain, or events such as Teresa's conversion,[9] or the experience of a particular group such as the life in the Convent of the Incarnation in Avila at the time of Teresa's conversion, or practices such as Teresa's own mode of prayer.[10]

Obviously, no one has direct access to any experience except perhaps one's own and many would maintain we do not even have direct, but only mediated, access to our own subjectivity. But in any case, we could all agree that we do not, because we cannot, study "raw" or immediate experience, that is, experience prior to interpretation and expression, if indeed such a thing exists (which I doubt). We access experience through its expression in "texts" broadly understood. Such texts may be written documents such as biographies, autobiographies, poetry, journals, and histories; literary, plastic, and musical artistic creations; conversations and other oral presentations; accounts of dreams and visions and prayers; works, movements, and whatever else serves to make personal experience inter-subjectively available: that is, to exteriorize it into the public forum. But the texts of interest to scholars of spirituality are texts that mediate the particular as particular rather than the texts that thematize and formulate, however tentatively, the tradition.

An extended example might help to clarify the difference I am suggesting between a research project in theology and one in spirituality. Both the scholar of spirituality and the theologian might be studying *conversion* and both might be focusing on the actual conversion of a particular person, say Teresa of Avila. The theologian's primary interest is in the phenomenon of conversion itself, of which Teresa's experience is a particularly interesting instance. What are the conditions of possibility of conversion? What precipitates it? What are its nature, structure, dynamics? Are there different kinds of conversion? What are its effects? Are there criteria of validity that distinguish genuine from ersatz conversion? The theologian may be drawing on biblical material, such as Paul's conversion recounted by Luke in Acts 9:1–19 in comparison with Paul's own account in Galatians 1:1–17; or on psychological analysis, such as William James supplies in *The Varieties of Religious Experience;*[11] or on theological analysis, such as Bernard Lonergan's theory of conversion.[12] Theological anthropology, the theology of grace, and other theoretical material will undoubtedly play a part. But even if the theologian is focusing on the conversion of Teresa of Avila, the theologian is seeing that particular personal event as an instance of a theological category, namely, religious conversion. The theological tradition will be used to analyze and judge Teresa's experience as it is recounted in her autobiography, while Teresa's experience of conversion may raise new questions to the theological tradition's understanding of this reality, helping to refine the tradition or enrich it. The theologian will be asking such questions as, Was this really a conversion? In what sense? Or was it simply an experience of profound repentance? And what is the distinction between conversion and repentance? Is a fundamental restructuring of consciousness à la Lonergan and as verified in Paul essential to conversion in the strict sense of the term? Was Teresa's conversion primarily intellectual or affective? And so on. What the theologian is seeking is a deeper and more adequate understanding of conversion itself by relating the theological data on the subject to a particularly striking instance of conversion from the history of spirituality.

The spirituality scholar is going to approach the same subject matter, Teresa's conversion experience recounted in her autobiography, differently and for different purposes. The object is not to understand conversion but to understand Teresa's conversion experience specifically. The focus is precisely on the "individual": that is, the particular experience of conversion as it occurred in the life of Teresa. This event in Teresa's experience is being interrogated not as a particular instance of a general category—that is, conversion—but precisely as an ingress into Teresa's particular and personal lived experience of faith—that is, her spirituality—in which her conversion is a particularly significant moment. It is not primarily conversion, but the religious experience of Teresa, that is the object of inquiry. Consequently, primary importance will be given to her historical, cultural, and religious context; her biography up to and after the experience; her autobiographical description and analysis of it; the theological, religious, and literary resources she had (or did not have) for interpreting her experience; the contribution that depth, developmental, or archetypal psychology can bring to an understanding of the dynamics of Teresa's experience; her aesthetic formation, which made the precipitating encounter with the statue so powerful for her; the effects on her consciousness of contemporary attitudes toward women as well as her own originality in regard to the feminine in relation to God; and so on. Theological and philosophical material on conversion may well figure in the interrogation of Teresa's conversion experience, especially if the study raises questions about her God-image, her theology of suffering, and her understanding of Church and ecclesial authority. But theology may or may not be the primary tool of analysis, and it is not the purpose of the study to understand better the theology of conversion or to directly contribute to the theology of conversion (although both of these might occur). The point of the study is to understand Teresa of Avila's experience of God, her spirituality, as it gave rise to, shaped, and was shaped by this experience.

So, is theology integral to this project in spirituality? Yes. Is the study primarily theological? Not necessarily. Theology is integral to any research project in Christian spirituality, as is biblical material and church history, not because the project is a study in spirituality but because it is a study in *Christian* spirituality and all Christian faith experience is suffused with and embedded in the theological tradition of the Church. Teresa's conversion, in other words, was not Buddhist enlightenment or psychological healing but a personally revolutionizing *prise de conscience* in Christ. So theology is relevant and integral to the research. But because it was a profound psychological experience, psychological theory is also integral to the project. Because her experience of conversion is mediated to us in a historically conditioned literary text, the history of sixteenth-century Spain and of the literary genre of autobiography are also relevant and integral. Because Teresa was a woman in a patriarchal Church and culture, feminist analysis is crucial. Because her experience of conversion precipitated a major religious movement, namely, the reform of the Carmelite Order, the history of religious life in the period of the Reformation is important. And so on. Which of these many disciplines, and perhaps others not mentioned, will more or less govern the research project depends on the purposes of the researcher. Someone primarily interested in the way gender affects religious experience will shape her study of Teresa's conversion one way. Someone interested in how literary genre and rhetorical agenda shape religious experience will construct his study differently. Someone defending the authenticity of Teresa's experience against theological skeptics might rely more on theology than someone interested in the role of aesthetic sensibility in religious experience.

In summary of this point, the object of study in theology may be either some topic or category of Christian tradition itself, for example, Christ's humanity or religious conversion, or some problem like the possibility of a just war or the meaning of salvation; and it may then be focused by some particular event like the emergence of the new cosmology, or Teresa's conversion, or the war in Iraq, or the recognition of the fact of religious pluralism. But the point is, finally, to understand the tradition itself better in order to integrate our experience and the tradition in a coherent and developing way.

The point of the study of spirituality, however, is to understand the religious experience as and in the "individual" or particular, whether that is an individual person, like Teresa; an individual movement, like Benedictinism; an individual commitment, like Martin Luther King's nonviolence; an individual charism, like Francis of Assisi's stigmata; an individual devotion, like that of Edward Taylor to the Lord's Supper; or an individual aspect of Christian life, like work. The purpose is finally to understand the particular as well as we can in order to expand and enrich our grasp of the relationship of humans with God, which is always an interpersonal and social encounter and, as relationship, is never "general." One might say, by way of analogy, that there are two ways to study humanity: one way is by studying what anthropology, psychology, sociology, and history teach us about human nature in order to relate this knowledge to actual humans; another is by studying concrete human beings in person and through literature and the other arts in order to understand more fully what humanity means. These approaches are not exclusive of one another nor unrelated to each other. Indeed they should be mutually enlightening. But in the first case, the object is to expand our *theoretical knowledge* of humanity so that we might understand actual humans better and be more adequate in our treatment of them. In the second case the object is to expand our knowledge of the *concrete experience* of being human so that, among other things, our theoretical formulations are more adequate to their subject matter.

In short, one might say that the "knowing" aimed at by theology is primarily conceptual, arrived at through the study of formulated expressions of the tradition in the classical and contemporary loci, and eventually expressed in second-order language that has applicability beyond the individual case. The "knowing" aimed at by spirituality is primarily personal and arrived at through the multidisciplinary analysis of thick description of the individual that remains concrete and specific even as it gives rise to constructive results that have, ideally, broad implications. Theology probably has more in common with philosophy, while spirituality has more in common with psychology or art criticism. In any case, it is probably as futile to try to eliminate all overlap between the two disciplines as it is to try to distinguish absolutely between systematic theology and historical theology, or between biblical criticism and biblical theology. A research project in spirituality is recognized not only by what it studies but by the way it is conceptualized, constructed, and prosecuted, and by the kinds of knowledge in which it results.

Approach to Study: Relationship Which Distinguishes

Let me turn more briefly to a second point of relationship and distinction between the two disciplines, namely, approach. Increasingly systematic theology understands itself as a hermeneutical and constructive enterprise rather than a deductive or even inductive science. Theology attempts to interpret the texts and traditions of Christianity in critical dialogue with the culture in which it is lived today, realizing that theological discourse is itself part of culture and therefore not fully separable from it. It seeks what Gadamer calls a fusion of horizons between the Christian faith tradition as thematized in theological loci and the cultural situation in which that tradition is lived and of which it is a part. The academic discipline of spirituality in its contemporary incarnation is also a hermeneutical enterprise. It seeks to interpret concrete and individual instances of the living of Christian faith as these are mediated to us in particular texts, practices, art objects, and so on. It seeks a fusion of horizons between the world of the scholar and the individual phenomenon being studied.

I would suggest, by way of hypothesis, that though both theology and spirituality are concerned with the *fusion of horizons* that Gadamer described, Ricoeur's notion of *appropriation* is realized differently in the two fields precisely because the object of study in one case is accessed through a body of thematized knowledge, and aims at ever-more-adequate second-order discourse, and in the other case is accessed through expressions of the particular, and aims at knowledge of the individual. The fully engaged theologian does not simply interpret the tradition objectively for the benefit of readers or listeners, but also appropriates what he or she illuminates as personal, existential—that is, spiritual—augmentation. In other words, appropriation for the theologian is, ideally and ultimately, not only increased knowledge but deepened personal spirituality or engagement with God. The fully engaged scholar of spirituality does not simply interpret concrete examples of human encounter with God but also understands this encounter as a particular participation in a living tradition that these individuals incarnate and mediate. In other words, appropriation for the scholar of spirituality means not only increased knowledge of the divine-human relationship but also enriched and deepened existential participation in the tradition in its contemporary realization.

CONCLUSION

By way of conclusion, I have my doubts about how much time and energy we should spend on trying to establish absolute, clear-cut differences between theology done well in the service of the faith life of the Church, and spirituality done well as theologically responsible study of the actual experience of living faith in the Church. Distinctions are indeed necessary, especially until it becomes clearer to all concerned that the contemporary discipline of spirituality is not an attempt to resuscitate the corpse of what was once called spiritual theology.[13] That version of theology of the spiritual life, exemplified by such works as Adophe Tanquerey's treatise on ascetical and mystical theology, was an effort to abstract from concrete religious experience a generalized "scientific" theory of the spiritual life generated by and expressed in the categories of dogmatic theology.[14] From this dogmatic theory could be deduced what the spiritual life should consist in and how, ideally, it should function. It was understood as a subdivision of moral theology, itself subordinate to dogmatics, and assumed to be applicable to all believers with allowances made for minor idiosyncrasies. It had a (non)relationship to real spirituality analogous to the relationship of what was once called rational psychology (which was really philosophical anthropology) to the psychic experience of real people as studied today by psychologists. I would suggest that systematic theology today does not play this defining and normative role in the contemporary discipline of spirituality, but that does not imply that theology is dispensable or unimportant to the new discipline.

Conversation on the relation of systematic theology to spirituality as an academic discipline would probably be facilitated if the theological participants could lay to rest any suspicion that spirituality as a discipline is either poaching on their territory or denigrating their work as intellectually abstract or spiritually vacuous. By the same token, scholars of spirituality need to renounce the suspicion that theology is trying to subjugate, supplant, or appropriate their field. Spirituality belongs in the theological household not as a dependent or minor but as a mature member of the family, distinct from but closely related to systematic theology as well as to other theological disciplines.

We may be witnessing yet another chapter in the story that began when biblical studies decided it did not need a theological "tutor," the natural sciences decided they did not want a "queen," and philosophy decided it was no longer interested in being a "handmaid." Mutuality among equals is a better model for productive conversation than rivalry, hegemony, or absorption. The more the members of the theological household talk to each other rather than at or past or down to each other, the richer the intellectual (and spiritual) fare the academy will be able to offer to contemporary seekers. Systematic theology is a critical participant in the work of spirituality studies, and spirituality as a discipline has much to offer to systematic theology. Both have much to offer to and much to learn from ethics, church history, practical theology, non-Christian religions, and their other colleagues in the theological academy. Furthermore, as in any healthy family, each member will also have partners and friends from outside the household that may or may not be equally interesting or attractive to other members of the family. I lament the fate of theological Humpty Dumpty, but his demise has bequeathed us a vastly expanded and diversified field of inquiry and challenged us to live in a wider interdisciplinary world. In my view, whatever the dangers of fragmentation or the frustrations of difficult communication, the contemporary adventure—intellectual and spiritual as well as social and religious—is more interesting and rewarding than life in the ghetto or even in a theoretically better ordered academy.

Notes

1. When I speak of "spirituality" or "theology" in this essay, unless otherwise specified, I mean Christian spirituality and Christian theology.

2. In some circles, notably more conservative settings, this branch of theology is still called *dogmatic theology,* emphasizing the prescriptive, positive, and normative understanding of theology. In more liberal settings, including most major Catholic academic settings today, the preferred term is *systematic theology,* emphasizing the hermeneutical, critical, and constructive character of the enterprise.

3. I have attempted in other places to define this primary meaning of spirituality in a more nuanced way: namely, as I have said in other articles and presentations, "the experience of conscious involvement in the project of life-integration through self-transcendence toward the ultimate value one perceives." This more descriptive definition rules out certain misunderstandings of spirituality (for example, social organizations like Nazism) while, by not specifying it religiously (for example, as Christian), allowing for interreligious discussion of spirituality as well as consideration of nonreligious spiritualities such as ecospirituality or some forms of feminist spirituality. However, for the purposes of this essay, the briefer and more general definition will do.

4. We should recognize that all disciplines are only relatively autonomous. The increasingly interdisciplinary character of most research today constitutes a questioning in practice of the Enlightenment model of nonoverlapping, radically distinct disciplines.

5. The history of the Church is an ever-expanding category. Scholars today would want to include in their understanding of history the artistic traditions (music, painting, architecture, etc.), as well as established spiritual traditions (for

example, Benedictinism), as well as the Church's ongoing self-definition through the relationships it has established by treaties, concordats, and so on with various and changing political and cultural contexts. And historians are increasingly challenged to incorporate the previously excluded data of "heterodox" material and the experience of marginalized or oppressed groups in their discourse.

6. I am avoiding the term *critical correlation,* although I continue to find it one helpful way of conceptualizing the work of theology because there are other valid ways of understanding theology today and I do not want to get into that discussion here.

7. For Catholic theology, the Platonic-Aristotelian-Thomistic philosophical tradition was considered virtually normative (although it was never exclusive, for example, among Franciscan theologians) until the first half of the twentieth century. Protestant theology was never as dependent on a single system but philosophy, since the Middle Ages, has played a role in theological exposition.

8. See Paul Ricoeur, *Interpretation Theory: Discourse and the Surplus of Meaning* (Fort Worth, TX: Texas Christian University, 1976), 78–79.

9. Teresa of Avila recounts her experience of conversion when she was confronted with a statue of the "Ecce Homo" in *The Book of Her Life* in *The Collected Works of St. Teresa of Avila,* vol. 1, translated by Kieran Kavanaugh and Otilio Rodriguez (Washington, DC: ICS Publications, 1976), ch. 9, pp. 100–101, with considerable detail about her spiritual condition prior to the event and subsequent to it.

10. For example, Teresa gives extensive teaching on the subject of prayer, its stages, the phenomena that characterize the stages, and so on, in both the *Life* and *The Interior Castle* in *The Collected Works of St. Teresa of Avila,* vol. 2, translated by Kieran Kavanaugh and Otilio Rodriguez (Washington, DC: ICS Publications, 1980), 263–451, notes pp. 480–99. But she also describes in detail her own individual experiences in prayer. The two are, of course, related. She says explicitly that in speaking about mental prayer, for example, "I can speak of what I have experience of" (*Life,* chap. 8, p. 96). But in the case of her teach-

ing about prayer, she is dealing with material applicable to different people in different ways, whereas in speaking of her own experience with all its particularities and idiosyncrasies, she is describing "the individual" or her "experience as experience" rather than as an instance of the general, even though she knows it is such.

11. William James, *The Varieties of Religious Experience,* introd. by Eugene Kennedy (New York: Triumph, 1991). [Originally the Gifford Lectures delivered at Edinburgh in 1901–02 and published by Longmans, Green.]

12. A brief presentation of Lonergan's theory of self-transcendence or progressive conversion is available in "Self-transcendence: Intellectual, Moral, Religious" in *Collected Works of Bernard Lonergan: Philosophical and Theological Papers 1965–1980,* edited by Robert C. Croken and Robert M. Doran (Toronto: University of Toronto Press, 2004), 313–30.

13. It should be recognized that some contemporary scholars who name their area of specialization "spiritual theology" are not using the term the way it was used from the late-eighteenth to the mid-twentieth century, especially in Catholic circles.

14. Adophe Tanquerey, *The Spiritual Life: A Treatise on Ascetical and Mystical Theology,* 2nd and rev. ed., trans. by Herman Branderis (Tournai: Desclée, [Society of St. John the Evangelist], 1932).

PART III

Major Published Works of Sandra M. Schneiders, IHM

BOOKS

Written That You May Believe: Encountering Jesus in the Fourth Gospel, 2nd ed., revised and expanded. With a Study Guide by John C. Wronski, SJ. New York: Crossroad, 2003. Originally published New York: Crossroad, 1999. Awarded second place, category of scripture, Catholic Press Association of the United States and Canada, 2000.

Selling All: Commitment, Consecrated Celibacy, and Community in Catholic Religious Life. Religious Life in a New Millennium, vol. 2. New York/Mahwah, NJ: Paulist Press, 2001. (Indian edition: Bandra, Mumbai, India: Pauline Publications, 2003.) Awarded second place, category of professional books, Catholic Press Association of the United States and Canada, 2002.

Finding the Treasure: Locating Catholic Religious Life in a New Cultural and Ecclesial Context. Religious Life in a New Millennium, vol. 1. New York/Mahwah, NJ: Paulist Press, 2000. (Indian edition: Bandra, Mumbai, India: Pauline Publications, 2003.) Awarded first place, category of spirituality—soft cover, Catholic Press Association of the United States and Canada, 2001.

With Oil in Their Lamps: Faith, Feminism, and the Future. 2000 Madeleva Lecture in Spirituality. New York/Mahwah, NJ: Paulist Press, 2000.

The Revelatory Text: Interpreting the New Testament as Sacred Scripture. 2nd ed. Collegeville, MN: Liturgical Press, 1999. Originally published 1991. Translated in French as *Le Texte de la Rencontre: L'interprétation du Nouveau Testament comme écriture sainte* by Jean-Claude Breton and Dominique Barrios-Delgado [Lectio Divina 161]. Paris: Cerf/Fides, 1995. Author's response to Review Symposium of *The Revelatory Text* appears in *Horizons* 19, no. 2 (Fall 1992): 303–9.

Beyond Patching: Faith and Feminism in the Catholic Church. 2nd ed., revised and expanded. Anthony Jordan Lectures, Newman Theological College, Edmonton, 1990. New York/Mahwah, NJ: Paulist Press, 2004.

New Wineskins: Re-Imagining Religious Life Today. New York/Mahwah, NJ: Paulist Press, 1986. Translated into Dutch as *Jonge Wijn in Nieuwe Zakken: Een nieuwe voorstelling van religieus leven vandaag* by Til Lagerberg. Aalsmeer: DABAR Boekmakerij Luyten, 1992. Awarded Book-of-the-Year by *Human Development* 8, no. 1 (Spring 1987).

Women and the Word: The Gender of God in the New Testament and the Spirituality of Women. 1986 Madeleva Lecture in Spirituality. New York/Mahwah, NJ: Paulist Press, 1986. Translated into Portuguese as *As Mulheres e A Palavra: O gênero de Deus no Novo Testamento e a espiritualidade das mulheres* by Grupo Solidário São Domingos. São Paulo, Brazil: Ediçes Paulinas, 1992.

How to Read the Bible Prayerfully. Pamphlet. Collegeville, MN: Liturgical Press, 1984.

The Johannine Resurrection Narrative: An Exegetical and Theological Study of John 20 as a Synthesis of Johannine Spirituality. 2 vols. Ann Arbor, MI: University Microfilms International, 1982.

CHAPTERS IN BOOKS

"The Gospels and the Reader." In *The Cambridge Companion to the Gospels,* ed. Stephen C. Barton, Cambridge: Cambridge University Press, forthcoming.

"Approaches to the Study of Spirituality." In *Blackwell Companion to Christian Spirituality*, ed. Arthur Holder, 15-33. Oxford: Blackwell Publishing, 2005.

"Biblical Foundations of Spirituality." In *Scripture as the Soul of Theology*, ed. Ed Maloney, 1–22. Collegeville, MN: Liturgical Press, 2005.

"The Resurrection (of the Body) in the Fourth Gospel: A Key to Johannine Spirituality." In *Life in Abundance: Papers Given in Tribute to Raymond E. Brown*, ed. John R. Donahue, 168–98. Collegeville, MN: Liturgical Press, 2005.

"To See or Not to See: John 9 as a Synthesis of the Theology and Spirituality of Discipleship." In *Word, Theology, and Community in John*, ed. John Painter, R. Alan Culpepper, and Fernando F. Segovia, 189–209. St. Louis, MO: Chalice Press, 2002. Also published as "Choosing to See or Not to See (John 5:1–18 and 9:1–44)," chap. 9 in *Written That You May Believe*.

"God Is the Question and God Is the Answer." In *Spiritual Questions for the Twenty-First Century*, ed. Mary Hembrow Snyder, 68–74. Maryknoll, NY: Orbis Books, 2001.

"Feminist Biblical Interpretation and the Renewal of the Church." In *Light Burdens, Heavy Blessings: Challenges of Church and Culture in the Post Vatican II Era. Essays in Honor of Margaret R. Brennan, IHM*, ed. Mary Heather MacKinnon, Moni McIntyre, and Mary Ellen Sheehan, 31–51. Quincy, IL: Franciscan Press, 2000.

"Spirituality in the Academy." In *Exploring Christian Spirituality: An Ecumenical Reader*, ed. Kenneth J. Collins, 249–69. Grand Rapids, MI: Baker Books, 2000.

"Biblical Spirituality: Life, Literature, and Learning." In *Doors of Understanding: Conversations in Global Spirituality in Honor of Ewert Cousins*, ed. Steven Chase, 51–76. Quincy, IL: Franciscan Press, 1997.

"Feminist Spirituality: Christian Alternative or Alternative to Christianity?" In *Women's Spirituality: Resources for Christian Development*, 2nd ed., ed. Joann Wolski Conn, 30–67. New York/Mahwah, NJ: Paulist Press, 1996.

"Feminist Hermeneutics." In *Hearing the New Testament: Strategies for Interpretation,* ed. Joel B. Green, 349–69. Grand Rapids, MI: Eerdmans, 1995.

"The Resurrection of Jesus and Christian Spirituality." In *Christian Resources of Hope,* ed. Maureen Junker-Kenny, 81–114. Dublin, Ireland: Columba Press, 1995.

"Contemporary Religious Life: Death or Transformation?" In *Religious Life: The Challenge of Tomorrow,* ed. Cassian J. Yuhaus, 9–34. New York/Mahwah, NJ: Paulist Press, 1994. Also appears in *Cross Currents* 46 (Winter 1996/1997): 510–35.

"The Bible and Feminism: Biblical Theology." In *Freeing Theology: The Essentials of Theology in Feminist Perspective,* ed. Catherine Mowry LaCugna, 31–57. San Francisco: HarperSanFrancisco, 1993.

"Women in the Fourth Gospel and the Role of Women in the Contemporary Church." In *The Gospel of John as Literature,* ed. Mark Stibbe, 123–43. New York: E.J. Brill, 1993. Originally published in *Biblical Theology Bulletin* 12 (April 1982): 35–45.

"Spiritual Discernment in the Dialogue of Saint Catherine of Siena." In *Horizons on Catholic Feminist Theology,* ed. Joann Wolski Conn and Walter E. Conn, 159–73. Washington, DC: Georgetown University Press, 1992. Originally published in *Horizons* 9 (Spring 1982): 47–59.

"Religious Life *(Perfectae Caritatis)*." In *Modern Catholicism: Vatican II and After,* ed. Adrian Hastings, 157–62. London: SPCK; New York: Oxford University Press, 1991.

"Spirituality in the Academy." In *Modern Christian Spirituality: Methodological and Historical Essays,* ed. Bradley C. Hanson, 15–37. Atlanta: Scholars Press, 1990.

"Scripture and Spirituality." In *Christian Spirituality: Origins to the Twelfth Century,* ed. B. McGinn and J. Meyendorff, 1–20. Vol. 16, *World Spirituality: An Encyclopedic History of the Religious Quest.* New York: Crossroad, 1985.

"The Effects of Women's Experience on Their Spirituality." In *Women's Spirituality: Resources for Christian Development,* ed. Joann Wolski Conn, 31–48. New York/Mahwah, NJ:

Paulist Press, 1986. Originally published in *Spirituality Today* 35 (Summer 1983): 100–116.

"New Testament Reflections on Peace and Nuclear Arms." In *Catholics and Nuclear War: A Commentary on "The Challenge of Peace," the U.S. Catholic Bishops' Pastoral Letter on War and Peace,* ed. Philip J. Murnion, 91–105. New York: Crossroad, 1983. Reprinted in *Ethical Issues,* ed. Terry Reynolds, 236–73. Belmont, CA: Thomson Higher Education–Wadsworth, 2005.

"New Testament Foundations for Preaching by the Non-Ordained." In *Preaching and the Non-Ordained: An Interdisciplinary Study,* ed. N. Foley, 60–90. Collegeville, MN: Liturgical Press, 1983.

"Prophetic Consciousness in the Contemporary Church." In *To Build a Bridge,* 14–27. Proceedings–Convergence II. Washington, DC: Leadership Conference of Women Religious/Conference of Major Superiors of Men, 1982.

"Conversion to Discipleship" (2 parts). In *Formation in the American Church: Proceedings,* 9–30. Washington, DC: Religious Formation Conference, 1982.

"Freedom: Response and Responsibility: The Vocation of the Biblical Scholar in the Church." In *Whither Creativity, Freedom, Suffering? Humanity, Cosmos, God,* ed. F. A. Eigo and S. E. Fittipaldi, 25–52. Vol. 13 of the Theology Institute of Villanova University. Villanova, PA: University Press, 1981.

"The Ministry of the Word and Contemporary Catholic Education." In *Ministry and Education in Conversation,* ed. M. C. Boys, 15–44. Winona, MN: Saint Mary's Press/ Christian Brothers' Publications, 1981.

"Towards a Contemporary Theology of Religious Obedience." In *Starting Points: Six Essays Based on the Experience of U.S. Women Religious,* ed. L. A. Quiñonez, 59–85. Washington, DC: Leadership Conference of Women Religious, 1980.

"Christian Spirituality in the Gospel of John." In *Scripture and the Church,* ed. R. Heyer, 14–20. New York/Ramsey/ Toronto: Paulist Press, 1978. Originally published in *New Catholic World* 219 (November/December 1976): 261–64.

"Did Jesus Exclude Women from Priesthood?" In *Women Priests: A Catholic Commentary on the Vatican Declaration*, ed. L. Swidler and A. Swidler, 227–33. New York/ Ramsey/ Toronto: Paulist Press, 1977.

"A Contemporary Theology of the Vows." In *Journeying Resources*, 14–27. Washington, DC: Leadership Conference of Women Religious, 1977.

"Symbolism and the Sacramental Principle in the Fourth Gospel." In *Segni e Sacramenti nel Vangelo di Giovanni*, ed. P. R. Tragan, 221–35. Studia Anselmiana 66. Roma: Editrice Anselmaian, 1977.

"History and Symbolism in the Fourth Gospel." In *L'Evangile de Jean: Sources, rédation, théologie*, 371–76. Bibliotheca Ephemeridum Theologicarum Lovaniensium 44. Gembloux/ Leuven: Duculot/University Press, 1977. Reprinted as "Geschichte und Symbolik im Johannesevangelium." Translated by E. Strakosch and J. Beutler. *Erbe und Auftrag* 52 (February 1976): 30–5.

ARTICLES

"Impact of *Classics of Western Spirituality* Series on the Discipline of Christian Spirituality." *Spiritus* 5, no 1 (Spring 2005): 97–102.

"Religion vs. Spirituality: A Contemporary Conundrum." *Spiritus* 3, no. 2 (Fall 2003): 163–85.

"Religious Life in a Postmodern Context." *Religious Life Review* 42 (January-February 2003): 8–30.

"Biblical Spirituality." *Interpretation* 56 (April 2002): 133–42.

"Charism and Formation." *Proceedings of the Twelfth National Congress of the Religious Formation Conference.* Silver Spring, MD: Religious Formation Conference (November 2001): 15–24.

"The Charism of Religious Life." *Proceedings of the Twelfth National Congress of the Religious Formation Conference.* Silver Spring, MD: Religious Formation Conference (November 2001): 7–15.

"Horizons on Spirituality." *Horizons* 26 (Fall 1999): 307–10.

"The Study of Christian Spirituality: Contours and Dynamics of a Discipline." *Christian Spirituality Bulletin* 6 (Spring 1998): 1, 3–12. Also appears in *Studies in Spirituality* 8 (1998): 38–57; and in *Minding the Spirit: The Study of Christian Spirituality,* ed. Elizabeth A. Dreyer and Mark S. Burrows, 5–24. Baltimore: Johns Hopkins University Press, 2005.

"Congregational Leadership and Spirituality in the Postmodern Era." *Review for Religious* 57 (January-February 1998): 6–33.

"Interpreting the Bible: The Right and the Responsibility." *Scripture from Scratch* (September 1997). Awarded Catholic Press Association "Best Article Originating with the Magazine," 2nd place, 1998.

"A Hermeneutical Approach to the Study of Christian Spirituality." *Christian Spirituality Bulletin* 2 (Spring 1994): 9–14. Also appears in *Minding the Spirit: The Study of Christian Spirituality,* ed. Elizabeth A. Dreyer and Mark S. Burrows, 49–60. Baltimore: Johns Hopkins University Press, 2005.

"Spirituality as an Academic Discipline: Reflections from Experience." *Christian Spirituality Bulletin* 1 (Fall 1993): 10–15. Also appears in *Broken and Whole: Essays on Religion and the Body.* 1993 Annual Volume of the College Theology Society, vol. 39, ed. Maureen A. Tilley and Susan A. Ross. Lanham, MD: University Press of America, 1994.

"Celibacy as Charism." *The Way Supplement* 77 (Summer 1993): 13–25.

"Scripture as the Word of God." *Princeton Seminary Bulletin* 14, no. 1 New Series (1993): 18–35.

"Living Word or Dead(ly) Letter: The Encounter between the New Testament and Contemporary Experience." In *The Catholic Theological Society of America: Proceedings of the Forty-Seventh Annual Convention Held in Pittsburgh 11–14 June 1992* 47, ed. Paul Crowley, 45–60. Santa Clara, CA: Santa Clara University, 1992.

"The Risk of Dialogue: The U.S. Bishops and Women in Conversation." *Journal for Peace and Justice Studies* 2, no. 1 (1990): 49–63.

"Spirituality in the Academy." *Theological Studies* 50 (December 1989): 676–97.

"Feminist Ideology Criticism and Biblical Hermeneutics." *Biblical Theology Bulletin* 19 (January 1989): 3–10.

"Religious Life: The Dialectic Between Marginality and Transformation." *Spirituality Today* 40 (Winter 1988, suppl.): 59–79. Also available online.

"Formation for New Forms of Religious Community Life." *The Way Supplement* 62 (Summer 1988): 63–76.

"Evangelical Equality: Religious Consecration, Mission, and Witness," part 1: *Spirituality Today* 38 (Winter 1986): 293–302; part 2: *Spirituality Today* 39 (Spring 1987): 56–67.

"Theology and Spirituality: Strangers, Rivals, or Partners?" *Horizons* 13 (Fall 1986): 253–74.

"Church and Biblical Scholarship in Dialogue." *Theology Today* 42 (October 1985): 353–58. Also appears as "The Church and Biblical Scholarship in Dialogue." *Circuit Rider* 18 (September 1994): 5–8.

"God's Word for God's People." *The Bible Today* 22 (March 1984): 100–106.

"Cultural Influences on the Project of Ministerial Collaboration." *Newsletter: The National Organization for the Continuing Education of the Roman Catholic Clergy* 12 (Special Resource, Collaboration in Ministry, 1984): 27–39.

"The Paschal Imagination: Objectivity and Subjectivity in New Testament Interpretation." *Theological Studies* 43 (March 1982): 52–68.

"Theological Trends: Ministry and Ordination I." *The Way* 20 (October 1980): 290–99; "Theological Trends: Ministry and Ordination II, The Ordination of Women." *The Way* 21 (April 1981): 137–49.

"From Exegesis to Hermeneutics: The Problem of the Contemporary Meaning of Scripture." *Horizons* 8 (Spring 1981): 23–39.

"Faith, Hermeneutics, and the Literal Sense of Scripture." *Theological Studies* 39 (December 1978): 719–36.

"Liturgy and Spirituality—The Widening Gap." *Spirituality Today* 30 (September 1978): 196–210.

DICTIONARY AND ENCYCLOPEDIA ARTICLES

"Christian Spirituality: Definition, Methods and Types," "Johannine Spirituality," "Spiritual Exegesis," "Spirituality and Scripture." In *Dictionary of Christian Spirituality*, ed. Philip Sheldrake. Louisville, KY: Westminster/John Knox Press, 2005.

"John of the Cross." In *The Encyclopedia of Religion*. 2nd ed. Ed. Lindsay Jones. Woodbridge, CT: Macmillan Reference USA, 2005.

"Feminist Spirituality." In *The New Dictionary of Catholic Spirituality* (1993), ed. Michael Downey, 394–406. Collegeville, MN: Liturgical Press, 1993.

"Vow, (Practice and Theology)." In *New Catholic Encyclopedia* 17. Supplement: *Change in the Church*, 696–99. Washington, DC: Publishers Guild; New York: McGraw Hill, 1979.

CONTRIBUTORS

JUDITH A. BERLING, is Professor of Chinese and Comparative Religions and Convener of Interdisciplinary Studies at the Graduate Theological Union, Berkeley. Her two most recent books are *A Pilgrim in Chinese Culture: Negotiating Religious Diversity (1997)* and *Understanding Other Religious Worlds: A Guide for Interreligious Education* (2004), both from Orbis Books. Her research interests include Chinese and Japanese religions, interreligious learning, and interdisciplinarity in theological disciplines and religious studies.

MARY C. BOYS, SNJM, is the Skinner and McAlpin Professor of Practical Theology at Union Theological Seminary in New York City. She is the author or editor of eight books, including three on Jewish-Christian relations: *One Woman's Experience* and *Has God Only One Blessing? Judaism as a Source of Christian Self-Understanding,* both published by Paulist Press, and *Seeing Judaism Anew: Christianity's Sacred Obligation* (Rowman and Littlefield, 2005). She is working on a book exploring ways of understanding the death-resurrection of Jesus Christ.

DOUGLAS BURTON-CHRISTIE is Professor of Christian Spirituality at Loyola Marymount University, Los Angeles. He has published several articles and *The Word in the Desert: Scripture and the Quest for Holiness in Early Christian Monasticism* (Oxford, 1993). He serves as editor of *Spiritus,* the journal of the Society for the Study of Christian Spirituality.

LISA E. DAHILL is Assistant Professor of Worship and Christian Spirituality at Trinity Lutheran Seminary in Columbus, Ohio. Her publications include *Truly Present: Practicing Prayer in the Liturgy* (Augsburg Fortress, 2005) and *Educating Clergy: Teaching Practices and Pastoral Imagination* (Jossey-Bass, 2005). Her research interests include Bonhoeffer, hymnody, gender and violence, and the spiritual formation of clergy.

JOHN R. DONAHUE, SJ, taught at the Jesuit School of Theology at Berkeley from 1980 to 2001, and from 2001 to 2004 was the Raymond E. Brown Distinguished Professor of New Testament Studies at St. Mary's Seminary and University, Baltimore. He is the author of *The Gospel in Parable: Metaphor Narrative and Theology in the Synoptic Gospels* (Fortress, 1988) and, with Daniel Harrington, SJ, of *The Gospel of Mark, Sacra Pagina, 2* (Liturgical Press, 2002). He is working on a study of the relation of the Bible to social justice and has been lecturing on topics of biblical ethics and spirituality.

ALEJANDRO GARCÍA-RIVERA is Associate Professor of Systematic Theology at the Jesuit School of Theology at Berkeley and core doctoral faculty member of the Graduate Theological Union at Berkeley. Several of his articles and his book *The Community of the Beautiful: A Theological Aesthetics* have received awards from the Catholic Press and the United Church Press. His current interests include theological aesthetics, theology and the arts, suffering and the human person, and interfaith aesthetics.

BELDEN C. LANE is Professor of Theological Studies at Saint Louis University. A Presbyterian theologian on a Jesuit faculty, he teaches the history of American Christianity and is particularly interested in connections between spirituality and geography. His books include *The Solace of Fierce Landscapes: Exploring Desert and Mountain Spirituality* (Oxford, 1998) and *Landscapes of the Sacred: Geography and Narrative in American Spirituality* (Johns Hopkins, 2001).

BRUCE H. LESCHER is Director of Sabbatical Programs and Lecturer in Spirituality at the Jesuit School of Theology at Berkeley. He has published articles on American Catholic spirituality and, more generally, on issues involving spiritual formation. He is currently working on a book on spiritual direction.

ELIZABETH LIEBERT, SNJM, is Professor of Spiritual Life at San Francisco Theological Seminary and a member of the faculty in Christian Spirituality at the Graduate Theological Union, Berkeley. She is the author or co-author of three books, including *The Spiritual Exercises Reclaimed: Uncovering Liberating Possibilities for Women* (2001) and *Retreat with the Psalms* (2001), both published by Paulist Press. She is currently at work on a book on spiritual discernment.

ROBERT JOHN RUSSELL is Professor of Theology and Science at the Graduate Theological Union, Berkeley, and Founder and Director of the Center for Theology and the Natural Sciences. Recent books he has edited include *Fifty Years in Science and Religion: Ian G. Barbour and His Legacy* (Ashgate, 2004) and *Quantum Mechanics: Scientific Perspectives on Divine Action* (Vatican Observatory Press and The Center for Theology and the Natural Sciences, 2001). His current research and scholarly interests include resurrection, eschatology and scientific cosmology; time and eternity in light of contemporary physics; Christian spirituality and the natural sciences; theological and philosophical elements in physics and cosmology; and interreligious dialogue and the natural sciences.

PHILIP SHELDRAKE is William Leech Professor of Applied Theology in the Department of Theology and Religion at the University of Durham, England. His published works include *Spirituality and History: Questions of Interpretation and Method* (Orbis Books, 1998) and *Spaces for the Sacred: Place, Memory and Identity* (SCM Press, 2001). He is a past president of the Society for the Study of Christian Spirituality. He is currently conducting interdisciplinary research on the spirituality and ethics of city-making. He is also writing on spirituality and theological method.

SANDRA M. SCHNEIDERS, IHM, is Professor of New Testament Studies and Christian Spirituality at the Jesuit School of Theology at Berkeley and at the Graduate Theological Union. Widely sought as a lecturer, she is the author of numerous works in New Testament studies, Christian spirituality, and contemporary understandings of religious life (see bibliography). She is currently at work on the third volume of *Religious Life in a New Millennium*.

Index of Names

INDEX OF TITLES